HELP
AT
LAST

HELP
AT
LAST

A Complete Guide
To Coping With
Chemically Dependent Men

by EDWARD KAUFMAN, M.D.

GARDNER PRESS INC.
New York   London   Sydney

The author is greatly indebted to Karen Thomas
for editorial services and Lisa Phillips and Vicki
Zucker for manuscript preparation.

Gardner Press, Inc.
19 Union Square West
New York 10003

Orders for Australia and New Zealand to:
Astam Books
27B, Llewellyn Street
Balmain, N.S.W., Australia

Library of Congress Cataloging-in-Publication Data
New York : Gardner Press Tradebook, 1990.
Gardner Press Tradebook,
CURRENT PPD: 9006

Kaufman, Edward,
Help at last :
1990.
ISBN: 0898761662

89-23285

To my beloved wife
Karen K. Redding
who taught me about
the "other half"
of co-dependency

Contents

CHAPTER 3
RECOGNIZING THE EFFECTS OF COMMONLY
ABUSED DRUGS   **34**

CHAPTER 4
UNDERSTANDING THE ADULT MALE ALCOHOLIC
AND HIS FAMILY   **63**

CHAPTER 5
UNDERSTANDING THE ADULT MALE DRUG
ABUSER AND HIS FAMILY   **80**

Preface

I have been working with alcoholics and drug abusers for more than 25 years. During this time, I have written over 100 professional articles, chapters, and books. However, this book is different from my other work. My decision to write it came about one day when a 32-year-old man visited my office with his wife and four-month-old baby. He was an alcoholic and drug abuser who had been denying the fact for four years. He finally admitted he was an alcoholic when his wife told him she would leave if he did not admit to his problems and accept the help he needed. This was a difficult decision for his wife, particularly because of her concerns about caring for her young child. She needed every means of support she could get to follow through on it.

Although the husband finally admitted he was an alcoholic and needed help, he was procrastinating about committing to treatment. His wife looked at the books on the shelf in my office, which I had written for professionals, and asked me if there was anything that she, a layperson, could read to help her through her difficulties. At the time I could only suggest that she attend Al-Anon, an outgrowth of Alcoholics Anonymous for families and friends of alcoholics. Unfortunately, I had nothing to give her to read that would provide the support and guidance she required to cope at this confusing—often painful—time in her life.* Even though I had been in similar situations before, this was the moment I decided to write this book—a book to address the questions and concerns of the layperson.

I really do not know why this particular couple served as the catalyst for my decision to write *Help At Last*. Perhaps it was this woman's poignant combination of strength and vulnerability. Perhaps it was because the husband so desperately needed her to take the seemingly impossible step of leaving him in order to reach the part of him that was aware of his dire need for help. Perhaps after more than 25 years in the field, I thought that my contribution would be of value to the more than *20 million American families* who must cope with the problems of severe drug and alcohol abuse on a daily basis.

Alcoholism alone has affected the lives of 81 million Americans on some level—whether you are a child, a husband, a wife, a parent, an employer, or a close friend of an alcoholic. Most are completely baffled by the behavior of those about whom they care so deeply. I felt there was a real need for a book providing clear, detailed information on those aspects of chemical dependency which are necessary for the survival of those who are close to the substance abuser.

---

*Since that time, I have become aware of a number of excellent helpful books by other authors, which are listed in the appendix of this volume.

The problems caused by alcohol and drug abuse in our society are enormous and, at times, they appear to be overwhelming. Yet we seem to be emerging from our "stoned" age. The abuse of almost every category of drug is decreasing, even among our young people. Alcoholism has stabilized at about 10 to 20 million people in the United States. The three-martini lunch is widely being replaced by a run or an aerobics class. Valium® is no longer the leading prescribed drug in America. Physicians are prescribing it less often and with greater caution. Family members are becoming more aware of the extent to which drug and alcohol abuse by loved ones also entraps them, perhaps for a lifetime. In recent years, approaches that show great promise for dealing with substance abuse within the family have been developed. This book describes these approaches and programs in detail, and it traces their origins using recent studies of the families of substance abusers.

Since an essential aspect of understanding chemical dependency is being able to recognize the physiological and psychological effects of alcohol and widely used drugs, these will be described completely, yet with an effort to be succinct.

It is impossible to live with an alcoholic or drug-abusing man and not become co-dependent to some extent. Therefore, a chapter on understanding and assessing the harmfulness of co-dependency is included. This is followed by a chapter on specific coping strategies for dealing with substance-abusing men while they are still actively using chemicals.

Help At Last describes available treatment programs, how to get the substance abuser to participate in them, and how to choose the appropriate treatment modality. And finally, the problems of coping with the chemically dependent person after sobriety is discussed.

When I first started to write this book, I planned to cover every substance-abusing family member—husband, wife, child—in a single volume. About halfway through, I realized that this was too much information for one book. Thus, this book is focused on the adult male substance abuser, his spouse, and his family. However, it should also be helpful to other relatives, particularly children and close friends.

Much of the material will be helpful for anyone who is intimately involved with a substance abuser regardless of age, gender, or the person's substance of choice. Many of the coping strategies presented are even relevant for anyone who is closely involved with a self-destructive, non-substance-abusing person. Counselors and therapists who work with substance abusers and their families will also find the perspectives included helpful in understanding their own co-dependency issues, as well as in many direct aspects of working with clients. Hopefully this book will provide hope to those who feel helpless in the face of dealing with chemical dependency in their male loved ones and to provide the beginnings of *Help At Last*.

▽   ▽   ▽

HELP
AT
LAST

C H A P T E R

1

Introduction

*I*t was 9 o'clock in the evening and dinner had been ready since 6 o'clock. Joan, 42-year-old wife and mother, sat at the kitchen table, waiting. Stan, her husband, promised he'd be home by 5:30 so they could spend some time together. He was late again, and Joan was disappointed—again. She had the feeling she'd been through it all before. Her thoughts drifted to the past. Recollections of her 10th birthday, an important soccer game, her graduation, promises of her father coming, promises of gifts, of smiles. So many broken promises from the two most important men in her life. Years of hurt and anger stored up, yet not showing the feelings because her father and Stan liked her better when she held them in. Joan had learned, above all, not to rock the boat.

Even as a child, Joan had always dedicated her life to a man; first her alcoholic father and then a cocaine-wasted brother. She had always hoped that her mother would rescue her from the hurt and disappointment she experienced over and over again, but mom was too needy herself. She wanted Joan to take care of her too. Now, mom, too, was drinking, almost as heavily as dad.

Despite Joan's greater success in school, it seemed that her brother, Carl, was always favored. She was furious at her mother and father for praising Carl and ignoring her. As a child, she was frequently confused by her mother's behavior toward her. Her mother's words twisted her first in one direction and then the other: "You are a good daughter. You are worthless. Love me. Love your father. Take care of me, but I won't take care of you."

When she was a young girl, her dad would often get "close" to her when he was drunk. She remembers vividly his sweaty body lying over hers, pressing her down in the dark night. Then he'd leave her bed, whispering hoarsely, "Nothing happened, remember, nothing happened." And Joan was a good girl—she never told.

Joan grew up being the perfect girl, taking care of everyone else and never getting her own emotional needs met. The only consistently loving person in her life was grandma, but she's been dead for 25 years. She still remembers her grandmother with fondness and she misses that stabilizing influence in her life.

Today, Joan is haunted by the feeling that her dad follows her; she thinks she sees him all the time, particularly when she drives near his favorite bar or liquor store. She still feels swallowed up by her mother and disappointed and violated by her father, so she avoids them as much as possible.

She knew when she married Stan that his father was alcoholic, but she thought that her love could remedy his childhood hurts. Besides, Stan was such a hard worker, so strong and dominating, and so much fun at parties. She literally worshipped him in the early years of their marriage. She thought that at last she had found someone who needed her, but who could also care for her. Now, after 20 years of broken promises, she was still waiting and hoping that Stan would change. Yet, deep down she knew he wouldn't, and that she would go on being hurt again and again. She wanted him to leave, but she was too frightened by the prospect of how she would survive without him to ask.

The children still needed her and their father, yet their home was in chaos. Becky, at 17 years old, was emotionally responsive and an intellectual over-achiever, stretched far beyond her means. Jordy, their son, was getting drunk regularly at parties. He was 16 years old. And Stan kept *promising* he'd change. He stopped drinking twice in the past year, but soon started again with the rationale that he'd proved he wasn't an alcoholic by being able to stop drinking. For Joan it was even worse when he stopped and started than when he drank all the time. It built up her hopes and then brought them crashing down again. If she mentioned his lateness or his drinking, Stan would blame her for starting a fight. If she ignored it, she felt she was condoning his behavior. She didn't know what to do. Joan saw a counselor who told her to leave Stan, but she couldn't. She just wanted a little help—she wanted some relief at last from her life long struggle.

Joan's story and others like it are being repeated in thousands of families all over America. But now for Joan and others like her, as well as for Stan, there is *help at last*. Perhaps you and your family are among those thousands.

We live in an overmedicated society in which alcohol and drug abuse* lead to serious problems in every aspect of contemporary life. The damage caused by alcoholism and abusable drugs does not respect age, sex, ethnicity, income bracket, geography, or legality. These chemicals are viewed benignly as our society's major means to relieve pain, fear, and boredom. Yet, one-third of

---

*Though alcohol is a drug, it is often considered in its own separate category. "Substances" and "chemicals" are terms used synonymously for "drugs." "Addiction" is a synonym for "dependence." Chemical dependency has emerged recently as a term that describes abuse of and dependence on either drugs or alcohol or any combination of both. "Abuse" may be used as a synonym for dependence or to denote a level of drug or alcohol use that is pathological, but not at an addictive level.

all Americans have alcohol problems in their extended families. Alcohol-related highway accidents kill over 25,000 people a year, including 10,000 young people between the ages of 16 and 24. Three hundred thousand other individuals are seriously injured yearly.

Alcoholism is the fifth leading cause of death in the United States. As a consequence of alcohol-related problems, at least $15 billion is lost yearly to the national economy. The overall risk of developing alcoholism has doubled in the past 15 years. Five percent of high school seniors drink alcohol daily. And alcohol, glamorized in magazines and on television, will take the lives of more young people than all other drugs combined. Prescription and black market barbiturates, tranquilizers, stimulants, and sleeping medications are widely abused. One out of every six teenagers and one of every 11 adult Americans suffer from a severe problem with abuse of drugs or alcohol.

The year 1979 marked a turning point toward the decreasing abuse of drugs by our youth as measured by a national survey of high school seniors. This trend continued steadily until 1985. In that year, however, the use of marijuana, tranquilizers, barbiturates, cigarettes, cocaine, PCP, and opiates other than heroin all increased. This increase was only partially balanced by a decline in the use of amphetamines, methaqualone and, to a lesser extent, LSD. The year 1987 was the first that cocaine use decreased, although there was an increase in the use of "crack," an easily prepared, potent form of cocaine. It appears that cutting off the supply of one drug often leads to increased use of other drugs.

Over 90 million prescriptions are filled yearly for minor tranquilizers. But the problems caused by their use are in many ways greater than those caused by heroin addiction in our society, despite the publicity given the latter. We think of heroin addiction as a debilitating, ugly and expensive habit. However, the damage done by pills, booze, and more recently by cocaine, is just as costly to each substance-abusing individual and his or her immediate family, and it is far more widespread than the abuse of heroin. Substance use and abuse continue to spread despite recent efforts to control the flow of drugs into the country and to educate the public about their dangers.

Some individuals are able to use, misuse, and abuse alcohol and drugs without becoming dependent or being defined as alcoholics or addicts. However, *all* drug use patterns affect physical health, cause family problems, lead to accidents, and result in destructive social behavior. Serious problems associated with alcohol and drug abuse are not limited to the individual users themselves. Alcohol and drug abuse affects everyone around the user.

Although alcohol bears many similarities to any other chemical that can be abused and is addictive, its widespread use is more supported by legal, personal, professional, social, and cultural sanctions. There is similar support for the use of prescription mind-altering drugs. There are few social rules or guidelines regarding the safe and proper use of alcohol or sedatives.

What Does the Term "Substance Abuse" Mean?

Some basic definitions are helpful in understanding substance use. Substance abuse is defined as the use of a psychoactive (affecting the mind) drug, alcohol, or a combination to the extent that it seriously interferes with an individual's physical health, social relationships, or vocational functioning. An individual who is involved in an automobile accident or who commits an act of violence while intoxicated is, by definition, a substance abuser. Most serious substance abusers are dependent on drugs and/or alcohol. For the purposes of this book, *dependence, addiction,* and *habituation* are used interchangeably. Substance dependence is defined by the presence of tolerance or withdrawal.† *Tolerance* is defined as the need for increasing amounts of a drug to experience the same or lessened effects. *Withdrawal* refers to the presence of serious physical and psychological symptoms when drug intake is lessened or discontinued.

Cross-tolerance results when use of one drug leads an individual to require greater than normal doses of another drug or drugs. This phenomenon occurs among all the sedative hypnotics, minor tranquilizers, barbiturates, and alcohol (see Chapter II). Cross-tolerance does not affect the lethal dose of a substance. This means that when drugs in combination are taken simultaneoslty by individuals who are dependent on one or more of these chemicals, they can act additively and produce toxic, often fatal reactions. For example, diazepan (Valium) is almost never fatal by itself, but it is frequently found as a contributing factor in deaths from combined Valium and alcohol ingestion.

Due to the similarities of effects among all of the sedating drugs and alcohol, these substances are frequently mixed together or substituted for one another, resulting in what is sometimes called "polydrug" abuse.

There are many individuals whose behavior is so obvious that they are clearly alcoholics or drug addicts. Unfortunately, this is all too often evident to everyone *but* the individuals themselves. More commonly, what we observe are degrees of alcohol and drug use that cause medical, psychological, and social harm. These consequences may range from mild to moderate to severe dysfunction. In order to determine if someone's use of a drug or alcohol is a problem, we must look carefully at many aspects of use.

---

†In the latter part of 1987, the American Psychiatric Association's official position on the criteria for the diagnosis of substance dependence shifted dramatically from the long-held reliance on dependence and withdrawal. Thus, according to their diagnostic reference (DSM-III-R) the diagnosis is made whenever at least three of the following criteria exist: (1) use in larger amounts or over a longer time than intended; (2) persistent desire or failed efforts to cut down; (3) great deal of time spent getting, using, or recovering from substance use; (4) frequent intoxication or withdrawal at times when it is destructive; (5) reduced social, occupational, or recreational activities; (6) continued use despite persistent problems; and (7) tolerance of at least 50 percent (e.g., increase from four pills daily to six).

The frequency, quantity, and circumstances in which persons use chemicals (alcohol and/or drugs) should be detailed. Four specific components must be explored: (1) Does the person feel different or experience himself or herself differently when drinking, smoking, or ingesting the drug? (2) Does the person's behavior change when he or she is under the influence of the drug? (3) Does the person demonstrate any adverse consequences of drug use in terms of physical, emotional, interpersonal, or vocational function? (4) Does the person's drug use affect those who are close to him or her? The person who uses alcohol or a prescribed drug in a moderate, low-risk fashion will answer negatively to these items, except perhaps under the most controlled of social circumstances. When individuals *require* the effects of alcohol or drugs for any reason, they are by definition involved in high-risk use.

Drug dependence can be psychological or physiological. The term "addiction" was once used to describe physiologic dependence only. Psychological dependence results from the use of drugs capable of changing the conscious state or mood of the consumer in one way or another, regardless of what change is produced. The addict relies upon this change in consciousness and feelings in an attempt to cope more effectively and to experience reality differently. Thus, drug-dependent people may switch from one particular drug or brand of alcohol to another, depending on drug availability, social desirability, or personal appeal, in order to achieve the desired state of mind that certain classes of drugs produce. Rarely do they stick with one drug or type of alcohol for years. The drug-dependent person has a psychological reliance on the effects of the drug that produces an altered state of consciousness or change of moods and feelings.

However, psychological dependence is not a requisite for a person to acquire physical dependence. Anyone can become physically dependent on almost any psychoactive drug without necessarily acquiring a psychic or psychological dependence. For example, after surgery, a person may develop a mild physical dependence on morphine which will be only temporary if the individual is not prone to addiction.

Drugs as Magic Solutions

"Better things for better living through chemistry" is an old advertising slogan used in the 1950s by a major chemical company. But it aptly describes the present-day American attitude toward instant relief of emotional or physical pain through magical pills or substances. Far too many physicians respond to their patients' needs by readily providing prescriptions for instant relief. Warranted or not, easy access to medication reinforces the public's desire for fast cures. This applies not only to tranquilizers and sedatives, but also to the public's demand for penicillin for a cold, or a potent pain reliever for a headache, or codeine for a cough. It takes only a few seconds to write a prescription. It can require far more time to determine what the real problem is and to provide the appropriate nonpharmaceutical medical solution. The media, as well, perpetuate the myth of the magic of the pill or tonic with their constant promotion of alcohol, over-the-counter (OTC) drugs, and even vitamins. Too frequently, it does not matter to people what the substance is as long as it is something that can be taken into the body. We are a society conditioned to believe that pills and potions can cure anything and everything that ails us.

Mechanisms of Drug Dependence

No single factor produces or maintains dependence on any psychoactive drug. Rather, drug dependence is the final outcome of biological, psychological, social, and cultural variables. People vary in their vulnerability to drug dependence and that vulnerability varies with heredity, time, and circumstances. An individual's potential for addiction is always in a state of flux.

There is no such thing as an "addictive personality." However, some people are more vulnerable than others and, therefore, are more likely to become drug dependent given a specific set of circumstances. Inherited factors alone cannot determine addiction, although they can lead to a biological predisposition. Currently, there is more evidence of increased statistical probability of developing alcoholism along genetic (inherited) lines than there is for drug abuse. Genetic differences may influence the degree and type of response to a drug. However, they do not produce drug dependence by themselves.

Although many people relieve stress through the use of alcohol and/or psychoactive drugs, most individuals are able to control and limit their use. Such controls and limits include: legal, moral, and religious constraints; social expectations and sanctions; cultural norms, and personal values about the relative merits and costs of drug and alcohol use. Most people establish a personal cost-benefit limit on how much they are willing to pay in exchange for the psychological relief. They set their balance by weighing the health and interpersonal costs against the psychological rewards of psychoactive drug use. Most substance-using individuals are able to live within these personal cost-benefit limits most of the time.

Under certain psychological conditions people may be unable to set such limits or may be unable to behave in accordance with personal value limits. These people may believe that the benefits outweigh the costs or, in order to maintain a pattern of drug dependence, they may develop distorted perspectives in which they believe that they are paying much less than they really are. These circumstances establish a setting for the development of drug dependence. Denial of serious consequences, particularly with minimization and projection of blame onto others, is one of the earliest signs of substance abuse.

Some persons who are highly vulnerable to developing drug dependence as a result of genetic, familial, or social factors, may be able to avoid such a possibility only through total abstinence. Recovering alcoholics and drug addicts learn from hard experience that a totally drug- and alcohol-free existence is necessary in order to maintain independence from drugs. Methods utilized to achieve total abstinence may be the result of therapeutic interventions or may have a self-help, legal, moral, religious, psychological, or social foundation.

Abuse of Drugs and Alcohol in Combination and in Several Individuals in the Same Family

This book deals with the combined problems of drug and alcohol abuse. In part, this is because so many people in our society now abuse both of them. In addition, the families of drug abusers and alcoholics have many similarities as well as differences. Often they are the very same families viewed from different generations. That is, many families with alcoholic parents have children who present themselves as drug abusers. The reverse is less often true.

People have used combinations of drugs and alcohol for centuries. However, starting in about 1970, a growing trend to alternate between or simultaneously abuse alcohol and a multitude of other drugs was observed. The literature on the families of alcoholics and the families of drug abusers and addicts emerged separately and appeared to describe these families very differently. However, when these families were examined more closely we learned that frequently we were dealing with the same family but focusing on different generations. Like the parable of three blind men touching different parts of an elephant and each describing the same animal differently, experts viewed the same family from different generational perspectives. During this period, the literature on the alcoholic family tended to focus on the older male alcoholic, his spouse, and his adolescent (often drug-abusing) children. Books and articles written about the families of drug abusers focused on younger men in their late teens or early 20s and their parents, one or both of whom who were alcoholic in at least half of the reported cases.

This book focuses on the three- or four-generation family system of the *adult male substance abuser*, whom we'll frequently refer to as the "SA" for purposes of brevity, regardless of the identified patient's substance or substances of choice. It is important to look at the impact of the SA on all members and generations of the family, including grandparents, parents, siblings, cousins, and children. *Every* family member is affected by the SA and everyone needs to be involved in treatment for his or her own sake, as well as for the good of the SA. Any additional family members who are included in treatment not only help us understand and assist the substance abuser, but receive important aid themselves. Reluctant family members usually require the help of a skilled therapist before they can be brought into treatment for the substance abuser or for their own benefit.

The progression of the development of illicit drug abuse in an individual indicates that drug abuse is preceded by alcohol and cigarette use. There are four stages of this progression: from beer to wine, or both, to cigarettes or hard liquor, then to marijuana, and then to illicit drugs. Neither alcohol nor marijuana use is truly a steppingstone to seducing a nonpredisposed individual down the path to "hard" drugs. Rather, these particular substances are both very commonly used in our society and are used and abused sequentially and more frequently by those who are predisposed to eventually go on to "harder drugs." It is understandable that behaviorally and biologically vulnerable individuals would first try the more available, less dangerous drugs like alcohol and marijuana before they try the less available and riskier drugs. Although marijuana and alcohol do not cause people to abuse drugs, their use opens the door (or gate) to more serious drug abuse. The steppingstone hypothesis has been replaced by the "gateway theory," which is currently a more acceptable viewpoint.

The common current usage of drugs by alcoholics and alcohol by drug abusers explains how studies of an alcoholic's family system at one point may be the same as evaluating the drug abuser's family at another time, or vice versa. The ubiquitous nature of inextricably woven drug and alcohol abuse compels us to look at both problems together, as well as to attempt to sift them apart.

There are several physiological and behavioral signs of drug and alcohol dependence that become manifest to a point where they can be readily recognized. These will be described in detail according to specific drugs and alcohol later in the book. However, there are also general patterns of behavior in SA's that will be summarized in the following sections.

Common Identification and Recognition Factors of Both Drug Abusers and Alcoholics

By now it is common knowledge that not all alcoholics are skid row bums and that not all drug addicts are stealing thousands of dollars daily to support their habits. Yet, surprisingly, I regularly interview drug-addicted persons and alcoholics who deny their dependence by rationalizing that they continue to hold high-level jobs, though often just barely, and don't break the law to support their habits. Only 7 percent of the people on skid row are alcoholic. The skid row alcoholic is most atypical. The more typical alcoholic is likely to be employed, married, a member of a church, lodge, or club, and a respected member of the community. Since he does not look or act like the cultural stereotype of the alcoholic, the condition is likely to be denied by everyone around him, not just the alcoholic himself.

Certain on-the-job problem behaviors are suggestive of alcoholics and drug abusers. These include difficulties with their families, friends, employers, the law, or problems with their physical and emotional health. Signs of substance abuse at work include frequent absenteeism, long breaks, tardiness, diminished efficiency, and impaired attitude toward co-workers and clients. Substance abusers are also heavily involved in on-the-job accidents.

The 10 most common signs of alcoholism at work, as reported by recovered alcoholic policemen, listed in their order of frequency of occurence, are:

1. Hangover
2. Nervous and jittery behavior
3. Edginess, anger, emotional instability
4. Procrastination
5. Red, bleary eyes
6. Sporadic work pace
7. High sensitivity to inquiries about drinking
8. Hand tremors
9. Avoidance of boss, company, physician, peers
10. Neglect of work details

Other warning signs include evidence of financial or domestic problems, unusual drinking habits, and any of the physical signs and symptoms associated with substance abuse and dependence described in the following two chapters.

Alcoholics rarely visit doctors with direct complaints of alcoholism. Rather, the alcoholic typically seeks medical care for major complications of alcoholic abuse, such as liver, stomach, heart, skin, or neurological complaints. Such people often do not consciously link these medical illnesses with their alcohol abuse. A large number of sedative abusers and alcoholics suffer traumas from frequent accidents that occur while in a state of intoxication. What physicians typically treat or see are bone fractures and head injuries that are caused by falls, burns from careless cigarette smoking, muscle weakness, or a variety of confused mental states. Some of these patients may recognize that their medical problems are linked directly to their drinking, but they are not likely to complain specifically about their alcoholism. A third group indirectly seeks medical help for their alcoholism by complaining principally of insomnia, nervousness, tremors, anxiety, anorexia, frequent colds, or stomach upset.

All too often, physicians miss the diagnosis of alcoholism or drug abuse in a routine physical examination. For many physicians, their first medical encounter with alcoholics takes place while they are residents training in large public hospitals, where the alcoholic patient may well be the prototype skid row bum. This initial encounter contributes to the stereotyped label placed on alcoholics that in turn creates a problem in the accurate diagnosis of alcoholism. Another contributing factor in clouding the issue of correct diagnosis is that many physicians themselves misuse alcohol and drugs, and thus may overlook the problems in their patients. For many then, a doctor's lack of concern about a patient's alcohol and drug abuse is not sufficient evidence to rule out the existence of a possible problem.

A questionnaire widely circulated by Alcoholics Anonymous is very helpful as a screening device for alcoholism, although a medical diagnosis should only be made by a physician. A facsimile of this questionnaire appears at the end of this chapter and is included for the reader's application to a suspected alcoholic or drug-abusing family member. The word "drug" can be readily substituted for the word "alcohol" in the questionnaire.

Identification of the Drug-Abusing and Drug-Dependent Person

Drug-related behavior is described in great detail in the chapters that follow. Two checklists for determining if someone you know might be drug dependent are also included in these chapters. Individuals often progress from controlled and moderate drug use in the early stages to heavy abuse in later stages. As this occurs, these individuals report more blackouts, episodes of out-of-control drug use, accidents, injuries, hangovers, and rebound depressions. Regular usage and expenditures for drugs tend to be rationalized as non-drug-related expenditures and usual responsibilities are neglected. The patient or family will report neglect of work or school, termination of friendships, acute anxiety attacks or panics, intermittent alienation from the family, and financial difficulties. Prior history may include abrupt onset of seizures and treatment for overdoses or detoxification. Suicide attempts, and a history of delinquency or driving offenses are also suspicious behaviors. Friends are limited more and more to those who use drugs, and the individual may become seclusive and furtive to hide drug use.

The language of drug users is pervaded by idioms of the drug culture, which shift rapidly as these terms are taken over by "normal" teenagers and by the mass communication media. Most drugs of abuse have nicknames that are determined by factors such as the color of the drug, the name of the manufacturer, or the real or imagined effect of the drug. Some examples are: "Reds"—secobarbital; "Cibas"—glutethimide; "Ups" or "Speed"—amphetamines; "Smack"—heroin, etc. Prescription drug abusers often refer to these drugs in their plural form: Valiums®; "Ludes"—Quaaludes®. Familiarity with the latest slang terms may reflect involvement with the drug culture.

Illicit drug abusers have little concept of time, except when keeping an appointment will result in obtaining drugs. Drug abusers frequently become deceitful, conniving, and resentful of authority. They become so accustomed to lying that they no longer know what is and is not true. Many drug abusers are obstreperous, challenging, angry, or violent when they do not get what they want or when they are on stimulants, sedatives, or in withdrawal. Although some individuals can maintain jobs even while regularly using heroin, sedatives, or stimulants, most serious drug abusers neglect work or school. This is in contrast to alcoholics, who frequently are able to maintain steady employment. Old friends become targets of manipulation and hostility and friendships slip away. Associations become limited only to other individuals who will share in drug taking or drug procurement. Sudden personality change frequently accompanies drug intake. There may be a history of acute anxiety attacks or panics, particularly from cocaine, stimulants, and hallucinogens. Drug abusers are very unreliable with money and bills as increasingly more of their funds are devoted to their drugs. Often, money and small articles are found missing from the home, and this may progress to theft of family valuables and possessions.

The children of drug abusers are subjected to a great deal of abuse and neglect. A history of child abuse is a frequent warning signal of parental drug and alcohol abuse.

How a patient relates to prescribed drugs may provide evidence of drug abuse. Any patient who returns to the doctor's office for a prescription renewal of an abuse-prone drug before the prescription should have been used up is suspect. Drug abusers can be very skilled in making up excuses for why they ran out of medication prematurely. Some examples include, ''My friend's mother died and I gave him some,'' ''I lost the prescription,'' and ''The pharmacist only gave me half because he didn't have any more in stock.'' Many drug abusers share and trade drugs with their friends and frequently sell prescription drugs at highly inflated prices.

Evidence from a pharmacist that a prescription has been altered is a definitive indication of drug abuse. Any individual who can tolerate therapeutic or large doses of a drug without experiencing the expected psychological or physiological effects is probably tolerant. Tolerance is proof of dependence on a particular drug or on a chemically related drug. Substance abusers are particularly skillful in asking for their drug of choice, and they have a multitude of stories to justify why they cannot be helped by nonaddicting drugs. The more mentally disturbed or desperate drug abusers will try to obtain any drug whatsoever to alter their mental state, even drugs that are not commonly abused or home remedies. One individual I treated when he was incarcerated in a federal prison was so desperate for an altered state that he injected a juice made from fermented ragweed pulp (which caused a severe bacterial infection in his bloodstream). An ''accidental'' overdose is a common sign that an individual is abusing or is dependent on a drug or a combination of drugs and alcohol. Definite suicide attempts and actual suicides are common in substance abusers.

The physical health of substance abusers invariably suffers from the direct and indirect effects of drug and alcohol use. These problems are discussed in detail in Chapters II and III. General indicators of these kinds of conditions or symptoms may include a pale or gray coloring to their faces, particularly around the eyes and mouth. They may also appear flushed, with heavy perspiration and warm or clammy skin. Alertness and attention diminish. Eyes appear dull, glassy, or inflamed. Speech is slurred and marked personality changes occur.

Common Family Patterns

When we first began to study them, the families of alcoholics initially appeared to be very different from the families of drug abusers, particularly when comparing first-generation alcoholics with second-generation drug abusers. At first glance, all families of alcoholics seem very similar, but when carefully scrutinized, there are actually many differences among them. Substance abusers create a kind of suction effect that either draws the entire family into their substance abuse and related behavior, or repulses them so that they withdraw. Thus, these families may either be overinvolved with and "stuck to" each other, or distant and aloof. Many families vacillate between these two extremes of relatedness.

Some families that rally to every crisis precipitated by the substance abuser may use this behavior to break the routine of isolation and inattentiveness to the problem. If repeated, this activation can serve to reinforce destructive behavior patterns as the family repeatedly uses crises to awaken them from their lethargy. Another common pattern is that anger in these families is frequently swallowed totally or only released explosively—one extreme or the other.

Individual Vulnerability to Substance Abuse

Several common categories of individuals who are vulnerable to drug and alcohol problems are adolescents, neurotics, the aged, female homemakers, chronic pain sufferers, stressed-out executives, medication-prone people, and those who live in urban ghettos and are subjected to an environment of high-density drug abuse. Specific vunerability and family interactions are summarized below. Details about adult male SA's are described in the chapters that follow.

The Adolescent

During the latter part of the 1960's, "adolescence" and "drug abuse" became virtually, though not necessarily fairly, synonymous. In adolescence, behavior that would be considered aberrant or even pathological during other stages of life occurs as part of the normal spectrum of growth and experimentation. The struggles toward sexual and personal identity that define adolescence are as extreme as the behavior elicited by these challenges. Mood swings are rapid and often inexplicable. A minor comment or event may precipitate severe turmoil leading to difficult, obnoxious, acting-out behavior. Drug abuse provides a destructive though partial fulfillment of many of the adolescent's psychological and social needs, while preventing the required completion of many developmental tasks required in adulthood.

The rebelliousness and impulsiveness that are so often a part of adolescence, combined with the overly punitive responses that such behavior frequently elicits, may render the adolescent vulnerable to the abuse of drugs through cycles of escalating defiance and punishment. Adolescent substance abuse is particularly dangerous developmentally and psychologically, because it prevents the formation of many necessary skills and coping strategies that may never be learned in later years. Table 1 at the end of this chapter lists some common signs of adolescent substance abuse.

The Neurotic

The most common neurotic symptoms that lead to the search for pharmacologic relief are depression and anxiety. Rapid relief may be provided by minor tranquilizers such as Valium,® Ativan,® Xanax,® or Librium.® However, we should be aware that these drugs are habit forming. Drugs commonly prescribed for sleep, such as Dalmane® and Halcion® are also habit forming. Neurotic individuals with a history of drug abuse, dependence, or alcoholism are especially susceptible to addiction even when a physician prescribes these drugs at recommended dosages.

The Aged

Losses of spouse, relatives, job, friends, and independence are major stresses in old age. Loneliness, chronic pain, disability, or anticipation of an undignified death further complicate an already difficult stage of life. These stresses may lead to hypochondriasis (excessive concern with one's health), anxiety, and depression. Alcoholism and drug abuse are readily available escapes. Habituation to sleeping pills and excessive use of prescription narcotics for chronic pain or tranquilizers are drug-use patterns common to the elderly. Abuse of over-the-counter (OTC) drugs, felt to be harmless, and the overuse of tonics for their alcohol content are typical geriatric problems too often overlooked. Sedative abuse in the elderly may be avoided if we are informed that as we age, progressively less sleep in needed. Also, elderly individuals generally require half of the usually prescribed dosage of mind-altering medications whereas customary therapeutic doses are often toxic to them.

The Female Homemaker ‡

Women tend to abuse prescription drugs more frequently than men. Studies show that unemployed homemakers use more sedative/hypnotics, antidepressants, diet pills, relaxants, and minor tranquilizers than the general population. The homemaker who is not employed outside of the home or engaged in a rewarding avocation may suffer from diminished self-esteem and a negative self-image. She may feel isolated. Everyday tasks and problem solving are regarded as unimportant, unfulfilling, and dull. She has no one with whom to share her daily financial, social, and familial stresses, and the resulting tension may be manifested as anxiety, depression, or physical symptoms. Self-treatment often begins with alcohol as it is easily available. Diet pills prescribed for weight loss, sedatives prescribed for insomnia, or tranquilizers for anxiety are equally accessible and commonly used self-remedies.

Unfortunately, the woman who manages a home and family and holds down a full-time job outside the home is even more vulnerable to alcoholism than her nonworking counterpart. This is no doubt related to having a doubled input of stress. Women with part-time jobs are also vulnerable, perhaps because they are expected to perform more easily the full-time tasks of homemaker along with their jobs.

The Executive

Individuals in this category use alcohol and drugs to cope with high levels of vocational, financial, and familial stress. Sedative drugs and/or alcohol are relied upon to relieve insomnia, anxiety, or somatic symptoms such as headache and back pain. Stimulant drugs such as amphetamines, Ritalin,® Preludin,® and cocaine may relieve fatigue and temporarily enhance work productivity before their use becomes destructive. Executives tend to hold on to high levels of work function even after alcohol or drugs have destroyed their family lives.

---

‡This section also applies to wives of substance-abusing men who resort to drugs and alcohol in order to cope.

The expanding group of female executives is particularly prone to these stresses because of the burden of being required to perform on the job and being expected to maintain the home as well.

Chronic Pain Patients

Those who suffer from chronic pain are quite vulnerable to becoming addicted to medications given to relieve pain such as codeine and other narcotics, Fiorinal,® Darvon,® or sedatives. Every attempt should be made to prevent these addictions and to provide nonhabituating methods of relief. The latter range from drugs such as Motrin® and the antidepressants to relaxation techniques, TENS units, and self-hypnosis.

The Medication-Prone Person

Anyone who firmly believes that any physical or emotional symptom can magically be relieved by the *right* drug is a potential drug abuser. The person who self-medicates most minor aches and pains with an OTC remedy or prescribed pill is more likely to misuse medication than one who can tolerate occasional discomfort. Crucial contributing factors in creating a medication-prone individual are the attitudes toward chemicals and pain relief that existed in the home where the patient was raised, and sibling as well as parental use and abuse of drugs and alcohol. A lot of individuals expect instant relief from the everyday demands of contemporary life. The average person often expects relief from the emotional pain that is associated with that stress. It is tempting, simple, and quick to ingest a pill in the hope that it will provide instant relief. The individual who experiences this immediate relief from a pill may be just the one who is getting started on the path to drug dependence.

Some people feel that they are entitled to the drug of their choice for what they consider to be "recreational" use. Even the word "recreational" is destructive when applied to drug use, since it perpetuates the myth of chemical solutions to personal problems and discourages the development of more meaningful forms of recreation. Furthermore, many so-called "recreational" drug users eventually become drug abusers and drug addicts.

The Ghetto Resident

In urban ghettos, rampant poverty and widespread drug availability lead to very high rates of alcoholism, drug abuse, and addiction. As one New York City black ex-addict stated, "In Harlem, even the buildings nod," meaning that in the ghettos, heroin is so plentiful that the buildings are filled with people drowsy from heroin at any given time.

Rural ghettos are not immune. However, drug abuse trends tend to be regional and to fluctuate every year or two. In 1985, in southern California ghettos, PCP (phencyclidine, "Shermans") was the drug of choice; in Chicago, it was T's and Blues (Talwin® and pyribenzamine); in Miami it was cocaine, and so on. In 1986 "crack" cocaine was rapidly emerging and growing in use on both coasts. In 1988, illegally manufactured amphetamines and LSD were making a comeback. In 1989, "ice," a cheap, smokeable form of methamphetamine gained in popularity and may eventually surpass "crack" in destructive potential.

Drug trends often originate in ghettos and the inner city, spread into middle-class, urban neighborhoods, and then to suburbs and rural areas. In a sense, we all live in semi-walled off environments and are vulnerable to regional drug trends and availability. Yet, in contemporary society many trends of substance use and abuse sweep across the country as rapidly as a highly advertised new consumer product.

This introduction to the problems that drugs and alcohol cause individuals, their families, and society should help us to recognize the substance abuser, particularly when he or she is a member of our own family. The following four chapters provide specific information that will aid in the recognition and understanding of substance abuse.

References

Kaufman, E., Polydrug abuse or multidrug misuse: It's here to stay. *British Journal of the Addictions*, 72:339-374, 174.

Kaufman, E., *Substance Abuse and Family Therapy.* Grune & Stratton, New York, 1984.

Pattison, E. M., & Kaufman, E., Alcohol and drug dependence. In E. Usdin & J. M. Lewis (Eds), *Psychiatry in General Medical Practice*, McGraw-Hill, New York, 1979, pp. 305-336.

▽   ▽   ▽

Table 1
Common Signs of Adolescent Drug or Alcohol Abuse

1. Increased defiance of rules, regulations, and directions.
2. Becoming more secretive, particularly with regard to trends and activities.
3. Sudden or gradual drop in school grades, attendance, interest in extracurricular activities, or behavior.
4. Different friends who have difficulties of their own.
5. Emotional highs and lows, short tempers.
6. Withdrawal from family functions.
7. Isolation in their own rooms.
8. Loss of initiative and energy.
9. Sleeping or eating more or less than usual.
10. Not caring for self or clothing.
11. Not telling parents about relevant school meetings.
12. Not coming home, or going to school or work late and making excuses.
13. Possessions, money, prescription drugs, or alcohol missing.
14. Selling possessions or unexplained availability of money.
15. Increased manipulations of parents and other authorities.
16. Defensiveness when confronted.
17. Legal problems including unpaid tickets, attendance at parties that the police must terminate.
18. Change in drinking habits.
19. Coming home intoxicated or with other signs of drug abuse (bloodshot eyes, smell of alcohol or drugs).
20. Evidence of drug paraphernalia.
21. Verbally or physically abusive to family members.
22. Increase in minor illness or injury.
23. Running away from home.
24. Increased lying and arguments about lying.

Table 2
Are You An Alcoholic?

To answer this question, ask yourself the following questions and answer them as honestly as you can.

1. Do you lose time from work due to drinking?
2. Is drinking making your home life unhappy?
3. Do you drink because you're shy with other people?
4. Is drinking affecting your reputation?
5. Have you ever felt remorse after drinking?
6. Have you ever been in financial difficulty as a result of drinking?
7. Do you turn to lower companions and an inferior environment when drinking?
8. Does your drinking make you careless of your family's welfare?
9. Has your ambition decreased since drinking?
10. Do you crave a drink at a definite time daily?
11. Do you want a drink the next morning?
12. Does drinking cause you to have difficulty in sleeping?
13. Has your efficiency decreased since drinking?
14. Is drinking jeopardizing your job or business?
15. Do you drink to escape from worries or troubles?
16. Do you drink alone?
17. Have you ever had a complete loss of memory as a result of drinking?
18. Has your physician ever treated you for drinking?
19. Do you drink to build up your self-confidence?
20. Have you ever been to a hospital or institution on account of drinking?

If you have answered YES to any one of the questions, it is a definite warning that you may be an alcoholic.

If you have answered YES to any two of the questions, the chances are that you are an alcholic.

If you have answered YES to three or more of the questions, you are definitely an alcoholic.

C H A P T E R

2

Recognizing the Effects
of Alcohol and Alcohol Abuse

*A*lcohol is the most commonly used and abused drug in our society. The breadth of the problem and its unique physical effects warrant this separate chapter devoted to recognizing alcohol's psychological and physical effects.

Alcohol has been used and abused since the beginning of recorded history. The discoveries of modern science have forced society to give up its earlier illusions about alcohol's healing properties. Ironically, the word "whiskey" comes from a Gallic word meaning "water of life." If abused, whiskey becomes instead the "elixir of death." Definitions of alcohol abuse and dependence were given in Chapter I. Now we're going to look at what it means to be diagnosed an alcoholic.

When I was a medical student in the late 1950's, syphilis and tuberculosis were the primary diseases used for teaching us about the body's components, because those diseases affected so many different parts of the patient's body. Today, those diseases are not nearly as important as alcoholism. If contemporary medical students learn all of the effects of alcohol upon the human body, they understand the physiology of every organ system. Alcoholism ravages not only the life of an alcoholic, but his or her body as well.

A person does not have to be living on skid row to be considered an alcoholic. In reality, a mere 7 percent of alcoholics meet the criteria for the skid row stereotype. Many people continue their own alcoholism by accepting only a very limited definition of the term, such as the skid row wino. They fool themselves by claiming "I can't be an alcoholic—I don't miss work," "I only drink beer," "I fill my glass with ice," "I don't shake," or "I don't drink in the morning." They may even stop drinking for days, weeks, or months as part of a fervent personal denial of their alcoholism. They may run 26-mile marathons to avoid recognition. An alcoholic's loss of control over drinking may be only periodic, yet it is ultimately progressive. The practice of controlling drinking periodically is actually evidence of the presence of the disease, not its absence. It is often true that when a person reaches the point at which he or she questions his or her drinking, the very presence of doubt is itself a red flag of warning. People who drink normally don't have to question their drinking habits or confirm their ability to control their drinking.

The repeated inability to drink without being able to stop prior to intoxication may be sufficient in and of itself to confirm the diagnosis of alcoholism. One 55-year-old female patient of mine has drunk alcohol less than 20 times in her adult life. Yet, every time she has drunk alcohol, she has become intoxicated. She is an alcoholic even though she has actually drunk far less alcohol in her life than the average social drinker. She has stayed sober for the past five years mainly because she has attended AA regularly.

The drinking histories and patterns of alcoholics are almost as varied as the kinds of alcoholic beverages on the market. Many pages could be devoted to describing all of these different kinds of alcoholics.

Behaviors and Characteristics Common in Alcoholics

There is no actual single entity known as "the alcoholic personality," but there are common behaviors and characteristics that help us identify alcoholics and recognize the disease. These characteristics are described in detail in Chapter IV. Some general, relevant behaviors are summarized in this chapter.

The denial that alcoholics use is such a major aspect of their personality, as well as the disease of alcoholism, that it cannot be overemphasized. Alcoholics deny how much they drink, how much their alcohol-related behaviors hurt everyone around them, and how devastating the impact of their drinking is on the lives of their families, friends, and employers. They constantly rationalize their behavior and lie to cover for themselves. At times lying, denial, and rationalization all become so fixed and confused in alcoholics' minds that they are truly not aware whether they are lying or not.

Alcoholics drink to satisfy hidden needs for nurturing that they cannot express as adults. They drink because they have learned that drinking brings them a great deal of power over others which they cannot obtain by direct means. However, it is risky to even briefly consider the underlying psychological reasons why alcoholics drink, because these very explanations can be and frequently are used by alcoholics as excuses to continue drinking.

Stated very simply, an alcoholic is someone whose drinking is out of control and who exhibits several of the following characteristics or signs: physical dependence with symptoms of withdrawal or tolerance; preoccupation with drinking; impaired work or career functioning and relationships; and health problems related to alcohol consumption. As the disease progresses, his or her entire life is preoccupied with alcohol and its effects. Frequent blackouts (periods of amnesia) are one common sign of early or pre-alcoholism. An early or pre-alcoholic is someone who, with a lower degree of the above characteristics, will most likely develop full-blown alcoholism in a matter of years. Pre-alcoholics place undue importance on drinking. However, they have not yet developed physical dependence or substantial impairment of any kind. In contrast, a nonalcoholic is someone whose use of alcohol is mild to moderate, causes no problems in his or her family, and shows *no* other signs of problems with alcohol. However, so-called alcoholic "characteristics" are not cast in iron. *Anyone* can *become* an alcoholic.

Alcohol is alcohol, and alcohol is a chemical. It has the same chemical formula (C_2H_5OH) regardless of whether it is fine aged red wine, a crisp California Chardonnay, champagne, scotch, beer, wine cooler, cheap Thunderbird, or rotgut. Alcohol's effects on the body are unique in contrast to its effects on the brain, where it acts very much like the sedative drugs. In fact, we often refer to sedative drugs such as Xanax®, Valium®, or other benzodiazepines as a "martini in a pill."

The psychological effects of alcohol are identical to those of the sedative and hypnotic drugs described in the following chapter. The sedative and disinhibiting (reducing or removing inhibitions) effects of alcohol last about four hours. In an alcohol-dependent person, when these effects wear off, withdrawal sets in. Withdrawal from moderate amounts of alcohol may last two to six hours and is characterized by nervousness and agitation. This is why drinkers awaken in the middle of the night and cannot get back to sleep. The irritability and restless sleep of withdrawal are strong contributors to the hangover experience. Severe withdrawal lasts about four days in alcohol-dependent persons and epileptic-type seizures can occur during this period. Severe withdrawal also causes mental confusion that may progress to delirium tremens (DTs) characterized by fear, shaking, disorientation, fever, and visual or the more rare auditory hallucinations. Full-blown cases of DTs are even fatal in about 15 percent of cases.

The subject of blood alcohol level (BAL) has received a great deal of publicity because it is generally considered to be verification of intoxication. To touch on this topic briefly, one ounce of 80-proof alcohol (the equivalent of one shot of hard liquor, one highball, six ounces of wine, or one can of beer) raises the blood alcohol level by approximately .02 percent. The average sized person metabolizes one drink every two or three hours. So the individual who stops drinking lowers his or her blood alcohol level by a little less than .01 percent every hour. Most individuals exhibit physical uncoordination at .06 percent. A BAL of .08 percent is considered legally intoxicated; .15 percent leaves most people staggering and incoherent; .40 percent renders a person comatose; and a BAL of .40 percent to .50 percent often results in death. These effects of BAL's vary according to body size and tolerance. A larger individual requires more drinks than a smaller person for a higher BAL. Tolerance is the amount of alcohol or drug that is consumed before intoxication is reached. An alcoholic who has developed a severe tolerance can appear to function normally at BAL's as high as .35 percent. Yet that same person may frequently have a period of amnesia despite apparently normal performance to the outside observer. This is called a blackout. In the later stages of alcoholism, tolerance is lost because the damaged liver becomes unable to metabolize alcohol, resulting in intoxication from ingesting relatively small amounts of alcohol.

Physiological Effects of Alcohol*

Digestive System

Alcohol affects and causes irritation to almost every organ in the body. Alcohol is absorbed by every cell in the human organism, particularly cells with a high moisture content like those in the pancreas. Within 20 minutes of ingestion, alcohol causes the stomach to secrete large amounts of hydrochloric acid. This acid eats away at the lining of the stomach causing irritation (gastritis). This irritation is first experienced as heartburn but can progress to ulcers or to multiple small bleeding sites in the stomach. Alcoholics continue to drink even after an ulcer develops. This is due in part to the fact that they don't feel the usual pain that is experienced with ulcers because of alcohol's local anesthetic effect. In addition, long-term excessive alcohol use deadens the nerve cells in the stomach, which further diminishes the body's ability to experience the warning signal of pain when an ulcer is present. Under these conditions, alcoholics may develop severe ulcers and, since they are also prone to abnormal bleeding, massive bleeding from these ulcers may result. In addition, the stomach of heavy drinkers loses tone so that the stomach does not totally empty after a meal. As a result, digestion takes longer and potentially dangerous vomiting is common. Gastric spasms can also lead to vomiting. This vomiting can lead to pneumonia or death through aspiration that takes place when vomit, instead of being expelled orally, passes into the airway blocking breathing and causing strangulation.

Acid may also be regurgitated into the esophagus, causing progressive heartburn, esophageal ulcers, and bleeding. In severe cases, the tissues of the

---

*See Table 1 for a summary of these effects.

esophagus can become so inflamed that the gastrointestinal tract becomes blocked or ulceration may progress to tearing of the stomach.

Ninety-five percent of alcohol is absorbed directly into the bloodstream in the stomach and upper part of the small intestine. The absorption rate is slowed down by food, so that after a meal the BAL rises more slowly. Once in the bloodstream, alcohol is absorbed by all the body cells, particularly the *pancreas*, as mentioned previously. In the pancreas, alcohol irritates cells, causing them to swell and block the passage of pancreatic digestive enzymes called amylase and lipase. These blocked enzymes then digest—literally eat up—the pancreas itself, causing a painful disease called pancreatitis. If the blood vessels of the pancreas are affected, this can progress to hemorrhagic pancreatitis. This life-threatening disease is long lasting, so that once an alcoholic has it, future drinking episodes will result in its recurrence. Pancreatitis can also lead to large, fluid-filled cystic tumors of the pancreas. Recurrent pancreatitis can also damage the insulin-producing cells of the pancreas, leading to diabetes.

Another digestive organ, the *liver*, is also irritated by alcohol. Alcohol causes cellular damage and swelling in the liver. This, in turn, blocks off the canals that carry a digestive juice called bile into the bowel. When this takes place, the breakdown products of bile back up into the bloodstream. This produces "yellow jaundice," which is characterized by the presence of yellow pigmentation in the skin and whites of the eyes. Alcohol's direct damage to the liver cells themselves is called alcoholic hepatitis. In some instances, this form of hepatitus may continue to progress even after the individual stops drinking. Repeated episodes of damage from hepatitis lead to long-term scarring of the liver tissue, known as cirrhosis. Even doses of alcohol as small as one drink causes sufficient irritation to the liver so that detectable, temporary increases of liver enzymes occur in the blood. These enzymes, SGOT and SGPT, are often measured in blood screens as part of a comprehensive physical examination. After several years of heavy drinking, liver cells are often so damaged that these enzymes stay elevated. This elevation is a sign that liver function is impaired. Breakdown of liver cells is a direct toxic effect of alcohol that is only partially spared by an adequate diet. Despite these common complications, only about one-third of alcoholics ever develop cirrhosis.

The healthy liver performs several functions affecting other parts of the body that are essential to normal health, which it cannot do when it is damaged by alcohol. The liver manufactures albumen, globulin, and prothrombin. Albumen helps each cell in the body maintain the fluid necessary for proper cellular function. Without albumen, every cell in our body loses fluids and begins to deteriorate (one more reason why an alcoholic's skin looks so sickly and gray). Globulin helps the body fight off infections. Prothrombin is necessary for the clotting of blood when there is a break in the skin or stomach lining. The lack of prothrombin caused by excessive alcohol intake is an important factor that contributes to gastrointestinal bleeding in alcoholics. This lack also leads to easy bruising of the skin from minor injuries. The lowered level of prothrombin can also lead to bleeding under the skull from minor head trauma. This dangerous, potentially fatal, bleeding is known as a subdural hemorrhage.

When the liver is irritated, the levels of cholesterol and fatty acids increase in the bloodstream. Some of this fat is redeposited in the liver, causing further damage to liver functioning and leading to continuous cycles of dysfunction and repeated liver damage.

Still another important function of the liver is compromised by chronic alcoholism. As the blood circulates through the body, it passes through the liver just before it returns to the heart. When "fatty infiltration," scarring, and inflammation cause swelling of the liver tissue, this causes constriction of the veins going through it. The resulting backup pressure on these veins causes them to swell (dilate) and lose their function (a condition called varicose veins). The veins that are particularly vulnerable are those in the legs, esophagus, and rectum. (This vein swelling in the rectum causes hemorrhoids.) The increased backup pressure, together with the decreased albumen, leads to a back flow of fluids outside of the veins that leads, in turn, to swelling in the feet, hands, and abdomen. It also causes the veins in the esophagus to swell. These dilated veins in the esophagus are very vulnerable to hemorrhage because of stomach acid which is regurgitated over them. A ruptured esophageal vein (called varix) is an ominous sign because it is associated with an 85 percent death rate over a five-year period, if the person persists in drinking alcohol.

One other function of the liver affected by alcoholism is its role in detoxifying drugs and alcohol, as well as other body toxins. Ninety-five percent of alcohol is broken down to nonalcoholic substances by the liver. Tranquilizers and sedatives are also detoxified in the liver. When the liver fails, the body is unable to adequately detoxify these drugs, and it cannot digest dietary protein. When this occurs, hepatic encephalopathy (brain inflammation) can occur, which can progress to fatal brain dysfunction. When liver function breaks down to the point that alcohol detoxification is impaired, a reverse tolerance occurs. Alcohol then stays longer in the system so that progressively smaller amounts of it cause intoxication.

Cardiovascular and Circulatory (Blood) Systems

The Cardiovascular System: Alcoholics have twice as much cardiovascular disease as nonalcoholics. This, in part, is due directly to the toxic effects of alcohol on this system. It is also because of other health risk factors and behaviors seen in alcoholics, including: heavy smoking, poor nutrition, and physical inactivity.

Alcohol has several direct toxic effects on the heart. These harmful effects far outweigh any cardiac benefits from the relaxing effects of alcohol. Alcohol leads to an increase in fat uptake by the heart muscle and small blood vessels in the heart. This effect occurs even in the presence of adequate nutrition and results in severely inadequate cardiac functioning. Alcohol affects the mineral balance in heart tissue, causing vital potassium to leave the cells of the heart. Alcohol also causes inflammation of the heart (cardiomyopathy). This is due in part to alcohol's direct inflammatory effects on the small blood vessels of the heart. An alcohol intake level of six ounces a day for two or three years is necessary to produce cardiomyopathy in an individual who otherwise has no heart disease. As the effects of alcohol build up in the heart, the heart muscle weakens and less blood is pumped through the system. Alcoholic cardiomyopathy can be fatal.

Circulatory System: Other blood vessels in the body become dilated and congested from alcohol. These dilated blood vessels can be readily observed in the facial skin of alcoholics (see the section on "The Skin"). Blood vessel walls thicken and degenerate with chronic drinking. Circulation is slowed and blood stagnates. This results in inadequate cellular nutrition and leads ultimately to deterioration of body tissues.

Alcohol also causes the blood pressure to increase and is a very common cause of high blood pressure (hypertension).

Alcohol causes the body to produce unusually large red blood cells (macrocytosis), which leads to a type of anemia. Alcohol damages the cells of the bone marrow. In alcoholics who have a deficiency of folic acid, a megaloblastic anemia develops with abnormally shaped red blood cells. Alcohol can shorten the life of red blood cells by as much as half of normal, which also causes anemia. Alcohol leads to lower levels of platelets and vitamin K, which impairs blood clotting. This deficiency also increases bleeding from peptic ulcers and weakened veins in the esophagus.

Cancer and Infectious Disease

Studies of heavy drinkers show an increased risk of cancer of the mouth, pharynx, larynx, esophagus, lungs, breast, thyroid, and liver, as well as melanoma (skin cancer). There may also be an association between the incidence of future cancer in children and the alcohol consumed by their mothers during pregnancy. This may be the result of a direct damaging effect on the baby's developing cells.

Recent experiments at University of California, Berkeley, have produced some test-tube results that show that at concentrations produced by only a few drinks, alcohol triggers a chemical chain reaction that might alter the genetic material of living cells. These chemical changes may cause cancer and occur when alcohol combines with its chief byproduct, acetaldehyde, to act like known cancer-causing chemicals.

Infections and infectious diseases occur more frequently in alcoholics than in the general population, particularly tuberculosis and pneumonia. This is due to the fact that alcohol impairs the ability of white cells to surround and destroy bacteria which invade the body. However, these infections themselves are often a consequence of personal neglect, as well as the effects of alcohol on the liver which also impair the body's defense system.

Sleep

Alcohol reduces the amount of time spent in the stage of sleep in which dreams take place, known as stage I or REM (rapid eye movement). After about five days of alcohol intake, REM sleep returns to normal baseline levels. When alcohol intake stops, there is a delayed rebound of dreaming sleep. This rebound is prominent at the time when DTs occur and may be related to triggering DTs. Stage I is a necessary part of the restorative aspects of sleep. Without it, a person experiences daytime anxiety and restlessness. But these very symptoms are often relieved by alcohol, which is a good example of one of the many cycles of cause and effect that force the alcoholic back to alcohol.

Normal sleep patterns in alcoholics are disturbed during alcohol intake, withdrawal, and even after a long period of abstinence. Alcoholics have difficulty falling asleep without alcohol. Their sleep is restless and characterized by decreases in stage IV, deep sleep. Disturbing nightmares and other awakenings are common. At times nightmares seem to continue when the alcoholic is awake and may be experienced as hallucinations. Withdrawal from alcohol is almost always associated with insomnia for a few days, but it may last for weeks or months. Acute withdrawal is also associated with frightening dreams and hallucinations. Long after withdrawal, recovering alcoholics have decreased stage I sleep and disturbances in normal sleep cycle patterns.

Nutritional Deficiencies

Alcohol produces many harmful nutritional effects on the body. It may decrease appetite, replace other nutrients in the diet as a provider of "empty" calories, and diminish the body's absorption, use, and metabolism of essential vitamins, minerals, and protein. An interesting and alarming statistic shows that alcohol provides 12 percent of the total calories consumed in the typical American diet. This is the same amount of protein calories that Americans normally consume. The effects of nutritional disorders in alcoholics range from vitamin deficiencies to protein and calorie malnutrition. On the other hand, male alcoholics of high socioeconomic status are often obese, because of their tendency to combine food and drinking. Alcohol is very high in calories (seven per gram).

Small quantities of alcohol imbibed by nonalcoholics stimulate the appetite and enhance the flavor of food. However, larger amounts of alcohol often reduce hunger. In alcoholics, the desire for food is decreased by the calories taken in from alcohol as well as by the stomach upset often caused by drinking. In addition, alcoholics generally don't want to spoil the intoxicating effects they are experiencing, therefore they don't eat because food slows down the rate of intoxication.

Alcohol inactivates vitamin B_1 (thiamin) and vitamin B_6 (pyridoxine). Thiamin deficiency, in turn, causes poor appetite. Changes in the small intestine and reduction of digestive enzymes from the effects of alcohol impair the absorption of food and vitamins. This combination of effects frequently leads to nutritional and vitamin deficiencies in chronic alcoholics and to full-blown malnutrition in the most severe cases. Lack of thiamin causes the most common vitamin deficiencies seen in alcoholics, particularly a complex syndrome called Wernicke-Korsakoff's. The symptoms of this syndrome include mental confusion, difficulties in balance, paralysis of eye muscles, amnesia, and confabulation (making up the past in an attempt to compensate for and cover up amnesia). Pellagra and scurvy are two vitamin-deficiency diseases that are very rare in modern society, but are still seen in alcoholics.

Folate and pyridoxine deficiencies lead to anemia. Lack of magnesium causes tremors, convulsions, and mental confusion. Low zinc concentrations in the blood lead to dermatitis, poor wound healing, and a decrease in the sense of taste.

Muscles and Bones

Alcohol has toxic effects on the muscles that are unrelated to alcoholic-induced malnutrition. Most chronic alcoholics have abnormalities in muscle cells that can be measured by electrical impulses (electromyography) and half have muscle cell damage that can be observed under a microscope. But despite these test findings, some alcoholics have no overt symptoms of muscle inflammation, called myopathy. The first overt phase of myopathy involves muscle swelling and tenderness, breakdown of flank muscle tissue, muscle paralysis, and kidney failure due to deposits of muscle tissue substances in the kidney. In chronic myopathy, there is a muscular wasting, causing muscle weakness. These changes may result from the direct effects of alcohol on muscle cell membranes or from mineral and nutritional deficiencies that affect the muscles.

The effects of alcohol on the bones result indirectly and mainly from the alcoholic's vulnerability to trauma while intoxicated. These traumas include falls, automobile accidents, and assaults. More directly, however, there can be bone loss from alcohol intake that weakens bones and can lead to fractures of the neck or legs, and can also contribute to hip diseases.

The Skin

Alcohol's effects on the skin are very obvious. Almost half of those alcoholics whose condition is severe enough for them to be admitted to hospitals have some active skin disease. W. C. Fields' trademark was his reddened bulbous nose, an enlargement called rhinophyma that is actually rare in alcoholics but, thanks to Fields, has become a stereotypical sign of the "funny" drunk. Puffy facial swelling is much more common and is prominent around the eyes of the heavy drinker. The alcoholic's complexion is often washed out, pasty and gray or reddish. Acne is common but improves when drinking ceases. The appearance of many dilated capillaries over the face, particularly the ears, cheekbones, and tip of the nose, is common. Spider nevi are dilated larger vessels (arterioles) about one-half inch in diameter and are indicative of severe liver disease. The conjunctiva (whites) of the eyes may be yellowed or infected and reddened. Eyes may be glazed, with a dull flat look. The tongue is often smooth and covered with a thick coating as both mouth and tongue may be inflamed. Late-stage male alcoholics may develop a feminine skin hair pattern that is also related to endocrine changes discussed in the next section.

The Endocrine System and Reproductive Organs

Alcohol stimulates the hypothalamus gland, which, in turn, stimulates the pituitary gland and then the cortex of the adrenal gland. All of these glands are part of the endocrine system. There are direct immediate effects of alcohol on the endocrine system, as well as long-term effects resulting from alcoholism's effects on other organs like the liver. Acute alcohol intake actually affects all of the body's endocrine glands, leading to conditions such as increased blood sugar and increased urination. Many of the effects of alcohol on the endocrine system are the result of liver damage. Male patients with cirrhosis may have an increase in female hormone production, which leads to enlarged breasts.

Alcoholism diminishes the secretion of the male sex hormone called androgen and increases the manufacture of estrogens, which are female hormones. Because of this hormonal imbalance, alcoholics have smaller testicles and decreases in testosterone production. The demasculinization effects of this imbalance include decreased sex drive, impotence, and infertility. Feminization is seen with enlarged breasts, more feminine fat and hair distribution, and redness of the palms of the hands.

Acute and chronic alcohol intake are both detrimental to sperm production. These harmful effects include impairment in the number, shape, and mobility of the sperm.

Chronic alcoholics have increased adrenal gland function with increased steroid hormones in the system. This condition is also seen in individuals who are anxious or depressed. All of the endocrine glandular effects of alcohol, fortunately, are reversible when alcohol intake is stopped, as long as long-term cirrhosis is not present, in which case damage is irreversible.

Genitourinary System

Alcohol speeds up urine production and excretion, causing dehydration. Beer, which advertising glorifies and our society values as a desirable thirst quencher at picnics and sporting events, rapidly leaves the drinkers thirstier than they were before they began working on the keg or six-pack. Alcohol is an irritant to the kidneys, which leads to loss of albumen (previously discussed in the section on "The Digestive System"). When the BAL starts to decrease, the brain secretes an antidiuretic hormone that causes body tissues to swell and retain fluids. Alcohol causes swelling of the kidneys, followed by fatty degeneration. The lining of the urinary bladder is also inflamed by alcohol. This irritation interferes with the bladder's ability to stretch, leading to frequent urination involving small amounts of urine.

In men, the prostate gland is also irritated by alcohol and becomes inflamed and swollen (prostatitis). This swelling narrows the passageway from the bladder, leading to difficulties in emptying the bladder. This swelling also affects the ability to have and maintain an erection. Prostatic swelling may interfere with the ability to climax during intercourse. As is well known, alcohol first stimulates the desire for sex, then rapidly leads to an inability to perform sexually.

The Brain and Nervous System

Those parts of the brain that have most recently developed from an evolutionary standpoint and are the brain's higher functions, like judgment and self-control, are the most sensitive to the effects of alcohol. Alcohol has direct damaging effects on the brain and nervous system. Chronic alcoholics show considerable brain shrinkage when their computerized tomographic (CT) scans are compared with those of nondrinkers. Some brain shrinkage is even seen in heavy social drinkers.

Brain damage in alcoholics is also consistently demonstrated by tests that evaluate neuropsychological impairment. These tests show impairment in the following areas: cognition, visual-motor speed, short term memory, and abstraction, but they do reveal normal tests of language function. The latter normal test may very well help the alcoholic to fool him or herself and others about his or her brain damage. The decline of blood flow to the brain that normally occurs with aging is accelerated in chronic alcoholics. Blood flow to more highly developed areas of the brain, such as the frontal cortex, is more affected than other areas.

There is a progressive decline in mental functioning in chronic alcoholics. This decline is first seen only in neuropsychological test batteries. Later it can be seen in routine psychiatric mental status examinations and on CT scans. All of these changes may partially resolve and return to normal after several years without drinking. Rarely does this brain damage progress to a full dementia (irreversible, severe deterioration of brain functioning). Other dementias associated with vitamin deficiencies such as Wernicke-Korsakoff's and pellagra were described in the section on nutrition in this chapter.

A number of other effects of alcoholism on the brain occur secondarily through the effects of alcohol on other organs. The prime example of this is impaired mental functioning as a result of liver disease. This results when, because of severe liver disease and/or backup pressure in the blood vessels, high levels of substances containing nitrogen reach the brain. The symptoms of this disorder, which is called hepatic encephalopathy, include: deterioration of mental functions ranging from mild to extreme; neurological signs, particularly tremors; and coma, which can result in death.

As a result of frequently reckless life-styles and the symptoms of alcoholism, alcoholics are vulnerable to a host of events that lead to brain damage from trauma. These include seizures, falls, assaults, and motor vehicle accidents.

Alcohol also affects the peripheral and autonomic nervous systems. Peripheral nervous system disease is common in chronic alcoholics and is characterized by diminished reflexes and sensation, and the impairment of motor functions such as walking and lifting. Antabuse® can also cause peripheral nerve disease, which is reversible by stopping intake. Autonomic nervous system (ANS) impairment caused by alcoholism may lead to an inability to sweat in affected local areas. Other symptoms of ANS dysfunction that are seen in chronic alcoholics include impotence and lowered blood pressure upon rapidly standing up, which can cause fainting.

This chapter has summarized the myriad variety of harmful effects of alcohol on the body. It is difficult to read this information without becoming wary of taking even a single drink. Given the predictable and understandable damaging effects of alcohol, it is surprising how many alcoholics show so few or even none of these damaging physiologic signs. This common lack of visible damage and impairment should not be used to deny the existence of alcoholism, particularly if other signs are present.

It is hoped that the spouse (or any co-dependent) of a male alcoholic will find this information useful without feeling pressure to assume responsibility for the alcoholic's health. However, any of the signs and symptoms of chronic alcoholism that have been described are certainly grounds for an immediate comprehensive treatment of the disease of alcoholism. How to help the alcoholic or abuser of chemicals admit his disease and obtain that treatment is the major topic of the rest of this book.

▽   ▽   ▽

References

Fort, J. *Alcohol: Our Biggest Drug Problem*. McGraw-Hill, New York. 1973.

Pattison, E.M., & Kaufman, E. *Encyclopedic Handbook of Alcoholism*. Gardner Press, New York. 1982.

Ritchie, J.M. The aliphatic alcohols. In A.G. Goodman, L.S. Goodman, T.W. Tall, & Murad, F. *ThePharmacologic Basis of Therapeutics*. Macmillan, New York, 1985, pp. 372-386.

Schneider, M. Some medical aspects of alcohol and other drugs of abuse, Max A. Schneider, M.D., Education Division, Santa Ana, Calif., 1985.

Tabakoff, B. Alcohol, drugs, and primary care: Physican education. *Substance Abuse*, 8(1):15-21, 1986.

Table 1
The Physical Effects of Alcohol on the Body

	ORGAN	SHORT TERM	LONG TERM
DIGESTIVE SYSTEM	Stomach	Heartburn, gastritis, vomiting	Bleeding ulcer, aspiration, pneumonia, death
	Esophagus	Heartburn	Esophageal ulcers
	Pancreas	Acute inflammation	Pancreatitis, diabetes
	Liver	Hepatitis	Cirrhosis, edema, decreased blood clotting, increased blood cholesterol
	Liver veins	Increased pressure	Dilated/ruptured veins in legs and esophagus
CIRCULATORY SYSTEM	Heart	Mild relaxation	Heart inflammation, increased fat uptake
	Small blood vessels		Widen and stagnate
	Blood Pressure	Mild to moderate increase	Hypertension
	Red cells		Enlarged, emptier cells
	Platelets		Decreased clotting

CANCER		Increase in mouth, larynx, esophagus, lung, breast, thyroid melanoma
SLEEP	Decreased dreaming stage	Marked general disturbance
NUTRITION	"Empty calories"	Thiamine and B_6 deficiency, protein, calorie malnutrition
MUSCLES AND BONES		Increased fractures, inflammation
SKIN	Flushing	Dilated capillaries, ruptured small vessels
ENDOCRINE GLANDS	Increased blood sugar and urination	Decreased androgen, increased estrogen
GENITOURINARY TRACT	Kidney irritation, bladder irritation, prostatic irritation	Swelling, degeneration of kidneys, cystitis, prostatis
NERVOUS SYSTEM	Decreased inhibition, normal language, inflammation of nerves	Brain shrinkage, decreased cognition and abstraction, muscle weakness and atrophy, decreased sensation

C H A P T E R

3

Recognizing the Effects of Commonly Abused Drugs

*I*n this chapter the most common and widely used drugs of abuse are described within the context of six separate categories as defined by pharmacologists: (1) narcotics, (2) stimulants, (3) depressants (sedative hypnotics and minor tranquilizers), (4) hallucinogens, (5) marijuana, and (6) inhalents (see Table 1 in this chapter for a summary of the effects of these drugs). A seventh section covers "look-alikes," designer drugs, OTC drugs, and drug combinations.

Knowledge of these drugs and their physiological effects is essential in understanding the risks of drug use and abuse. Just the physical consequences alone of using these drugs are often devastating. However, awareness of these far-reaching results should not serve as justification for the family to become or remain overinvolved in protecting the drug abuser from the consequences of his own actions. Rather, this knowledge should be used to help the family recognize and understand the range of issues involved in substance abuse. Once recognized, the family has the choice of responding in constructive and appropriate ways by implementing the intervention and coping strategies described in this book.

The focus here is on signs and symptoms of drug use, abuse and intoxication, dependence, withdrawal, medical complications, and pharmacological (drug) treatments of abuse and overdose. This last topic, which includes the substances customarily used in detoxification of the various drugs, is described more fully in Chapter 9.

The legal definition of cocaine as a narcotic is somewhat confusing. For our purposes, we use a pharmacologic definition of a narcotic instead, which focuses only on drugs that relieve pain and cause drowsiness. Therefore, cocaine appears in the discussion of the stimulant drugs to which it is pharmacologically related.

Narcotics

When we think of people with narcotic problems, most of us immediately visualize the hardcore heroin addict. Although hardcore heroin addicts receive the most publicity among users of narcotics, many narcotic abusers do not fall into that category, but instead are individuals who appear to be functioning well in middle- and upper-class households and occupations. This is particularly true of users and abusers of prescription narcotic drugs such as codeine, Darvon® (propoxyphene)*, and Talwin® (pentazocine). Heavy abusers of stronger narcotics such as methadone (dolphine), Demerol® (meperidine), Dilaudid® (hydromorphone), Vicodin® (hydrocodone), and Percodan® (oxycodone) fall somewhere between heroin addicts and abusers of milder narcotics in their adoption of a stereotypical hardcore, heroin-oriented life style. Recently, the spread of cocaine sales into the middle and upper classes has also introduced these social classes to heroin, which is often sold by the same pushers who sell cocaine.

A new form of heroin, called "black tar," is produced in northern Mexico. Black tar is up to 40 times more potent than usual street heroin and consequently is exceedingly habit forming and dangerous. Even mild drugs like Paregoric® and Lomotil® (diphenoxylate) are narcotics that are potentially addicting.

Some individuals are introduced to prescription narcotics by physicians and become addicted after surgery or painful medical problems. Heroin addicts tend to progress from tobacco, marijuana, alcohol, and inhalents to heroin as a result of strong peer influences in their teens. Abusers of strong prescription narcotics like Demerol® and Percodan® may follow either the medical introduction or peer influence route. Methadone abusers are mainly individuals who have previously used or been dependent on heroin and, having experienced the potency of pure methadone during detoxification or methadone maintenance treatment, wind up addicted to the treatment agent. Although methadone does not lead to as intense a high as heroin, its effects are longer acting and withdrawal is more gradual.

Signs and Symptoms of Use and Abuse

All narcotic drugs have three basic effects; analgesic, soporific, and euphoriant. Therefore, individuals under the influence of these drugs will have a higher tolerance for pain, will feel sleepy or drowsy, and will have a false sense of well-being.

---

*The names that appear in parentheses after trade names used throughout this book are the generic, pharmacologic names for these drugs. Trade names are always followed by an ®.

Physiological Effects and Dependence

Generally speaking, narcotics are addicting after two to four weeks at the level ordinarily prescribed to relieve pain (e.g., three to four 30 mg codeine or 65 mg Darvon® tablets daily). As a rule, addicted individuals increase their dosage after the first month.

Narcotics directly stimulate a trigger zone in the brain that initially causes nausea and vomiting. Most individuals experience these unpleasant side effects the first time they take narcotics. With such objectionable side effects, it requires a good deal of peer support and positive expectations to be willing to try taking narcotics again. Narcotics trigger the release of a chemical in the body called histamine, which is responsible for allergies and causes itching and sensualized scratching, redness of the eyes, and lowered blood pressure.

The central nervous system (CNS) is depressed by narcotic use, leading to a decreased cough reflex, drowsiness, and impaired breathing. Pupils become small, even in the dark. Narcotics cause constipation and difficulty in starting urination. Although tolerance is built up to the euphoriant effects of narcotics, little tolerance to their constipating and pupillary constricting effects occurs. The rush or initial euphoria lasts for a few minutes after intravenous use. After oral use, the onset of effects take longer—and they last longer—but they are less intense. This stage is followed by a pleasant "nodding" drowsiness with magical dreams and fantasies interrupted by frequent awakenings. The intoxicated state for most narcotics lasts three to six hours.

Psychological States† and Behaviors

Narcotics rapidly relieve worries and anxieties. They frequently are used to wipe out anxieties about assertion and socializing. The rush or high from intravenous (IV) use feels warm and powerful and has been descibed by addicts as equivalent to a sexual orgasm. Narcotics create a basic state of placid, "homeostatic" organization that helps the user feel content, integrated, and centered. Narcotics initially slow down or prevent ejaculation, which may, in part, explain their use by young men who are troubled by premature ejaculations. However, after addiction is well established, the sexual drive diminishes almost totally.

Certain specific behavioral changes occur in individuals who become dependent on the narcotic drugs. They are easily frustrated and lose interest in people except as providers of drugs or the money to purchase them. They manipulate others, using whatever means they can to get their way and they

---

†How the drug is experienced in the mind.

have a distorted view of the world in which drugs are the only priority. Narcotics users are also quite self-destructive.

Since these behaviors are frequently seen in people addicted to narcotics, it is difficult to determine the extent to which these personality characteristics may have already existed prior to drug use and abuse. Narcotics serve to wipe out severe buried or overt anger. Although use of narcotics generally dampens emotions, the drug can sometimes have an activating or agitating effect. Thus, part of continued narcotic use involves blotting out of emotional states.

Withdrawal

As with any drug, a dependent person experiencing withdrawal from narcotics exhibits behavior marked by frantic, desperate, manipulative attempts aimed at obtaining the drug of choice or a suitable substitute. Withdrawal begins as soon as intoxication ends, peaking at 36 to 72 hours (the cycle is longer with methadone). Physiological withdrawal symptoms include runny nose and eyes, and excessive perspiration. Yawning is frequent when awake, yet sleep is restless and unrefreshing. The user's skin feels prickly, which is known as goose or turkey flesh (the origin of the term "cold turkey"). The CNS rebounds from the depressing effects of the drug, causing reverse symptoms of dilated pupils, and higher pulse and blood pressure, involuntary muscular twitching, and kicking (the origin of "kicking the habit"). Tremors or shaking, severe muscle pains, and cramps in the abdomen, legs, and back are quite common. Although the acute stage of withdrawal is over in a week, an extended withdrawal persists that can last six to 12 months. This prolonged withdrawal can be documented by continued changes in blood pressure, pulse, body temperature, and sleep patterns. If not attended to and treated, the effects of withdrawal can drive an individual back to drugs to relieve the physical discomfort even in the absence of craving the drug. Craving, however, may last a lifetime.

Former addicts rapidly develop tolerance to, and dependence on, narcotics when they are taken for any purpose. These are among the many reasons why former narcotic addicts must fight to stay off of drugs every day for the rest of their lives. Former addicts can be given narcotic drugs in appropriate doses for medical reasons, as in a postsurgical state, but caution should always be exercised. In such cases, physicians must be made aware of the past history of addiction.

Medical Complications

In their pure, unadulterated state, narcotics cause fewer damaging effects to the body than other classes of drugs, with the notable exceptions of the effects of coma and lethal overdoses. High doses may cause pulmonary edema (fluid backup in the lungs), which is often fatal. Respiratory depression and coma, as a result of narcotic overdose, are associated with a diminished oxygen supply to the brain. This can lead to chronic brain damage with diminished mental functioning.

Most of the long-term, negative physical effects of heroin are actually related to the use of contaminated needles for IV use of the drug, rather than the drug itself. The difficulties associated with contaminated needles are almost too numerous to mention. Liver infections (hepatitis) occur in 80 percent of IV heroin addicts. In my study of Ivy League university student heroin addicts, I found that they had all contracted hepatitis from repeatedly using dirty needles. Heroin addicts often have false-positive blood tests for syphilis which is related to the effects of hepatitis on the testing process.

In IV users, veins become irritated from frequent injections and grow scarred and thickened. As a result, bluish-black, hard raised streaks, known as "tracks" occur on the skin over the veins. Tracks are most frequently seen on the inner bend of the elbow, but they can be found anywhere, including on the hands, feet, back of the knees, penis, or over the jugular vein in the neck. Abscesses can form over the site of intravenous or subcutaneous (just below the skin) injections. The veins themselves can become infected (thrombophlebitis), which leads to a common complication where lumps of bacteria and debris, called emboli, break off and circulate in the bloodstream. The emboli may lead to clots in the brain and strokes, or to clots on the heart valve that lead to infections of the inner lining of the heart (endocarditis).

Very serious infections in the bloodstream (septicemia) may also result from contaminated needles. Tetanus, malaria, and AIDS (acquired immune deficiency syndrome) are also commonly transmitted to IV drug users through unsterile needles. AIDS is plaguing heroin addicts throughout the country and in New York City it has already reached epidemic proportions. Two formerly rare diseases are being increasingly seen in IV heroin addicts: fatal kidney failure following a rapid breakdown of muscle tissue, and severe progressive Parkinson's disease. The latter is associated with the use of the designer drug MPTP, which is marketed as synthetic heroin or "china white."

Pharmacologic Treatments of Abuse and Overdose

The administration of Narcan® (naloxone) is the usual treatment for narcotic overdoses. This is a specific antidote because of its narcotic antagonist effects. However, its effects last only two to three hours whereas the effects of most narcotics last for three to six hours and the effects of methadone last for 24 hours. Thus, someone suffering a narcotics overdose may initially appear to recover after the administration of Narcan®, but then sink back into fatal coma.

Detoxification is done by administering methadone in special programs only, or by clonidine, a non-narcotic substance that is effective but not addicting. Methadone maintenance and narcotic antagonist administration may be very helpful if accompanied by a full range of other treatments. Methadone maintenance often lasts for several years. Methadone detoxification usually only lasts for 21 days. New legislation encourages an intermediate form of methadone maintenance of 180 days' duration, which presents a viable alternative to long-term maintenance. Naltrexone, which blocks the high of narcotics without inducing euphoria, can also be used to facilitate rehabilitation.

Stimulants

Caffeine is the most commonly used and abused stimulant in our society, but the two major stimulants generally associated with drug abuse are cocaine and amphetamines. These two drugs have very similar behavioral effects as they both stimulate the CNS and the sympathetic nervous system (SNS). However, there is no cross-tolerance between the amphetamines and cocaine, implying that each of these drugs has separate and unrelated receptor sites in the brain. The main physiologic difference between the two drugs lies in the fact that a physiologic tolerance rapidly and consistently develops with the use of amphetamines, but is irregular with cocaine use.

Before the major abuse stimulants are discussed, a few words about caffeine are indicated in light of its widespread presence in popular beverages and foods. Caffeine is ubiquitously found in coffee, tea, and soft drinks, as well as, to a lesser extent, in food products containing chocolate. Psychological dependence and tolerance both occur with the use of caffeine. "Caffeinism" or excessive caffeine intake is associated with anxiety, irritability, agitation, lethargy, and headache, all of which are relieved by ingesting more caffeine. Caffeine withdrawal leads to headache and depression. Caffeine use can lead to medical complications, including stomach and heart problems. It is strongly advisable that decaffeinated beverages be substituted if any medical or psychological problems arise.

Cocaine

For centuries, Peruvian natives have been chewing cocoa leaves to increase their energy and tolerance for hard labor at high-mountain altitudes where they live and work. For the same general reasons, cocaine was an active ingredient in CocaCola from 1896 to 1903 at a time when it was thought to be relatively harmless.

Sigmund Freud experimented with the drug on himself and attempted to use it to treat opiate dependence and depression in others. Like many present-day users of cocaine, Freud described the exhilaration and euphoria, the ability to work without food and sleep, and the aphrodisiac effects of the drug. Freud's infatuation with cocaine came to an end when he realized his own psychological dependence. However, he deleted any reference to his use of cocaine from his autobiography. Today, cocaine's only accepted use is as a topical anesthetic. Unfortunately, its medical availability is one factor that helps make it a common drug of abuse among physicians and nurses. Despite the vast amount of cocaine being used in the United States, relatively few addicted individuals sought treatment until very recently. Over the past few years, more and more cocaine-dependent individuals have entered treatment. Cocaine is now the fourth most common drug of abuse in our society. As more individuals use cocaine, an increasing number encounter serious problems. Deaths from cocaine are skyrocketing. Fortunately, effective methods for treatment of cocainism are just evolving. Two helpful, recent adjuncts are the national hotline for referrals (800-COCAINE) and CA (Cocaine Anonymous).

Amphetamines

The first evidence that amphetamines were being abused in this country appeared in about 1935 when they were readily extracted from OTC nasal inhalers. Until about 1976, amphetamines in pill form were widely prescribed by physicians for appetite suppression and weight loss. However, tolerance to this effect of the drug develops rapidly, leading those who take the pills to increase their dosage and eventually to abuse. As a result of physician education and legislation, this use of amphetamines has been gradually eliminated. Amphetamines are available as Benzedrine® (amphetamine), Dexedrine® (dextroamphetamine), and methamphetamine or Desoxyn® (methadrine). Methadrine is often used intranasally or intravenously by addicts. Ritalin® (methylphenidate) and Preludin (phenmetrazine) can be as dangerous as amphetamines, particularly if the user erroneously assumes that they are relatively safe. Several recently developed appetite suppressants have similar effects—and only slightly less abuse potential. These include Tenuate® , Plegine®, Presate®, Didrex®, Ionimine®, Voranil®, Sanorex®, and Apidex®. Amphetamines and other stimulates are addicting in doses over 30 mg daily for more than two weeks. Amphetamine addicts often use over 2,000 mg a day!

Signs and Symptoms of Use and Abuse
(Including Physiological Effects)

In low doses, both of the major stimulant drugs cause a euphoria (a heightened, and often false, sense of well-being). Both cocaine and the amphetamines stimulate the SNS, which governs "fight or flight" responses. In moderate doses, there is an elevation of blood pressure, increased blood sugar, a rise in respiration rate, and heightened alertness and vigilance. There is improved concentration and decreased fatigue and boredom, along with the mild euphoria, increased sociability, and increased talking. Both drugs dilate pupils, and cocaine raises body temperature. On the other hand, the drugs can cause irritation, restlessness, insomnia, heart palpitations, confusion, and even violence. When ingested nasally, cocaine causes a numbness and tingling in the mouth.

In higher doses, commonly observed effects are confusion, panic, paranoia, extreme violence, and hallucinations. Amphetamines tend to lead more often to full-blown schizophrenic psychosis, a mental disorder marked by paranoid delusions and a retreat from reality. Cocaine tends to produce a more pure paranoid state, characterized by abnormal feelings of persecution and mistrust. Irregular heart beat and epileptic-type seizures occur more commonly with cocaine.

Individuals who inject cocaine intravenously can experience all of the difficulties and medical complications associated with contaminated needles that were described in the section on heroin use. The effects of intoxication with IV use of cocaine are very similar to those seen with smoking cocaine paste or the free-base form of cocaine.

A form of base called "crack" first gained popularity in 1985. Crack is a potent, extremely dangerous and relatively inexpensive form of cocaine. Immediately following IV use or base (crack) smoking, there is an intense euphoric "rush" and then about 20 minutes of arousal. This stage is followed by restlessness and an uncomfortable mood, which lead to repeated ingestion every five to 20 minutes in order to recapture the euphoria.

Base smokers may have specific, unique symptoms related to the smoking process, including coughing and a black or bloody expectorate, dry lips, excessive thirst, and a weak, wispy voice. Other signs of base smoking are related to the process of preparation and smoking, which involves using ammonia, flammable solvents, and heating with torches and lighters. During this preparation process there may be chemical burns, fires, and explosions. Deep inhalation techniques that are used to reach very high cocaine blood levels may result in breathing difficulties. Many physiologic problems associated with base smoking are similar to those seen with nasally ingested cocaine. However, the very high blood levels of cocaine achieved from smoking result in much greater anxiety, paranoia, and addiction.

Psychological States and Behaviors

At low to average doses, the stimulants often lead to a powerful euphoria, with increased self-confidence and enhanced self-image. Users experience high levels of alertness, energy, and attention. There is decreased appetite and diminished need for sleep along with a postponement of fatigue. Individuals on stimulants feel active, powerful, arrogant, and talkative. Sensory awareness generally increases. Sexuality is initially stimulated, with free access to primitive, varied, often perverse fantasies that are frequently acted out with a cocaine-using partner. Conversely, after chronic use sets in, sexuality becomes unimportant and impotence and frigidity are common. Even at low doses, many individuals experience a combination of both pleasurable and uncomfortable effects. Undesirable effects include anger, anxiety, insomnia, a desire to commit aggressive acts, suspiciousness, and paranoia.

At moderate doses, the negative and undesirable psychological effects of stimulant use begin to outweigh the positive, with increased irritation, restlessness, anxiety, confusion, and paranoia. Self-confidence turns into megalomania, a grossly exaggerated feeling of self-worth and importance.

There is a limit to how much the CNS can be overstimulated by stimulant drugs. There comes a point when depression, fatigue, and loss of motivation eventually set in. As the CNS rebounds after prolonged use, the individual on cocaine or amphetamines will often go into an extended period of sleep ("crash"). With high doses of stimulants, we often see panic, delirium (a confused state of intoxication), homicidal rage, paranoia with delusions of persecution or grandiosity, visual and auditory hallucinations, and a syndrome, or cluster of symptoms, indistinguishable from true schizophrenia. In some cases, this drug-induced schizophrenia is irreversible. However, it is doubtful that stimulants cause schizophrenia in people who do not have a hereditary predisposition toward that disease.

Dependence and Withdrawal

There is no question that rapid physiologic tolerance develops with amphetamine use. Amphetamine users soon need to increase their dosage in order to counteract tolerance and again achieve many of the drug's desired effects ranging from appetite control to euphoria. When the drug dose is increased, so too is the risk of experiencing anxiety and paranoia. Users of high doses of amphetamines are prone to violence because of these high-dosage effects. In Japan, shortly after World War II, more than half of all murders committed in the country were related to rampant amphetamine use.

Because the withdrawal syndrome from amphetamines is mild compared with many other drugs, its addictive properties were once minimized. However, there is a definite withdrawal syndrome from amphetamines with the following symptoms: insomnia with restless sleep and nightmares, or a prolonged sleep of up to 24 hours; headaches; hot and cold sweats; muscle cramps; and feeling fatigued yet at the same time being jumpy. Brain waves are abnormal during amphetamine withdrawal but return to normal when amphetamines are used again.

Cocaine is unique among drugs for several reasons. It is the most psychologically addicting of all abuse drugs yet there is little of the tolerance associated with other powerful drugs and physical withdrawal is minimal. However, cocaine is so psychologically addicting that most cocaine users cannot turn down progressively higher doses. Given free access, most cocaine users would never stop.

In dramatic laboratory experiments, monkeys were subjected to a variety of commonly abused drugs that they could self-administer at will. The only drug that they self-administered until they died was cocaine. Despite suffering horribly painful symptoms in the process, including self-mutilation, convulsions, and collapse of the cardiovascular system, these monkeys used cocaine in a frenzy that finally proved to be fatal.

One reason that cocaine is particularly addicting is the misleading and dangerous myth that it is not habit forming. The myth of controlled use is a totally unrealistic and frightening aspect of cocaine use. Dr. Mark Gold has labeled the cocaine user's belief in his or her ability to control cocaine use, "the cocaine delusion." The high monetary cost of cocaine is the one aspect that may serve as a deterrent to using progressively more and more cocaine, just like the doomed monkeys.

It is not unusual for a cocaine user who inherits a large sum of money to find that it is gone in no time at all. Even a million dollars can be lost in a few months. Wealthy cocaine users talk frequently of how many Rolls Royces they have snorted up their noses.

The issue of tolerance to cocaine is controversial. In animals, a definite tolerance to the physical effects of cocaine exists, evidenced in laboratory experiments. In human chronic cocaine users, a kind of reverse tolerance can occur. This may occur with long-term use, when progressively lower doses of the drug are necessary to achieve euphoric effects. This phenomenon may be the result of a depletion of the brain's neurotransmitters (natural antidepressants), causing a lowered threshold to the effects of cocaine as well as a depressed state. This reverse tolerance phenomenon can be misleading if interpreted as an indication of the safety of cocaine.

The physical withdrawal from cocaine is also comparatively minimal, but it is greater with free-base and IV use. Withdrawal symptoms include: anxiety, insomnia, paranoia, depression, fatigue, sweating, chills, nausea, and vomiting. It is interesting to note that anxiety and paranoia occur during withdrawal as well as during intoxication.

Medical Complications

The medical complications of amphetamine use have been known for some time. In high doses, amphetamines can cause headaches, chest pain, irregular heart beat, collapse of the cardiovascular system, and coma. "Meth is death" was a drug culture phrase of the late 1960s that reflected the popular attitudes about the drug that helped to reduce the widespread abuse of methamphetamine, which is a form of amphetamine. Amphetamines do cause brain damage with prolonged use and, as mentioned previously, can precipitate or mimic paranoid schizophrenia. This brain damage may occur as a result of drug-induced high blood pressure, a direct effect of amphetamines on brain cells, or from direct damage to blood vessels in the brain. Cocaine also leads to brain damage, caused by increases in blood pressure and spasms of blood vessels.

Another common, though recently dispelled, myth about cocaine use was that it was relatively free of medical complications. The most common medical effects of cocaine are the toxic effects on the nasal area produced by ''snorting'' the drug through the nose, where inflammations (rhinitis) are caused. Over time there is erosion of the mucous membrane in the nose and ultimately perforation of the nasal septum (wall) between the nostrils. These holes in the septum can be repaired with plastic surgery, but not without a great deal of difficulty. Chronic cocaine use leads to marked weight loss, pale sweaty skin, dehydration, and a fine tremor or quivering. The complications of needle use and the pulmonary difficulties attributed to smoking the base form of the drug have already been discussed. Long-term base smoking can also lead to bronchitis. Cocaine stimulates the heart so that it beats faster and, at times, irregularly. This may lead to the heart actually stopping and to death unless there is immediate medical care. Death from cocaine overdose may also occur due to a rebound failure of the heart to function following overstimulation of the cardiovascular, respiratory, or central nervous system.

There is recent evidence that cocaine can cause long-term as well as acute heart disease. Grand mal (epileptic) seizures can result from cocaine use, as can hallucinations, like the sensation of bugs on the skin. In rare cases, grand mal seizures become repetitive and can be fatal. Irreversibly high body temperature may occur, which can also be fatal.

Pharmacologic Treatments of Abuse

No drugs are necessary to facilitate withdrawal from the stimulant drugs per se, although Valium® or Ativan® may be used to ease the crash. The abuse of stimulants exhausts the body's own supply of natural antidepressants through overstimulation. Antidepressant drugs such as Tofranil® (imipramine) or Norpramine® (desipramine) have been used with little success for some years. However, recently there has been a new wave of successful treatment with antidepressants. It now appears that imipramine and desipramine may even block the craving for cocaine. Part of the recent success of antidepressants may be due to several physicians having combined them with precursors of brain neurotransmitters (L-tyrosine and L-tryptophan) along with comprehensive treatment. Ritalin® has also been used with some success in treating cocaine addicts, but only those who were hyperactive as children. Lithium® may also be helpful, particularly in treating those suffering from true mood cycles (bipolar affective or manic-depressive disease).

Depressants: Sedative-Hypnotics and Minor Tranquilizers

These drugs are grouped together because of their many similarities, including medical usage, pharmacological effects, psychological experience, cross-tolerance, mode of abuse, dependence syndrome, and withdrawal symptoms. Alcohol can also be included here because of its similar basic effect on the CNS.

Most individuals who are dependent on these drugs have become so after first having them prescribed by a physician. At times they are purchased on the street illegally where they may have been redirected from legitimate pharmaceutical companies or illegally manufactured.

The drugs that fall into this category include the barbiturates, the potent barbiturate-like substitutes, and the benzodiazapines. Barbiturates may be short acting like Amytal® (amobarbital), Seconal® (secobarbital), and Nembutal® (pentobarbital), or long acting like phenobarbital.

The barbiturate-like substitutes were developed as drugs that were supposedly safer and had less abuse potential than the barbiturates. Ironically, however, they have been found to be even less safe and to have a much greater abuse potential than barbiturates themselves. These substitutes include Doriden® (glutethimide), Noludan® (methyprylon), Placidy® (ethchlorvynol), and Quaalude® (methaqualone).

The benzodiazepines include Librium® (chlordiazepoxide), Valium® (diazepam), Tranxene® (clorazepate), Dalmane® (flurazepam), Serax® (oxazepam), Ativan® (lorazepam), and Xanax® (alprazolam). Two other drugs also in this class are Equanil® (meprobamate) and Noctec® (chloral hydrate).

Signs and Symptoms of Use and Abuse

The drugs in this pharamacologic category act as depressants on the CNS. They cause slowed thought, speech, and comprehension. Speech is slurred and balance is affected. Memory and judgment are also impaired, and emotions change quickly with easily triggered crying, laughing, anger, paranoia, and suicidal thoughts. Rapid, repetitive eye movements (nystagmus) are often present, though drowsiness and sleepiness occur, which can lead to accidents. All of these drugs reduce the ability to make accurate judgments and decrease the ability to control body movements.

Physiological Effects

Early toxic symptoms include mild nystagmus (rapid eye movements), drowsiness, and loss of fine balance. With greater degrees of toxicity, nystagmus is more obvious and drowsiness is more marked, and walking turns into a stumbling gait (ataxia). At still higher doses, breathing and blood circulation are impaired. At this point, the toxic effects on these vital body functions can progress rapidly to coma and death.

Psychological States and Behaviors

The wide popularity of the sedative-hypnotic and minor tranquilizer drugs is a result of their ability to relieve anxiety and provide a sense of well-being. Like alcohol, the sedatives may initially produce behavioral excitation, stimulation, and lack of inhibition rather than the usual sedation effect. This "high" is a result of a release of inhibitions, which varies with the personality of the user and the expectation of the drug's effects. For example, if the expectation is sleep, drowsiness sets in. If the person is at a party and expects a euphoric state, then inhibitions are lowered and a high is experienced. By reducing restraint and lowering inhibitions, these drugs also provide a kind of false courage that permits a release of aggression and anger. Sedative drugs obliterate pain, and feelings of loss and failure, and may neutralize the user's feelings of rage, shame, and jealousy. They decrease sexual inhibitions but, once drowsiness or tolerance develops, sexuality greatly diminishes. They alleviate anxiety about self-assertion, particularly with authorities at work. They have been known to increase depression, and their psychological effects are similar to alcohol and narcotics in that they depress the CNS. All of these drugs severely impair a person's ability to operate machinery or drive a car.

Dependence

Dependence occurs whenever an individual regularly exceeds the therapeutic dose level of a sedative-hypnotic or minor tranquilizer or combines it with other CNS depressants, particularly alcohol. Dependence may even occur over a period as short as two to four weeks at doses normally prescribed by physicians. Placidyl® is marketed in a therapeutic dosage as high as 750 mg in a single capsule with 1,000 mg being the minimal addicting dose. Valium®, frequently prescribed by physicians at doses of 40 mg daily, may be addicting at doses as low as 10 or 15 mg daily, particularly with long-term use. Xanax® (alprazolam), now widely prescribed for anxiety, panic disorders, and depression, is the fourth most prescribed drug in the United States, and may be even more addicting than Valium® at doses of only 2–4 mg daily.

Early signs of the dependence syndrome to these drugs are anxiety and irritability, which can progress to aggressive, destructive behavior. Most individuals who are dependent will occasionally appear intoxicated, particularly when they increase their dose as dependent individuals invariably do.

One serious problem with the sedative drugs is that because of the grogginess they produce, it is easy to forget how many pills have been taken. It is common for sedative-abusing individuals to repeatedly take "just" a few more pills with a few more drinks and to lapse into a coma that may be irreversible and prove fatal.

One reason that dependence on these drugs is so widespread is that sedatives and tranquilizers, particularly benzodiazepines, are so readily available in our society. Given that hundreds of millions of these drugs are legally prescribed by physicians and that tolerance builds up so rapidly, it is surprising that dependence and abuse are not even more common. Even if a person is not prone to drug and alcohol abuse, no drug in this category should be taken for more than a few weeks at a time because of the inherent difficulty involved in stopping use.

Withdrawal

Mild or early symptoms of withdrawal from depressant drugs include anxiety, weakness, hand or body tremors, dizziness (from a drop in blood pressure), hyperactivity, nausea, cramps, vomiting, hyperactive reflexes, insomnia, and nightmares. With shorter-acting drugs like secobarbital, withdrawal symptoms begin 12 to 24 hours after use is stopped and are over in about three days. With longer-acting drugs like Valium®, withdrawal may not begin for two to three days after ending use and it may last seven to 14 days. Some individuals seem to have even longer periods of withdrawal symptoms that are actually related to a return of the anxiety for which the drugs were originally taken, rather than true withdrawal. However, prolonged physiologic withdrawal of several months' duration is also common, particularly after long periods of use and abuse.

More severe symptoms that tend to occur from one to seven days after use is stopped include confusion, muscle spasms, and epileptic-type seizures. Seizures can also occur as late as 14 to 30 days after cessation of use, but in these cases there may be a preexisting, underlying seizure disorder. In three to seven days, delirium may result, much like the delirium tremens of alcohol withdrawal. This often follows one to two days of poor sleep. In this state of delirium, the addict is quite confused about the realities of time, place, and person. The level of consciousness may fluctuate from a stupor to drowsiness to alertness. There may be hallucinations that are more often visual than auditory. Some individuals experience both delirium and seizures. This severe withdrawal resembles the symptoms of a serious infection and, therefore, physicians may miss the correct diagnosis if they do not know the individual's history of substance abuse. Seizures and other serious symptoms associated with drug withdrawal can occur during prolonged dependence even if fewer than usual drugs or doses are taken.

There are several rules of thumb about withdrawal symptoms that can help predict their severity and nature:

1. The higher the dosage, the more intense the withdrawal symptoms.

2. The longer the period of time the drug is used, the more intense the withdrawal symptoms.

3. Short- and intermediate-acting barbiturates and the more potent hypnotics produce a more intense withdrawal syndrome.

4. Multiple drug abuse, particularly the practice of combining both long- and short-acting drugs or alcohol, results in more intense withdrawal symptoms and a greater variety of symptoms including a two-stage withdrawal— the first stage peaking in one to three days, and the second stage appearing in three to seven days.

5. Individuals with a low seizure threshold, or histories of seizures are much more likely to experience withdrawal seizures.

6. Individuals with disturbed personalities prior to drug abuse are more likely to experience severe psychotic symptoms that are often exaggerations of their underlying psychological difficulties.

Medical Complications

Many of the toxic effects and withdrawal symptoms described above present themselves as medical or psychiatric complications; for example, irritability, anxiety, insomnia, confusion, or seizures. Falling asleep at inappropriate times while intoxicated may lead to accidents and fires. Heavy drug use over extended periods may lead to long-standing brain damage, in part through overdoses that directly lead to brain damage because of lowered oxygen supplies to the brain.

Long-term use of sedatives may also have a direct damaging effect on the brain even without documented overdoses. These effects include impaired reasoning, memory, learning, and speed of response. These damaging effects clear up rapidly during the first three weeks of sobriety. However, even after this three-week period, some brain damage remains that continues to clear up gradually over a period of one to three years.

Barbiturates are often used intravenously, generally by hardcore drug users. All of the medical complications associated with other IV drug use pertain to IV barbiturate use. In addition, local leakage of barbiturates at the site of injection is particularly painful and frequently causes infections.

Pharmacologic Treatments of Abuse

Drug-free methods of relieving withdrawal symptoms such as anxiety are always preferable to the use of any drug in treating addictions. Among methods that have proved effective are: biofeedback, meditation, yoga, self-hypnosis, acupuncture, relaxation techniques, and exercise programs.

An important point to keep in mind about outpatient pharmacologic treatments is that substitution of a supposedly less addictive sedative for a more addictive one rarely works. All too frequently, when a drug like Valium® is prescribed to a barbiturate or Quaalude® addict, the Valium® creates a more intense and mixed addiction rather than permitting the patient to switch to Valium® alone. If the switch could be made successfully, Valium® would be safer than the other drugs with equivalent doses. Benadryl®, Vistaril®, or Atarax® may alleviate insomnia without risk of dependence. Every benzodiazepine drug that has been developed is capable of being abused and can lead to dependence. Xanax®, Ativan®, and Halcion® are every bit as addicting as Valium®, if not more so. A new drug, Buspar® (buspirone), is currently being marketed and may relieve anxiety without risk of dependence. However, it takes several weeks to take effect. The major tranquilizers such as Thorazine®, Haldol®, Mellaril®, and Navane® have been used in low doses in some cases to relieve anxiety without risk of addiction. However, the extreme side effects of these drugs have restricted their use recently to all but psychotic disorders.

Hallucinogens

Drugs in this category produce hallucinations. The popularity and use of hallucinogen drugs peaked in the mid-1960s and diminished with the fading out of the quest for consciousness expansion movement in the early 1970s. The major exception to the pattern of decrease in hallucinogen use after this time is the drug phencyclidine in forms such as PCP, angel dust, Shermans, and cannabinol, whose use has continued into the 1980s. LSD use is again increasing in some regions of the country.

PCP is not purely an hallucinogen; it also has stimulant and depressant qualities. Its popularity, compared with other hallucinogens, is related in part to its wide range of psychological effects. PCP is also popular because it is inexpensive and easy to manufacture in home laboratories. Because of its uniqueness, PCP is described in this section separately from the other hallucinogenic drugs.

Signs and Symptoms of Use and Abuse

The word hallucinogen, when used for this classification of drugs, is a bit of a misnomer. These drugs are more "illusionogens" in that they more often cause a misperception of existing reality rather than a fabrication of reality. They are also called psychomimetic drugs because they mimic psychoses, and psychedelic because of their alleged mind expansion effects.

With prolonged use, these drugs cause an euphoria or a dreamy lethargy. Pupils become dilated, except with PCP, and the face becomes flushed. There is irregular breathing and trembling. There may be drug-induced panic particularly if the user is in an uncomfortable or unfamiliar situation or is not accustomed to the effects of a specific drug. Panic symptoms include feelings of terror, confusion, and fear of loss of control. Panic can progress to random running about, injury, disrobing, and paranoia. Grandiosity—such as believing that one can fly—is not uncommon. Hallucinations, illusions, and feeling bizarre changes in one's body are also frequent. Sensations that change from one sensory perception to another, as from sound to sight (synesthia), often occur. Fears of bodily disintegration and total loss of control are common. Time perception is affected and time appears to pass slowly. Thoughts and memories become frighteningly alive and threatening.

Physiological Effects

Hallucinogens have many different physiologic and psychological effects depending on their particular chemical structures. In addition to experiencing the kinds of effects associated with hallucinogens, abusers of these drugs may also show signs similar to users of amphetamines, atropine, scopolamine, and ergot compounds, when the hallucinogens are chemically related to these drugs. (Ergot compounds are a naturally occurring group of drugs that are used to treat migraine headaches.) Therefore, if a hallucinogenic drug is related to amphetamines, it may have a stimulating effect; if similar to atropine, there may be inhibition of the parasympathetic nervous system; when related to scopolamine, it may produce dreamy sleep or arterial contraction. Many hallucinogens, such as LSD, DMT, PCP, and psilocybin, mimic the functioning of the SNS so that there are tremors and increases in heart rate, blood pressure, and temperature.

Psychological States and Behaviors

Under the influence of hypnotic drugs, all sensory input may be misperceived with a heightened awareness of colors, sounds, and textures. As in *Alice in Wonderland*, objects appear to become very large or very small. Walls and ceilings seem to recede or close in and objects seem wavy or amorphous. The world may be seen as through a kaleidoscope or a piece of fine lace. The user may experience enhanced self-awareness. Concentration may be impaired or shortened; the individual may focus on an object or piece of music for hours at a time. Images are often seen even after the eyes have been closed.

Not surprisingly, hallucinations are common, particularly with the eyes closed. Fantastic visions occur frequently to which the user may react with fear or pleasure. Emotional disturbance is common and varied; there may be depression or elation, anxiety or euphoria, with rapid increases in the intensity of feelings or shifts from one mood to another.

Flashbacks or "free trips," which are recurrences of earlier experiences on hallucinogens, can happen months or even years after the last ingestion of these drugs. They can be triggered by smoking marijuana, drinking alcohol, stress, or even blinking lights. Other long-term after effects of hallucinogens include continued perceptual disturbances, mood changes, depersonalization (feeling unreal), confusional states, phobias, and body image changes.

Dependence and Withdrawal

Tolerance rapidly develops to the euphoric and psychedelic effects of hallucinogens, so that progressively higher doses are often used. However, a protective tolerance does not develop to the psychosis-producing effects that tend to worsen with repeated usage. As users of hallucinogens tend repeatedly to take higher doses of these drugs, they become more likely to experience psychotic symptoms. Withdrawal symptoms do not occur except for the lingering effects described above, such as flashbacks and possibly depression.

Special Aspects of PCP (Phencyclidine)

Many of the effects of PCP are similar to those of the other hallucinogens. However, PCP produces some unique effects.

PCP is most often smoked by mixing it with marijuana or normal tobacco, particularly *Shermans*. It can also be snorted (intranasal ingestion), taken orally, or injected intravenously. Because of its anesthetic properties, PCP causes symptoms that resemble drunkenness—slurred speech, slow reflexes, numbness, and disorientation. Balance is impaired, and there is a floating feeling of euphoria, particularly if the drug is taken in calm surroundings. PCP users under the influence may tolerate high pain levels. Even small doses may produce intense anger, agitation, irritability, perceptional distortions, paranoia, and hallucinations. With higher doses, there may be even greater paranoia, psychotic symptoms, and displays of violence. Users may be unable to control their body movements. They may exhibit the effects of sedation, stupor, coma, or convulsions.

PCP causes sympathomimetic (mimicking the SNS, which governs the "fight or flight" response) symptoms such as increased blood pressure, pulse, and respiration, and sweating and flushing of the skin. It also causes constriction of the pupils and may lead to repetitive eye movements and droopy eyelids. This grouping of symptoms involving the eyes of the PCP user during intoxication is unique. Movements, thoughts, and speech are slowed dramatically. Another unique aspect is that PCP intoxication may be very long lasting with acute effects lasting for weeks and long-term effects lasting months.

Pharmacologic Treatment of Abuse and Overdose (With Emphasis on PCP)

Physical treatments for abuse of hallucinogenic drugs involve treating the drug-induced anxiety and psychotic symptoms. In addition, there are measures that can be taken to speed up the excretion of PCP from the body, because it lingers in the tissues for weeks. Anxiety is treated with benzodiazepines (Valium®, etc.) and psychotic symptoms with major tranquilizers (Haldol®, etc.). Elimination of PCP from the body is enhanced by acidifying the urine. Cranberry juice, formerly thought to be helpful in this respect, does not get the urine sufficiently acidic to alter excretion, so a physician's involvement is necessary to facilitate elimination. Large doses of vitamin C, as high as 10 grams, or ammonium chloride may be necessary to acidify the urine sufficiently. Gastric (stomach) suction may even be used to remove recycled PCP from the body up to a week or more after ingestion.

Marijuana

Marijuana usage decreased in the early 1980s after 10 years of rapid, widespread, increasing use that peaked in 1979. Nationwide, the proportion of high-school seniors who used marijuana at all during the year prior to being surveyed decreased from a high of 51 percent in 1979 to 36.3 percent in 1987. Daily use of marijuana by high-school seniors fell from 10.7 percent in 1978 to 3.3 percent in 1987. This decrease in use appears to be a result of the successful campaign against drug use and abuse conducted by federal agencies, including the National Institute of Drug Abuse. However, 1985 was the first year in the past six years that there was no decrease in marijuana use; since then it appears to have plateaued.

The decrease in marijuana use has occurred despite—or perhaps because of—the great increase in potency of most marijuana sold today. The caution of America's young people about marijuana use appears to be attributable to their increased awareness and concern about the damaging psychological and physical effects of the drug. Most physicians, researchers, and other leaders in the field of substance abuse did not begin to recognize and report the dangers of marijuana use until the late 1970s. The national publicity and dissemination of recent findings about the dangers of marijuana has also helped turn the tide against marijuana use. The decrease in cigarette smoking, associated with some of the same preventive health factors, has no doubt also contributed to the decrease in marijuana smoking. In 1987, 73.5 percent of high-school seniors stated the belief that regular marijuana smokers run a great risk of harming themselves. In 1978, only 35 percent expressed that view.

Nevertheless, we should not become overconfident about having solved the marijuana problem. About 57 million Americans have reported using marijuana at least once. There are an estimated 20 million current marijuana users in the United States. Five percent of young people who report using daily, tend to use very heavily (three and a half joints daily on the average). Even though marijuana use appears to have declined in some segments of society, the more potent marijuana available in the past few years is far more dangerous than the weaker pot of 10 or 20 years ago. Hashish, a concentrated and very potent form of marijuana, is also often abused.

A major problem with marijuana is its relationship to the use of other drugs. There is increasing evidence of an association between regular marijuana use and heroin use. Though considered less dangerous than heroin, marijuana is certainly a harmful substance in its own right. The confusion about it results in part because it is relatively safer than other drugs and alcohol. There is no question that statistically even a single use of marijuana predisposes an individual to the use of other drugs. Furthermore, the more frequently marijuana is used, the more likely the individual is to abuse other drugs. Almost 100 percent of daily marijuana smokers use other drugs. Dupont has called marijuana a "gateway" drug along with alcohol and cocaine. Although these three drugs are considered by young people to be harmless and controllable, they are all dangerous and addicting. They open the gate to a lifetime damaged by serious drug dependence. Using an illegal drug, even one as common as marijuana, breaks the moral barrier against more dangerous illegal drug use. Just the fact that marijuana is illegal may also put the purchaser in contact with someone who sells other illegal drugs and may contribute to the progression to more potent and dangerous drugs.

Signs and Symptoms of Use and Abuse

The effects of marijuana, like those of any drug, depend on dose, setting, expectation, and personality. The intoxicated state produced by marijuana is most often characterized by a pleasant euphoria and contented drowsiness, although anxiety occurs in over 50 percent of users. Relaxation rapidly sets in for most users as does giddiness.

Physiological Effects

Physiologically, marijuana produces dizziness, tingling, and an increased thirst, the latter is often satisfied by alcoholic beverages. There may also be odd food cravings, usually for sweets. Pulse rate and blood pressure are increased. The whites of the eyes are reddened and the pupils are dilated and may be sluggish in responding to light. Arms and legs may feel heavy. There may be nausea and faintness, particularly when rising from a reclining position or when getting out of a hot bath or spa.

Psychological States and Behaviors

Under the influence of marijuana, absurd and ludicrous things are experienced as hilarious, and dull, mundane events become extremely interesting. This effect of the drug to distort and exaggerate reality contributes to the "amotivational syndrome"; if trivia is so interesting, and infantile humor so hilarious, why progress to the pursuit of anything more complex or difficult to obtain? Signs of this syndrome include a loss of drive and ambition, an increase in passivity and dropping out of the "establishment." Frequent users of marijuana lose their motivation to participate and compete in everyday work pursuits and schooling.

It has not been definitely established that the amotivational syndrome is directly caused by marijuana rather than both marijuana use and amotivation being the result of some other common stimulus. There is evidence that marijuana will overwhelm individuals with preexisting low levels of motivation, but will not diminish achievement in those who are highly motivated. A laboratory study by Brady in 1984 showed that already moderate users, when under the influence of marijuana, curtailed future planning for the sake of immediate gain.

Marijuana greatly distorts the user's sense of time, generally making events seem longer. On the other hand, amnesia may result so that memories of a particular evening will fade quickly. There is loss of inhibitions, but not to the extent that marijuana intoxication leads to violence. Marijuana-induced anxiety may progress to extreme confusion and paranoia, particularly about being arrested for using pot. This fear is called "pot paranoia."

Marijuana users have difficulty in communicating with those who are "straight" and enjoy hiding their usage. They feel that only someone else who is "stoned" can really understand them. Those who are not intoxicated often experience the marijuana user as boring, irrational, or incomprehensible.

Marijuana is often classified as an hallucinogen. However, hallucinations are rare. What the marijuana user experiences are really illusions, visual distortions, and synesthia (transfer from one sensory modality to another). A lack of sense of self, called depersonalization, and a state of derealization, in which the world feels unreal, also frequently occur.

Potent marijuana is capable of precipitating a psychosis in a vulnerable individual. In anyone except those who are extremely prone to schizophrenia, these episodes of severe mental disturbance generally resolve and disappear within 24 hours of use. In someone who, for example, has had a prior schizophrenic episode, psychotic breakdowns may be triggered that run prolonged courses before resolution. These episodes begin with pronounced anxiety that increases to panic, fear of death, and fear of insanity. In a one-year period during the Vietnam war, 12 cases of marijuana-induced psychosis were seen among 250,000 American troops who allegedly smoked marijuana. In only two of those 12 cases had any prior personality disorders been noted. All of these servicemen were able to return to duty within one week of their psychotic episode.

Long-Term Psychological Manifestations

Marijuana is stored in body tissue, therefore, it is not rapidly eliminated from the body. Consequently, marijuana may continue to exert direct effects for several weeks after ingestion. These long-term effects may contribute to the prevalence of the "amotivational syndrome" seen in regular marijuana users.

Dependence and Withdrawal

The common myth that there is no tolerance built up to marijuana is an unfortunate one. The myth probably came about because, in the initial phases of smoking marijuana, the user needs progressively less as he or she learns to tune into and utilize the effects of the drug. However, after this period, a rapid tolerance develops. More than 90 animal studies have clearly demonstrated the many effects of marijuana to which tolerance develops. One such study demonstrated a *6,000*-fold increase in dose requirement to achieve effects. Tolerance occurs in humans after three to six consecutive days of use. A substantial degree of tolerance is lost 24 hours after termination of chronic use. Marijuana has some degree of cross-tolerance with alcohol, opiates, and sedatives, but does not show cross-tolerance with LSD or stimulants. Cross-tolerance means that tolerance built up to one drug may also cause a similar tolerance to a drug that has never been taken before.

In my own clinical experience with users, the withdrawal symptoms that occur after cessation of marijuana smoking are generally minimal, consisting of mild to moderate anxiety or depression. However, monkeys who were given high daily doses of marijuana intravenously for 36 days developed an intense opiate-like withdrawal that lasted five days. Clinical studies of men who smoked potent hashish over long periods of time showed severe withdrawal with symptoms of sweating, disturbed sleep, tremor, muscle weakness, and depression. Abdominal cramps, nausea, and increased heart rate have also been noted in withdrawal from potent marijuana.

Medical Complications

Marijuana definitely impairs visual perception and coordination, speeds up heart rate, and slows reaction time. Although these effects are transient, they frequently lead to automobile or other kinds of accidents. The evidence of marijuana's damaging effects on the lungs and related structures is clearer than its effects on any other system in the body. Bronchitis is a very common consequence of marijuana use. Marijuana smoke contains 50 percent more carcinogenic hydrocarbons than tobacco. About three marijuana cigarettes are as carcinogenic as an ordinary pack of 20 cigarettes. Since it is so potent and is inhaled more deeply than tobacco, it is quite damaging to lung tissue. It causes respiratory disease and may lead to lung cancer.

The other major physiologic effect of marijuana is on the reproductive system. Testosterone is lowered, leading to decreased sperm production and increased sperm mortality in adult males. In male adolescents, lowered testosterone can lead to feminization. These effects of marijuana are readily reversible, however, when ingestion stops. Marijuana may also inhibit the female reproductive system. There is evidence that it causes genetic abnormalities and tumors, and inhibits the immune system. There is no present evidence that it causes brain atrophy.

Marijuana has two legitimate medicinal uses. It decreases the nausea and vomiting of anticancer drugs, and reduces eye pressure in cases of glaucoma, an eye disease involving increased fluid pressure within the eye that poses a threat to vision.

The Inhalents

Young teenagers make up the largest group of users and abusers of the most commonly abused inhalents, which are glue, paint, and spray can aerosols. Adults may abuse totally different categories of inhalents, such as anesthetic gases, like ether, nitrous oxide, and chloroform.

One inhalant that was popular several years ago was amyl nitrate or "poppers." Amyl nitrate is classified with the inhalents because of its mode of administration. It is available in ampules that require snapping or popping just prior to inhalation—thus the slang terms "snappers" and "popper." It may also be poured into a capped vial that can be opened and inhaled intermittently. Butyl and sodium nitrate are similarly used. Their duration of action is very short and these drugs are frequently used to heighten sexual pleasure at the point of orgasm. Medically, amyl nitrate is used to relieve a heart condition called angina. Although its side effects are few, they include aggravated glaucoma, headaches, low blood pressure, and fainting. There are a few documented reports of death associated with the use of amyl nitrate, and at one time it was thought to be a cofactor for contracting AIDS. There is recent evidence, however, that disputes this.

The euphoria produced by inhalents is related to their highly toxic effects on the brain. They cause a confused mental state or delirium in which there may be visual and auditory hallucinations, grandiose delusions, body-image distortions, and micropsia or macropsia (feeling little or big).

Tolerance to inhalents does develop so that increasing amounts are used to achieve desired effects. Psychological craving for repeated use also occurs. A mild withdrawal syndrome may be experienced, with restlessness, anxiety, and irritability. A desire for relief of these withdrawal symptoms also leads to repeated use. Death can occur from suffocation when a user loses consciousness while using a bag over the head for inhaling. Death can also result from explosions caused by smoking and inhaling gasoline fumes at the same time. Sudden heart failure has also lead to death.

Repeated exposure to inhalents can lead to paralysis of peripheral and cranial nerves, grand mal seizures, and damage to the liver, kidneys, and bone marrow. Heavy use can also cause brain damage with severe difficulties in intellectual functioning.

Look-Alikes, Designer Drugs
and Over-the-Counter Drugs

Look-alikes, which resemble many of the drugs of abuse in appearance and effect, are now widely marketed and easily available. However, most look-alikes sold are meant to resemble the stimulant drugs like pseudo-cocaine, pseudo-amphetamines, or pseudo-speed. As the manufacture of legal amphetamines diminished drastically (from 12 billion in 1971 to less than two million in 1981), the market for substitutes has grown. Most of these stimulant look-alikes contain ephedrine, caffeine, or phenylpropanolamine, all of which have some stimulating, amphetamine-like qualities. They are used to help individuals to work beyond their normal capacity. They also lead to a "high" that may be facilitated and enhanced by drinking alcohol. Although these look-alike drugs are safer than amphetamines, there are serious medical and psychological problems that can result from continuous or high dose usage. Phenylpropanolamine frequently causes high blood pressure in doses of 50 to 85 mg.

Designer drugs encompass a broad range of new compounds that are synthesized in hidden, often very sophisticated, laboratories. These drugs may be given new names like "Ecstasy" in order to help market them widely. When they first are manufactured and sold, they are not illegal, because law enforcement agencies are unaware of their existence. Use may become rampant before a drug is specifically identified and placed under federal control. For example, Ecstasy became widely used and abused in 1985 until controls were placed on it following several months of notoriety and therapeutic claims. Similarly, it took a while before MPTP, marketed as a potent synthetic heroin called "China white" that frequently produces severe, progressive Parkinson's disease, to be identified and recognized so that its production, sale, and use could be controlled.

Many designer narcotics are variations of fentanyl-like products that are similar to, but more potent than, heroin. These extremely dangerous substances frequently result in overdose and death. Unfortunately, analogs of PCP are easy to synthesize and are as dangerous as the actual drug itself.

OTC Drugs: Any drug that can be sold without a physician's prescription falls into this category. The use of these drugs is part of a long-standing American tradition. At the beginning of the 20th century, cocaine and opium were actually OTC drugs. Many mind-altering nonprescription drugs are readily available, most with limited effectiveness for the condition they are purported to help, but considerable potential for abuse. There are thousands of different OTCs, and they are often used and abused in combination with other drugs to enhance desired effects.

OTCs are not innocuous or without severe abuse potential, particularly by euphoria-seeking youths and the elderly. They are widely advertised in the media and are consumed by those who are media responsive. The general categories of mind-altering OTCs are hypnotics, antianxiety agents, analgesics, and stimulants.

Most common sleep-aid/OTC drugs, including Sleep-Eze® and Sominex®, contain scopolamine. These drugs produce toxic effects, including dilated pupils, dry skin, rapid pulse, delirium, and, in extreme cases, psychoses. All sleep-aid/OTC drugs contain antihistamines. They are often used and abused for their sedative properties, and when used in combination, may increase the effects of prescribed sedative drugs, leading to serious overdoses.

OTC sedatives such as Compoz® are not really effective relaxants, but they do have some harmful effects. OTC analgesics (pain relievers) usually contain aspirin, phenacetin, or acetaminophen (aspirin substitute) and caffeine. These drugs do not have toxic psychological effects unless they are taken in very high doses. However, they are frequently involved in overdose suicide attempts.

Codeine-containing cough syrups are available as OTCs in most states. A four-ounce bottle of one of these products can contain as much as 240 mg of codeine, which, if consumed all at once, is very potent, and if repeated, can lead to narcotic dependence. The stimulant OTCs described under "look-alikes" often contain caffeine. No-Doz® contains 100 mg of caffeine per tablet, equal to the amount of caffeine in a few cups of coffee. OTC weight-control products are actually ineffective and frequently contain phenylpropanolamine.

There are also many psychoactive (mood-altering) substances occurring naturally in herbal preparations as well. They are found in Mormon tea (ephedrine), periwinkle (indole alkaloid, an hallucinogen), snakeroot (reserpine, a tranquilizer), and others.

Drug Combinations

Obviously, there are millions of possible combinations of drugs used by drug-dependent people. Alcohol is frequently mixed with sedatives and the total depressant effect is often more than the sum of the two taken independently. Sedatives taken together are generally additive as are sedatives and narcotics. This means that the effects of one drug are added to the effects of the other drug. Stimulants are often taken with depressants to balance out effects. However, stimulants generally are relatively ineffective in relieving sedative-induced drowsiness. Sedatives combined with alcohol may facilitate sleep or relieve the edginess produced by stimulants. Thus, for example, there is a great deal of alcohol use, abuse, and co-dependence in cocaine abusers. The combined use of amphetamines and barbiturates may produce a greater elevation of mood than either drug taken alone. Capsules containing a combination of these two substances were formerly widely marketed, but became illegal in the late 1970s.

References

Brady, J. V., Griffiths, R. R., Heinz, R. D., Biglow, G. E., et al. *Abuse Liability and Behavioral Toxicity Assessment: Progress Report from the Behavioral Biology Laboratories of the Johns Hopkins University, School of Medicine.* NIDA Research Monograph Series 49. DHHS Publication No. ADM84-1316, U.S. Government Printing Office, Washington, D.C., 1984.

Cohen, S. Marijuana: A new ball game? *Drug Abuse and Alcoholism Newsletter*, 8(4), 1979.

Marijuana and Health: A government view. *Focus on Alcohol and Drug Issues*, 1(2):28-29, 1978.

Marijuana and Youth. NIDA Research Monograph 40. U.S. Government Printing Office, Washington, D.C., 1982.

Dupont, R. L. *Getting Tough on Gateway Drugs.* American Psychiatric Association Press, Washington, D.C., 1984.

Gold, M. S., & Verebey, K. The psychopharmacology of cocaine. *Psychiatric Annals*, 14(10):714-723, 1984.

Dougherty, R. J. Pseudo-speed: Look-alikes or pea-shooters. *New York State Journal of Medicine*, pp. 74-75, 1982.

Nicholi, A. M. The inhalents: An overview. *Psychosomatics*, 24(10):914-921, 1983.

Schuckit, M. *Drug and Alcohol Abuse: A Clinical Guide to Diagnosis and Treatment.* Plenum Press, New York, 1985.

Smith, D. E., & Wesson, D. R. *Uppers and Downers.* Prentice-Hall, Englewood Cliffs, N.J., 1973.

Willford, B. B. *Drug Abuse: A Guide for Primary Care Physicians.* American Medical Association, Chicago, 1981.

Hoffman, F. G. *A Handbook on Drug and Alcohol Abuse.* Oxford University Press, Toronto, 1985.

$\triangledown \quad \triangledown \quad \triangledown$

Table 1
Effects of Commonly Abused Drugs

DRUG TYPE

NARCOTICS:	
Opium (Paregoric), Morphine, Heroin ("smack"), Hydromorphine (Dilaudid), Meperidine (Demerol®), Methadone (Dolophine), Codeine. Others: (Percodan®, Talwin®, Darvon®, Lomotil®)	**SIGNS OF USE:** Euphoria, drowsiness, nodding, respiratory problems, depression, constricted pupils, nausea, obliterated drives and worries, complications of needle use. **SIGNS OF OVERUSE:** Slow, shallow breathing, clammy skin, coma, possible death. **SIGNS OF WITHDRAWAL:** Watery eyes, runny nose, loss of appetite, irritability, muscle tremors and jerks, chills, sweating, cramps, restlessness, panic, yawning, dilated pupils.

STIMULANTS:
Cocaine ("snow,"
"flake," "coke,"
"rock," "crack")
Amphetamines
("speed," "uppers,"
"ice") (Dexedrine,
Desoxyn) (Preludin)
Methylphenidate
(Ritalin®)

SIGNS OF USE: Increased alertness, excitation, euphoria, increased pulse rate and blood pressure, insomnia, loss of appetite, grandiosity, suspiciousness.

SIGNS OF OVERUSE: Agitation, hallucinations, convulsions, increase in body temperature, compulsive rituals, schizophrenia, death.

SIGNS OF WITHDRAWAL: Apathy, somnolence, depression, irritability, disorientation, prolonged sleep (crash).

DEPRESSANTS:
Chloralhydrate
("knockout drops")
Barbiturates
("downers," "reds,"
"yellow-jackets")
Glutethimide (Doriden)
Methaqualone
(Qualude®, Sopor)
Noludar®, Placidyl®
Benzodiazepines
(Valium®, Librium®,
Halcion®, Serax®, Dal-
mane®, Ativan®,
Xanax®, Miltoun®
(Meprobamate)

SIGNS OF USE: Poor judgment, drowsy, inattentive, slow, disinhibition, euphoria, slurred speech, disorientation, drunken behavior without alcohol.

SIGNS OF OVERUSE: Impaired memory and learning, shallow respiration, cold and clammy skin, dilated pupils, weak and rapid pulse, coma, death.

SIGNS OF WITHDRAWAL: Anxiety, insomnia, tremors, delirium (confusion), convulsions, fever, possible death.

HALLUCINOGENS:
LSD ("Acid")
MDMA ("XTC"),
Mescaline, Peyote
("buttons")
Psilocybin
Phencyclidine ("PCP,"
"angel dust," "hog")
Shermans

SIGNS OF USE: Hallucinations, illusions, time distortion, dilated pupils, *nystagmus (vibrating eye movement), *lid lag.

SIGNS OF OVERUSE: Psychosis, intensified trip, flashbacks, panic, *slowed movement and speech, *violence, panic, death.

SIGNS OF WITHDRAWAL: Edginess, crashing (withdrawal signs are minimal).

*These signs are characteristic of Phencyclidine (PCP) only.

MARIJUANA:
("pot," "grass,"
"reefer")
Tetrahydrocannabinol
(THC)
Hashish ("hash")

SIGNS OF USE: Rapid heart beat, euphoria, relaxation, increased appetite, disorientation, perceptual disorders, anxiety.

SIGNS OF OVERUSE: Psychosis, paranoia, fatigue, amotivational syndrome.

TABLE 1 *(Continued)*

SIGNS OF WITHDRAWAL: Insomnia, hyperactivity, decreased appetite.

INHALENTS:
Ether, Cloroform,
Nitrous Oxide,
Paint Thinners,
Lighter Fluid, Gaso-
line, Glues, Toluene,
Aerosols, "Poppers,"
(Amyl nitrate)

SIGNS OF USE: Excitement, euphoria, drunken behavior, disorientation, confusion, hallucinations.

SIGNS OF OVERUSE: Hypoxia (lack of oxygen to the body tissues), nerve paralysis, irregular heartbeat, respiratory problems, depression, sudden death.

SIGNS OF WITHDRAWAL: Anxiety, irritability (withdrawal signs are mild).

Table 2
Pharmacologic Treatments

Drug Type	Pharmacologic Overdose	Detoxification	Long Term Treatments
NARCOTICS	Narcan®	Methadone Clonidine	Methadone Naltrexone
STIMULANTS	Life support	Valium® (optional) Ativan® (optional)	Tricyclic Antidepressants (Desipramine), (Tofranil®) with L-tyrosine and L-tryptophane
DEPRESSANTS	Life support	Valium®, Ativan®	Vistaril (optional) Buspar (optional)
HALLUCINO-GENS	Valium®	—	Haldol (for psychotic symptoms after the first week)
PCP	Quiet Environment, urine acidification	Urine Acidification, gastric suction	Haldol (for psychotic symptoms after the first week)
MARIJUANA	—	—	—
INHALENTS	Life support	—	—

4

Understanding the Adult Male Alcoholic and His Family

*D*espite many similarities, there are enough differences between alcoholics and drug abusers to warrant devoting a separate chapter to each. It should be kept in mind that factors such as social class, ethnicity, and employment circumstances are powerful determinants in shaping individual roles and family function and, as such, they often outweigh the particular substance of choice, be it alcohol or drugs, in importance as a family shaping factor. In addition, many of the behavioral differences between alcoholics and drug abusers develop secondarily, after the substance-abusing pattern sets in, and may be attributable in large part to the fact that alcohol is a legal substance whereas drugs such as heroin, cocaine, and the hallucinogens are illegal. In other words, the lifestyle of a man who develops an illegal drug habit, and its impact on his family, present unique factors by virtue of the fact that the addict's substance of choice happens to be illegal. This fact alone thrusts him into a different lifestyle than the alcoholic male, with serious consequences both to himself and his family.

Before dealing with the specific aspects of the personality of the alcoholic male and what his family is like, a brief section on the commonalities seen in alcoholics and drug abusers is presented.

Psychological Similarities Between Alcoholics and Drug Abusers

Most alcoholics and drug abusers use similar defense mechanisms. The most important and powerful defense mechanism they share is denial—a hallmark of both illnesses. The term "denial" is used in the substance abuse treatment field in a much broader way than its common meaning or its usage as a key psychological defense mechanism. Substance abusers (SAs) not only deny the obvious reality about the extent and frequency of their substance abuse, but the behavioral consequences as well. SAs emotionally and verbally deny how much they have manipulated and hurt their family and friends. They deny how self-destructive their behavior has been, as well as the very real threat their continued substance abuse poses not only to their health but to their very lives. They deny a whole range of tactics that they use to hide, justify, or protect their substance abuse, minimize the consequences of their behavior, and prevent treatment.

Although denial is an unconscious mechanism, conscious lying is common to all SAs. There are times when, because of being in a substance-induced confused state, the SA doesn't really know if he is lying or not. Lying becomes so much a part of his life that he genuinely is not able to discriminate fact from fiction. Other defense mechanisms common to all SAs include projection (blaming others), regression (childish behavior), and rationalization ("If you didn't nag me so much, I wouldn't have to drink!").

Three key personality traits common to male drug abusers and alcoholics have consistently appeared in the scientific literature about substance abuse. These traits are impulsivity (the inability to tolerate frustration and the need to act quickly), repeatedly behaving in a manner that has inevitably led to negative results, and placing the need for immediate euphoria and relief from pressure or stress before long-term relief.

Drugs and alcohol are both used in attempts to decrease anxiety about assertiveness, particularly in work and social settings. Alcohol and sedative drugs are used to wipe out anger and hostility. However, the effects of these substances can boomerang and serve to release anger rather than suppress it. SAs are typically unable to handle tension or frustration. Their moods cycle rapidly, both on and off chemicals, swinging up and down from elation to depression. SAs engage in a constant inner battle—on one side they feel weak, dependent, and passive; and on the other, they try to be aggressive and totally deny any dependency needs. Drugs and alcohol are both initially used to overcome sexual fears and stimulate sexual fantasies and performance. However, over time sexual desire and performance greatly diminish with the long-term use of drugs and alcohol.

Only a minority of SAs are severely mentally ill and use alcohol and drugs as a form of self-medication in an unsuccessful attempt to treat their psychiatric disturbances. Another group of slightly less psychopathological SAs use alcohol and drugs to provide an otherwise lacking sense of self and internal stability (homeostasis). This phenomenon is very common in "borderline personalities," a complex psychiatric personality diagnosis often seen in substance abusers.

Alcoholic Personality Patterns

The focus of this section is on the alcoholic's behavior as he interacts with others in the family. The behavior of most abusers of prescription drugs, including pain pills, and that of mild to moderate, non-addicted abusers of marijuana, cocaine, and the hallucinogens is quite similar to that of the alcoholic. Individual alcoholic personality types are presented in order to help recognize, understand, and cope with the alcoholic's behavior. There is no such entity as a specific "alcoholic personality," but there are some common characteristics that can help us in identifying alcoholics and recognizing their behavior. For example, there are clusters of behavioral characteristics that are frequently seen in some male alcoholics, but not in others. There are also defense mechanisms, gender issues, and underlying psychodynamic conflicts that are common to many alcoholics.

Society has condoned and even glorified male drinking for centuries. It has long been considered a sign of masculinity to be able to "hold your liquor." Getting drunk is often a male adolescent rite of passage. Men drink together in clubs and bars to feel like they are "one of the boys." Drinking enhances identification, companionship, and closeness with other males. It is difficult for many men to communicate deeply and at length without getting drunk together. On the darker side, drinking also bonds men together in hostile and inappropriate sexual advances toward women, which may even progress to rape.

Any social and psychological explanations for the etiology of alcoholism are in no way meant to deny or minimize the importance of genetic factors in alcoholism, which scientific studies have repeatedly demonstrated to play a large role. It has been shown that the children of alcoholics are four times more likely to become alcoholics than offspring of nonalcoholics, even if they are adopted at birth and raised in homes without an alcoholic parent.

As pointed out before, alcoholics use denial more than any other defense mechanism to avoid recognizing their alcoholism. They deny not only their destructive drinking, but their manipulative behavior. When this denial is confronted, they become furious. If they accept the confrontation as valid, they become emotionally devastated and acutely depressed. Another common defense mechanism is projection. Alcoholics project the source of their problems from themselves onto those around them, often onto those closest to them.

Alcoholics often have a strong, relentless conscience that demands a great deal from them, driving them to experience excessive guilt and shame, even when sober, and often propelling them to compensatory overachievements. Never quite capable of fulfilling their own unrealistic demands, alcoholics are left depressed. Only a small minority of alcoholics are antisocial personalities who have little or no conscience and interact with others only to manipulate them for personal gain.

Dependency is another key issue in male drinking and alcoholism. Men are raised to believe that they must be self-sufficient and independent. To be openly dependent is extremely threatening and intolerable to male alcoholics. Yet at the same time, they have an unspoken belief that their emotional and physical well-being is the responsibility of women—wives, mothers, sisters. This belief leads them to feel *entitled* to being taken care of and nurtured by women without asking for it.

Yet.men deny that they need this care or that they are greatly dependent on being cared for by others. They are taught early on that feeling dependent or having warm or needy feelings is feminine and must be denied and avoided at all costs. Drinking allows the man to express these feelings and to be dependent. It allows him to experience his deep underlying need to be helpless and cared for as he was when he was a little boy. When intoxicated, it permits him to be undressed and tucked into bed, to sleep late, and to be coddled and protected from the demands of a world that expects him to always perform as a strong, responsible male adult.

The drinking or alcoholic man further denies and hides his dependency by acting masculine and independent around other men. On the other hand, he can be irrational, very emotional, hypersensitive, and shift from the role of emotional distancer to that of pursuer. So alcohol permits the male to express his emotional side, but it ultimately provides reinforcing punishment through guilt and remorse "the day after."

Some alcoholics deal with their dependency needs by denying that they have such needs and trying very hard never to appear dependent. Under the influence of alcohol, they act bossy and aggressive, even hostile and violent. Alcoholics may also become furious at their spouses when these buried and denied dependency needs are not met. The taboo against violence toward the "weaker sex" then may be broken, and the alcoholic will be physically violent to his spouse when he is drunk.

Another inappropriate response to buried dependency is for the male alcoholic to turn to his daughter(s) to fulfill these needs. He may even break the incestual taboo when intoxicated and seduce or force his daughter(s) or, more rarely, sons to meet his sexual demands.

Under the guise of bravado, most alcoholics have a deep and pervading lack of self-esteem and poor self-image. For some alcoholics, low self-esteem and lack of confidence are limited to selected facets of their life, such as in business or on the job but not at home, or vice versa. Their drinking is triggered by stresses affecting those areas in which they feel most inadequate. They then proclaim, "I wouldn't be drinking if business wasn't bad last year." Alcoholics often put responsibility for their behavior or feelings of inadequacy onto their spouses (projection). Arguments over responsibility often lead to sadistic violence. On the other hand, alcoholics are often quite self-punishing and masochistic. They commonly use alcohol to diminish their anxieties about self-assertion in communicative, social, and family settings. Alcohol is used to obliterate anger and hostility, which are eventually released during the later stages of intoxication and withdrawal.

Alcoholics, like drug abusers, suffer from a very low tolerance to frustration and an inability to deal effectively with anxiety or tension. They harbor repressed or conscious feelings of omnipotence, grandiosity, and extreme narcissism (self-love), which are all in stark contrast to their self-defeating inability to persevere and complete tasks. The male alcoholic experiences a constant inner battle between passivity and aggressiveness. Conscious or unconscious rebellion, a tendency to act out aggressive and sexual impulses, and strong unmet dependency needs inevitably lead to tremendous frustration and violent mood swings. Their experience of deprivation leads to depression and despair or to hostility, rage, and fantasies of revenge against those whom they perceive to be the cause of their frustration. The target is often the wife, children, or boss. The alcoholic is often described as a Dr. Jekyll and Mr. Hyde character. Puritanical, self-righteous behavior is prominent when sober, and vicious, aggressive actions predominate when intoxicated. Some angry alcoholics reverse this and become more docile when drinking.

The Families of Adult Male Alcoholics

Numerous books on the male alcoholic and his family have been written for the general public. A majority of the scientific investigations into alcoholism have been conducted on male alcoholics. Despite the broad knowledge in this area, much of what has been presented to the lay public has not been based on scientific studies, nor has it reflected recent developments in the study of families of alcoholics. Science has now shown that not all alcoholics are alike and, therefore, recommended coping strategies for families must vary according to the specific type of alcoholic involved and the specific family patterns that result.

Mansell Pattison and I have categorized male alcoholics and their families into four types: functional, enmeshed, separated, and absent. The discussion that follows on each category primarily describes a family consisting of husband, wife, and children, in which the husband is the alcoholic.

The "Functional" Family

The members of functional alcoholic families are so able to wall off and absorb the alcoholic's behavior that they rarely seek out books or other relevant information regarding the effects of alcohol on their family. These families appear to be stable and happy, but they carefully avoid any information or awareness that might challenge their denial of the existence of a problem or that might expose a conflict. Some of these families are able to isolate themselves or detach from the alcoholic's behavior throughout the years of the family's existence. Other families deteriorate into more reactive or separated family systems. However, these reactive families operate with less overt conflict than the enmeshed families described later.

The alcoholic's drinking in functional families evolves primarily as a response to social strains or personal neurotic conflict, not as the result of family stresses. Excessive drinking most often occurs outside the home, on trips, at parties, or at bedtime. The wife and alcoholic husband in a functional family maintain an overtly loving relationship with an adequate though gradually diminishing sexual life. They are successful as parents, and their children are reasonably well adjusted, experiencing good relationships with each other and with their peers.

Although such families function well, they are usually not psychologically oriented. They are functional, but not introspective or insightful. They are responsive to external change, but resistant to internal change. Because the family functions fairly well, there is little obvious conflict. Nevertheless, the focus of family concern is likely to be on the alcoholic husband and father, rather than on other family members. The emotional balance of the family is generally positive, with a desire to retain and rehabilitate the alcoholic, rather than to reject and expel him from the family.

If you suspect that your family falls into the category of remaining highly functional despite an alcoholic member, the best approach to implement is to ask the alcoholic to see a physician who thoroughly understands the psychological and physiological aspects of alcoholism. This knowledgeable doctor can investigate the extent of the drinking and its physical implications and prescribe a treatment program that can be followed just like any treatment recommended for a chronic disease. Intensive individual and family-oriented psychotherapy programs are usually not indicated, and they probably would be refused if suggested. If the alcoholic will not follow the physician's prescribed program, then a return visit in about a year is indicated. If medical complications do develop, this type of alcoholic is generally motivated to seek and follow treatment, particularly through a medically-based program. Treatment with Antabuse® or aversion techniques (see later chapters) may be successful. At this stage of their development, these families may respond favorably to an educative approach that emphasizes the teaching of new rules, roles, and behaviors that permit a more open and enlightened response to the alcoholic.

The Enmeshed Family

These are the families about whom most of the medical literature on the alcoholic family has been written. Alcohol use plays a critical role in their day-to-day behavior. It is the central organizing principle around which most family interactions are focused. Drinking behavior interrupts normal family tasks, causes conflict, and shifts roles. New responses are constantly being demanded from family members who do not know how to respond appropriately. In addition, marital and family styles, rules, and conflict may evoke, support, and maintain the husband's alcoholism as a symptom of family system dysfunction, or as a coping mechanism to deal with family anxiety. The husband's alcoholism is more severe in these families and creates physical problems, including sexual dysfunction and debilitating cardiac, hepatic, and neurological diseases in the alcoholic that, in turn, produce further marital conflicts and the demand for family role realignments. Alcohol is used to contend with family anxiety and anxiety increases when the alcoholic drinks, intensifying the family's disturbed behavior. Drinking to relieve anxiety, and the resultant family anxiety in response to drinking, continue to feed off of each other until a crisis develops.

Stresses on any single family member will immediately affect the entire family with a great sense of urgency. Communication among family members is often directed through a third party (triangulation) rather than face to face. Everyone in the family feels guilty and responsible for each other, particularly for the alcoholic and his drinking.

Such alcoholic marriages are often highly competitive. Each partner sees himself or herself as submitting to the other. The partner who yields loses his sense of self and is vulnerable to drinking. After the pattern of alcoholism is established, such couples continue a highly competitive relationship. The alcoholic attempts to control his spouse and avoid responsibility through passive-dependent techniques. In turn, the spouse tries to control by being forceful, active, blunt, and dominating or by suffering and becoming a martyr. Neither partner ever clearly becomes dominant, and the struggle continues indefinitely.

Fighting constantly occurs as the spouses blame each other for the family's problems. This dual projection blinds each partner to his or her own responsibility for creating problems, making change difficult. The couple fights endlessly about who is to blame and they readily bring their conflicts to others. As a result of constant friction, members of these families feel distant and alienated from one another. Yet they remain quite enmeshed, continuing to need each other and to react to one another.

The alcoholic may relinquish his role as a parent as well as a responsible husband. His role as the family breadwinner is the last to go, and loss or near loss of job may be necessary before the alcoholic will participate in treatment.

Since this type of enmeshed responsiveness is so common in alcoholic families, it is described in further detail later in this chapter.

The Separated Family

What we call separated families have a long history of repeated contact and conflict leading to separation. These marriages and families have fallen apart and separated only after the inability to overcome the multiple consequences of severe alcoholism and related behavior. They have not yet totally severed contact or given up hope of being reunited. The families in this category have been "burned" repeatedly by unkept promises and false starts made by the alcoholic.

If physically living apart, hostilities and arguments that hurt everyone and damage the alcoholic's already low self-esteem ensue when the alcoholic and family are brought together. The "separated family" should not meet for intensive therapy during the early phases of rehabilitation. Early treatment should focus primarily on the alcoholic. Potential ties to spouse, family, relatives, and friends should be explored early in treatment, and contact should be permitted if desired, in order to enhance the effects of later efforts for greater closeness. However, there should be no assumptions that any familial ties will be fully reestablished.

When abstinence and personal stability have been achieved by the alcoholic over several months time, more substantive family explorations can be initiated to reestablish parental roles, and family and kinship relationships, though it must still be understood that there is no guarantee of reconstitution. Intensive family therapy should be avoided until the alcoholic's vocational and social behavior have improved sufficiently and consistently to convince the family that a major positive change in the alcoholic's behavior is actually possible and is not just another empty promise.

Nonalcoholic members of these families should seek a support group such as Al-Anon or Alateen. Even decades after moving out of the household, children of enmeshed or separated alcoholic families can benefit from an ACA (Adult Children of Alcoholics) group.

The Absent Family

With this type of family, the alcoholic loses contact with parents and siblings early in his or her drinking "career." Some enmeshed or separated alcoholics may eventually deteriorate to the point of total loss of family. The alcoholic men in this group generally have never married, or have had only fleeting relationships. They rarely have close friendships, and they have minimal social or vocational skills. Significant others are limited to boarding home operators or "bottle gang" buddies with whom they share cheap bottles of wine.

Though estranged physically from him, parents of this type of alcoholic may continue to suffer the loss of their child to alcoholism for many years. These alcoholics may father children, in brief marital relationships, who suffer because of their absent father. The best approach to dealing with both types of loss is to disengage by emotional detachment or through the grief and mourning process, just as though the alcoholic son or father had died. The realization that this relative has been lost to the family and may never be returned can be quite liberating. This kind of acceptance fosters a sense of finality wherein family members can get on with their lives instead of waiting hopelessly for the alcoholic to return.

After becoming abstinent, a few of these alcoholics—particularly younger males—may respond positively to intense socialization in helpful peer groups such as Alcoholics Anonymous, church fellowships, and recreational and vocational rehabilitation. They are often able to develop positive new social skills, and they may even become able to engage in satisfactory marriage and family life. They may ultimately make an effort to reestablish some kind of contact with their parents and children or even, from a distance, resume or initiate the role of father to their children.

A word of caution. Many functional, enmeshed, or separated alcoholic families deny the alcoholism in their families by fallaciously considering the ''absent family'' category to be the only one that meets their own criteria for describing an alcoholic man and his family. For example, no man is an alcoholic until he has reached skid row so we have no alcoholic in our family.

More About the Enmeshed Family

The rest of this chapter is devoted to a detailed description and discussion of the emotionally overinvolved family system of the male alcoholic called the enmeshed family. It should be noted that these families do not stay fixed in their behavioral patterns, but alternate between phases of enmeshment and disengagement. At times, what is actually hostile enmeshment appears to be disengagement, particularly to family members themselves.

Regardless of the type of family system being discussed, alcoholism is a major stress on a family. It is an economic drain on resources, it threatens job security, and it interrupts normal family roles and tasks. Alcohol causes conflicts and demands behavioral changes and adjustments from family members who may not know how to respond appropriately. Alcoholism creates a series of escalating crises in the family that is ultimately capable of bringing the family system to a critical point at which its very existence is threatened.

In addition to the psychological consequences, alcoholism creates the many physical problems descibed in Chapter 2, which also stress the family. The sexual impotence or dysfunction so frequently produced by alcoholism in turn creates further marital conflict. The opposite also occurs. Marital and family conflict may evoke, support, and maintain alcoholism. Drinking may be a symptom of family dysfunction and a consequence of dysfunctional family styles, rules, and patterns of alcohol use. Therefore, alcoholism is both the cause and the effect of family dysfunction. Nevertheless, the alcoholic is always held responsible for every drink he takes.

Review of Studies of the Male Alcoholic and His Family

Early studies of alcoholic families focused on the personality structures of husbands and wives, assuming that conflicts based on individual differences between them were the basic problem. Most of these studies focused on the male alcoholic and his nonalcoholic wife. It was often implied that the wife was neurotic and chose an alcoholic husband in order to meet her own needs to dominate a man, or because she was dependent and she was frightened that a nonalcoholic husband who didn't *need* her would leave her.

Even more misogynistic than these theories was an earlier hypothesis that proposed that the wife "drove her husband to drink." The majority of these wife-blaming hypotheses were abandoned in the 1970s as a result of the emergence of the scientific study of communication patterns in alcoholic couples that emphasized the mutual, reciprocal responsibilities of both partners in marital dysfunction. These new studies indicated that male alcoholics used responsibility-avoiding messages excessively. In addition, the studies revealed that male alcoholics feel submissive not because their wives are dominant and force them into submission, but because they feel entitled to have power over others and because meeting the demands of a close relationship is innately threatening.

The alcoholic's wife may appear dominating because she is often a very responsible and direct person. Despite the appearance of domination, she is actually unable to control her husband. Each spouse becomes frustrated by the realization that the other will never change. Both the alcoholic and his wife are highly competitive, employing "one-up" messages more often and co-operating less than nonalcoholic couples. They blame each other, put each other down, turn each other off, and compete for dominance. Constantly side-tracking the other, neither spouse is able to develop solutions to family problems, which eventually causes communication to be terminated. This usually leads to the alcoholic's fleeing the scene to drink. Negative interactions characterize communication patterns in alcoholic couples, even when the husband is sober. Not surprisingly, these interactions become even more negative when the alcoholic is intoxicated.

Studies show that wives of alcoholics give and receive little affection, they use few positive adjectives to describe their husbands, drunk or sober, and they anticipate that their husbands will use extremely angry adjectives or phrases to describe them. Alcoholic fathers demonstrate less leadership, assertiveness, and problem-solving behavior with their spouses and children than non-drinking fathers.

One remarkably consistent finding in recent studies is a high incidence of alcoholism in the alcoholic's family of origin (his mother, father, and siblings). There is also a high rate of alcoholism in the family of origin of the spouse.

Women with alcoholic fathers tend to marry alcoholics, even in successive marriages. It may be that this setup for failure in marriage is an attempt to prove that their father's alcoholism could have been prevented or cured by love.

Birth of a Problem Drinker

Most people in our society choose spouses who are about equal to themselves in ego strength, but who have very different ways of dealing with stress. This tendency may be the source of the common saying "opposites attract." Frequently, a rigid, hard-working, unemotional man will marry a mischievous, frivolous, highly emotional woman. The former marries for vitality and the latter for security, and the never-ending war between the extremes begins on the wedding day, if not before.

In such relationships each person eventually sees himself or herself as yielding to the other. The one who submits most often loses his or her sense of self and is vulnerable to a drinking problem. If it is the husband, he becomes increasingly burdened by his responsibility to his job, wife, and children. Consequently, he increases his social drinking, particularly at home, but manages to carry on functioning at work for many years. Even after a pattern of alcoholism is established, these couples continue in a highly competitive relationship, with neither partner becoming clearly dominant. The ongoing struggle is characterized by each partner blaming the other for the family's problems. This dual projection prevents the couple from accurately seeing their respective roles in creating problems. They fight endlessly about "who started it," and they often bring in an outsider in the hope that the third party will render a judgment as to who is right and who is wrong.

Another pattern in these marriages is for the sober partner to "give up" and to let the drinking partner set the rules, to follow his or her lead, to cease trying to communicate, and to withdraw. Withdrawal involves long periods of silence and, in the long run, leads to the escalation of negative feelings and distrust that go unexpressed until they ultimately result in explosive expressions of anger.

Common Alcoholic Family Systems and Dynamics

As stated earlier, drinking can be a symptom or an expression of stress created by conflicts within the family system. Drinking in response to stress frequently triggers anger in the drinker and provokes others, which then causes further anger and provocation despite attempts by the alcoholic to absorb the anger by drinking. Drinking contributes significantly to incidents of verbal abuse and physical violence.

Communication patterns are strongly affected by drinking and drunkenness, which leads to other problems. Trying to communicate with a drunken spouse is exasperating and attempts at communication frequently lead to anger. The wife who tries to talk to a husband who has had more than a few drinks feels as though she is talking to a bottle rather than a person. Exceptions to this pattern occur when tolerance to alcohol has developed and communication patterns require alcohol as a facilitator.

Triangulating family systems are common in alcoholic problem families. In triangulating family systems, conflict or distance between two parties is automatically displaced onto a third party such as an in-law, lover, therapist, or child. Spousal interpersonal conflicts are also projected onto another issue or use of a substance (alcohol or drugs). This type of negative triangulation is in contrast to the productive use of a threesome in which each member can interact freely and without interference from the other two.

The male alcoholic leaves his spouse starved for attention and affection. Early in the marriage he expresses love through sex and the giving of material possessions. Since the alcoholic often believes that the act of having sex absolves all transgressions, particularly drinking, the wife—being aware of her husband's belief—withholds affection, because it leads to sex, which implies forgiveness. As alcoholism progresses, the alcoholic becomes more and more disabled sexually, and the marriage becomes increasingly asexual.

The alcoholic loses the spousal role in other areas as well. He gives up much of his role as parent. Other roles, such as taking care of household chores and maintenance, are rapidly abandoned. The nonalcoholic wife may encourage the oldest son to take over the responsibilities abdicated by the father, placing the son in overt competition with his father. As nonalcoholic members take over full management of the family, the alcoholic is relegated to the status of a child, which perpetuates his drinking. Closeness begins to develop between the nonalcoholic spouse and her children, parents, or in-laws, and the alcoholic feels more excluded. These alliances tend to foster a growing distance between the alcoholic and his family. The subsequent loneliness and estrangement are dealt with through continuing bouts of alcoholic drinking.

Male alcoholics tend to hold onto their jobs tenaciously through a great deal of covering up, denial, and manipulation so that the role as the breadwinner is the last to go. Actual job loss is often necessary before they will seek treatment. Employers with knowledge and awareness of alcoholism, particularly those with alcoholism-conscious EAPs (Employee Assistance Programs), will usually insist on treatment long before their employee bottoms out at work.

Co-dependency

A great deal of our present focus on the substance abuser's family is now viewed using the concept of co-dependency, which is also called co-alcoholism.

This issue is discussed in Chapter VI. Co-alcoholism is the term used to describe a disease in which nonalcoholic family members' lives revolve around the alcoholic, yet their responses to the alcoholic provoke, perpetuate, and protect the alcoholic's drinking and related behaviors. The term co-alcoholism is used when the SA primarily abuses alcohol. For our purposes here, we will use the words "co-alcoholic" and "co-dependent" interchangeably. Co-alcoholics are also referred to as "enablers" because their behavior enables the alcoholic to continue drinking. Co-alcoholics feel that they are in a no-win situation, and they are right. If they hide or pour out alcohol, the alcoholic becomes furious and drinks even more. If the alcoholic is going into withdrawal and has uncomfortable symptoms, the co-alcoholic/enabler feels compelled to purchase alcohol to relieve his discomfort.

Mutual Alcoholism

Some alcoholic men are married to women who are alcoholic, but whose alcoholism is primary rather than a later development of prolonged co-alcoholism. Early in these marriages there may be a playful period of having pleasant, childish fun together. Ultimately, each party struggles endlessly and in vain for the other to take care of him or her. They may even take turns with one being sober and responsible and caring for the helpless dependent partner. Arguments often focus on who is alcoholic and who is not, who drinks more and who can stop. This focus on alcohol permits both people to deny that their unmet need for dependency is the real issue. In the end, both parties become so alcoholic that neither can ever care for the other. At this point, one person becomes more willing to enter treatment, and it is usually the one who has become the most helpless. To avoid dealing with his or her own alcoholism, the other partner will generally insist on staying home to manage the house, or to take care of the kids, etc. to avoid participation in treatment. However, it is essential that both partners enter treatment together or within a few weeks of the other, because if only one is treated, the untreated spouse will rapidly pull the temporarily sober one back into mutual alcoholism.

Minor and Adult Children of Alcoholics

The early literature on alcoholism and the family focused primarily on the marital partners. The effects of alcoholism on the roles and functions of the children in the family were completely neglected. Margaret Cork referred to these offspring as "the forgotten children." The children in the alcoholic family are often the most victimized and damaged. They have growth and development problems, school, learning problems and emotional problems, and they frequently suffer from significant behavior dysfunctions.

Recently the problems and difficulties of children of alcoholics have been likened to those of individuals suffering from post-traumatic stress disorder (PTSD). PTSD is a syndrome usually seen in individuals who have been exposed to the severe stress of war combat. The symptoms include anxiety, depression, emotional overreacting, nightmares in which an event is relived, and flashbacks or reexperiencing of the original trauma. Flashbacks may be triggered by nonspecific anxiety or by any situation that reminds the individual of the original trauma. A patient of mine who is an adult child of an alcoholic father still suffers from severe anxiety attacks every time she sees her father, particularly if she meets him accidentally.

The reactive behavior patterns of children of alcoholics are generally a mixture of the following four kinds of responses: emotional overreactivity, emotional withdrawal, behavioral overcompensation, and behavioral withdrawal. These patterns have been described and named by several observers. Wegscheider observes that children of alcoholics adopt one of the following four roles: hero, scapegoat, lost child, or mascot. Black describes three roles: responsible, adjuster (passive and detached), and placator (emotional overfunctioner). Black emphasizes that these children are taught not to talk about the real problem, not to trust, and not to feel. Some children may adopt aspects of more than one of these roles and may shift roles as the family matures through its life cycle. These old childhood rules and roles greatly affect adult behavior.

Children of alcoholics are likely to (1) experience serious illnesses or accidents, (2) run away, (3) have problems with the police or courts, (4) become high-school dropouts, (5) have temper tantrums, and (6) have diagnosable mental illness during childhood. As already pointed out, children of alcoholics have a very high incidence of alcoholism and drug abuse in adolescence and adulthood. They are often subject to gross neglect and physical and sexual abuse. Children whose parents' alcoholism begins during their adolescence rather than in the early childhood years are not immune to these adverse consequences, though they are often considered less vulnerable. The inconsistency and unpredictability of parental support and expectations erodes the child's sense of trust, security, self-esteem, and confidence in others. This leads to a diminished sense of personal identity, a fear of intimacy, and an inability to form positive relationships. Socialization may be hampered by identifying with and acting out the alcoholic parent's lack of acceptance of society's rules and taking responsibility for their own actions.

Conversely, the child of an alcoholic may become overly concerned with assuming responsibility and caring for others because he has so frequently adopted this role with the alcoholic. These overly responsible children do not have time to play with their peers, which leads to difficulties with socialization and the ability to have fun. They feel responsible for fixing everyone, and when they discover that they cannot, they are disappointed and often feel rejected. They tend to be very controlled emotionally, and they attempt to control those who are close to them and any situation in which they feel challenged or threatened. Overly responsible children have a great deal of difficulty meeting their own needs in relationships and achieving intimacy in adulthood. Female children in these families tend to marry alcoholics, sometimes again and again. Their co-dependence in these marriages is very intense and difficult to alleviate.

Not all children of alcoholics are affected in these ways. Some survive rather well through the cushioning influences of siblings, adult friends, teachers, and extended family who can meet their emotional needs. A number of children of alcoholics grow up to become "survivors" in adulthood, able to cope effectively with stress and to use their caretaking abilities to advantage in appropriate ways. However, with most children of alcoholics, the harmful effects are long lasting and persist into adulthood.

In the past few years, a great deal of attention has been focused on recognizing the difficulties of adult children of alcoholics and addressing their needs. Many support and therapy groups are springing up based on the shared pain of being raised by alcoholic parents. One of these groups is called Adult Children of Alcoholics (ACA). This group uses the 12 steps of AA in a modified way to help members realize that they are not responsible for the alcoholic's behavior and to teach them to let go of their past pain. ACA groups may be based solely on the AA model or be led by a trained therapist who is often an ACA. Children of alcoholics are now being recognized and offered preventive services and special programs are being developed to meet their needs. Alateen and in some locations Alatot and Alafam are resources for the teenage and younger children of alcoholics. New ACA groups are spreading in order to reach out to the large numbers of grown-up children of alcoholics.

Children of alcoholics often play a critical interactive role in the family dysfunction that leads to and perpetuates alcoholism. Generally, I must see the couple and all of their children before I can understand or attempt to treat an alcoholic family. Children play an important part in the family disease, regardless of age. Some real and poignant examples are: the alcoholic's wife desperately clinging to their one-year-old severely retarded child throughout a family session, thereby excluding the newly recovering alcoholic; a seven-year-old girl telling her mother she wanted her to drink because that was the only time the mother showed affection; a 10-year-old boy encouraging his father to drink in the hope that violence would be avoided or attenuated; a delinquent teenager provoking a cycle of drinking and violent arguments between his parents, rendering them unable to follow through on enforcing rules of behavior and setting limits; and a "typical" teenager who would avoid doing his daily chores by focusing on his alcoholic father's negligence of family responsibilities. Alcoholic parents are often frustrated by their inability to cope with their children, and they deal with this frustration by drinking or claiming it as an excuse to drink. One alcoholic father told his marijuana-smoking son that the next time the son smoked pot, he would get drunk. The son promptly obliged by smoking pot, and the father went on a binge that ended in hospitalization.

This chapter has attempted to summarize the family patterns common in families with a male alcoholic. Many members of alcoholic families will recognize patterns that apply to them and their family. Often merely recognizing these patterns and realizing that they are related to alcoholism is extremely helpful to a family.

References

Bepko, C., Krestan, J. *The Responsibility Trap*. Macmillan Free Press, New York, 1985.

Black, C. *It Will Never Happen To Me*. M.A.C. Publishing, Denver, Col., 1982.

Bowen, M. Alcoholism as viewed through family system theory and family psychotherapy. *Annals of the New York Academy of Science*, 233:115-122, 1974.

Cork, M. R. *The Forgotten Children*. Addiction Research Foundation, Toronto, 1969.

Cotton, N. W. The familial incidence of alcoholism: a review. *Journal of the Studies of Alcohol*, 40:89-116, 1979.

Davis, D., Berenson, D., Steinglass, P., & Davis, S. The adaptive consequences of drinking. *Psychiatry*, 37:209-215, 1974.

El-Guebaly, N., & Orford, D. R. The offspring of alcoholics: A critical review. *American Journal of Psychiatry*, 134:357-365, 1977.

Fox, R. The alcoholic spouse. In V. M. Eisenstein (Ed.), *Neurotic Interaction in Marriage*. Basic Books, New York, 1956.

Gorad, S. L. Communicational styles and interaction of alcoholics and their wives. *Family Process*, 10:475-489, 1971.

Howard, D. P., & Howard, N. T. Treatment of the significant other, in S. Zimberg, J. Wallace, and S. B. Blume (Eds.), Plenum Press, New York, 1978.

Jacob, T., Faverini, A., Meisel, S. S., & Anderson, C. N. The alcoholic's spouse, children, and family interactions. *Journal of Studies on Alcohol*, 3(7):1231-1251, 1978.

Jacob, T., Richey, D., Evitkovic, J. F., & Blane, H. T. Communication styles of alcoholic and nonalcoholic families when drinking and not drinking. *Journal of Studies on Alcohol*, 42(5):466-482, 1981.

Kaufman, E., & Pattison, E. M. Differential methods of family therapy in the treatment of alcoholism. *Journal of Studies on Alcohol*, 42(11):951-971, 1981.

Kaufman, E. *Substance Abuse and Family Therapy*. Grune & Stratton, Orlando, Fla., 1985.

Paolino, T. J., Jr., & McCrady, B. S. *The Alcoholic Marriage: Alternative Perspectives*. Grune & Stratton, New York, 1979.

Steinglass, P. A life history model of the alcoholic. *Family Process*, 19:211-226, 1980.

Wegscheider-Cruse, S. *Choicemaking* Health Communications, Inc., 1985.

C H A P T E R

5

Understanding the Adult Male Drug Abuser and His Family

*T*his chapter deals mainly with men we identify as "hardcore" drug abusers. By "hardcore" we mean those men who are addicted to heroin, those who are heavy users of cocaine (particularly regular smoking of free base and IV use), those who are heavy regular users of amphetamines (including IV administration), and abusers of any other illegal or controlled substances that are repeatedly obtained through criminal behavior.

The more an individual on the road to addiction resorts to illegal behavior to support his habit, the more he acquires the traits of an antisocial personality (ASP). It is this antisocial behavioral development that becomes the criterion for defining hardcore drug abusers. Once the addict reaches the point at which antisocial personality patterns are established, using and obtaining his drugs have become the driving force in his life and are placed far ahead of any other aspect of his relationships with others. In order to get drugs and the money to pay for them, he falls into a pattern in which he lies to family and friends, cheats them, steals from them, and even physically attacks and beats them.

A much smaller percentage of alcoholics than drug abusers are antisocial personalities. Evidence shows that some of these alcoholics had already developed antisocial personalities prior to the onset of alcoholism, whereas others developed the behavior and traits typical of ASPs after its onset. Antisocial alcoholics are very often drug abusers as well as alcoholics.

The Adult Male Drug Abuser's Behavior and Personality Traits

Although there is no specific personality syndrome that can be said to be distinctive to men who are hardcore drug abusers, there are many behavioral characteristics that are predominant and occur frequently enough so that they quite clearly distinguish most drug abusers from normal people as well as alcoholics. The high incidence of ASPs among drug abusers and the related behavior as a distinguishing characteristic was discussed above.

ASP drug abusers become involved in personal relationships only for what they can get out of them, but they give as little as possible in return. Antisocial behavior may have been evidenced as far back in an individual's life as before the age of 15, when multiple skirmishes with the law and very unstable personal and family relationships were seen.* ASPs can be quite charming and seductive, but these initially appealing qualities are generally fleeting and before long ASPs begin to overreact to any frustrations with extreme rage. Because of their pathological self-involvement and self-centeredness, they are extremely detached from others. This detachment and an inability to genuinely love is often mistaken for strength of character, which some women find attractive. It is easy then to understand why these men typically have a history of multiple relationships that may include several marriages and divorces.

Another distinguishing trait of ASPs is that they are more violent than alcoholics even when they are not using drugs. ASPs have weak superegos or consciences, both of which function to control antisocial behavior in normal people. However, some of them have "Swiss cheese" kinds of superegos—rigidly moral and punitive in some areas but lax in others.

Psychological tests done on polydrug abusers (those who use different drugs simultaneously or sequentially) and heroin addicts show that men in both categories experience high levels of depression, confusion, denial, and grandiosity they resent authority and are very cunning. In these tests, the polydrug abusers scored higher on the presence of these traits than heroin addicts. These and other tests generally indicate that severe polydrug abusers have more mental illness than heroin addicts. Heroin addicts are often preoccupied with anger and rage, and use heroin to neutralize these powerful feelings.

It is difficult to associate a certain personality type or specific distinctive personality conflicts with an abuser of any particular drug. However, one distinction that can be made is between those addicts who clearly choose either uppers or downers. Men who prefer and use uppers, like amphetamines and cocaine, use the drugs to feel active and powerful in an environment that they perceive as threatening and hostile. With progressive use of stimulants, this desired effect of feeling powerful backfires, and they begin to feel more and more threatened, even in relatively harmless circumstances. Cocaine users,

---

*In fact, ASP cannot be diagnosed unless this behavior existed before the age of 15.

on the other hand, are often intensely competitive men who take risks in order to be successful. They find that cocaine helps drive them to this success.

Those who prefer downers, like heroin and other narcotics, feel the need to dampen their sexual desires, as well as their anger, and to reduce the stress of external stimuli. What they seek is a dramatic calming effect that produces tranquil feelings and a sense of peaceful existence in the world. This may also be true of prescription drug abusers who are dependent on narcotic drugs like codeine, Darvon®, and Percodan®.

Sedative abusers repeatedly exhibit behavior that seems to tempt fate to destroy them and perform extremely risky life-threatening acts. The drugs they choose provide a passage to oblivion that allows for the denial of personal failures and the release of inhibitions. They frequently experience a selective loss of memory that lets them forget fights and accidents and helps them avoid feelings of guilt or responsibility for their actions. Hallucinogens are typically used by sensation seekers to counteract boredom. Marijuana in contrast permits the user to relax and withdraw from competitive pressures.

One aspect that users of both uppers and downers have in common is that they both are used to alleviate depression, feelings of helplessness, and anxiety, without regard for or concern about any possible long-term, harmful consequences of their drug abuse.

Almost all classes or types of drugs are used to deal with problems and anxiety about sexual identity and performance. Alcohol and the sedative drugs relax or remove sexual fears and permit the user to overcome sexual inhibitions that often are unconscious. Methaqualone (Quaalude®) is thought to have a specific sexual stimulatory effect, which is probably a myth. Heroin does retard and delay ejaculation, which may be helpful in the initial sexual efforts of teenage boys who are often prone to premature ejaculation. Conversely, when heroin addiction sets in, the user's need for any sexual contact is often totally obliterated by the effects of the drug. Stimulants initially enhance a male's sexual fantasies as well as performance but, just as with heroin addicts, stimulant addiction ultimately leads to the eradication of the drug abuser's sexual desires.

Many drug abusers do not have a particular drug of choice. They will use anything that helps them alter or change their moods or cloud their thoughts. In the jargon of the drug world, these users are sometimes referred to as "garbage heads." Some SAs only have a proclivity to become addicted to downers, and some only to uppers, but many have the potential of becoming addicted to any type of drug.

As discussed earlier, the effects of any drug on a particular person depend on the user's expectations and the setting in which the drugs are taken. If sleeping pills are taken with an expectation of sleep, then they produce somnolence. If they are taken at a party to release inhibitions, then they initially produce activation, but eventually cause sedating effects. The specific psychological effects of commonly abused drugs were described in detail in Chapter 3.

The Adult Male Drug Abuser's Family

Family of Origin

The most consistent finding in studies of the families of drug abusers is the presence of an alcoholic father in up to 50 percent of the cases. When we look at families of younger drug abusers, we see more fathers who are themselves drug abusers. Fathers who have died or abandoned the family when the drug abuser was young are also quite common. However, in certain ethnic groups, such as Italians and Jews, the fathers of drug abusers neither abandon their families nor are they substance abusers themselves.

In contrast to other ethnic groups, Jewish and Italian fathers are often emotionally overinvolved with and overreactive if they have a drug-abusing son. When Jewish and Italian male SAs are married, they are so close to their family of origin that loyalty to spouse versus family is a consistently critical issue in the dynamics of the family. Most of the Italian and Jewish fathers of heroin addicts with whom I have worked were very hard workers who set high performance standards for their sons. But these standards were not met or even approached by the sons. Many Italian sons worked directly for their fathers and, as a result, were frequently protected from having to meet the usual demands of employment outside the family-run business. Perhaps coincidentally, several of these fathers suffered disabling physical injuries after the onset of their son's drug dependence, which prevented them from continuing to work.

Although a large number of adult male drug abusers appear to be uninvolved with their parents, a closer examination of their contacts with parents reveals that they are quite enmeshed and overinvolved despite many futile attempts at individuation (the process of developing individual identities and autonomous lives). Experience shows that mothers are very close to their adult drug-dependent sons. This has been the case in every family with which I have worked regardless of ethnicity. The mothers in these families go through stages of co-dependency that are similar to those experienced by the wife of an alcoholic (described in detail in the following chapter). Hence, the mother's reactivity from her overinvolvement with the drug-abusing son ranges from denial to overprotectiveness to total preoccupation with to withdrawal from.

These enmeshed mothers think, act, and feel for their drug-abusing child. Several mothers with whom I have worked regularly took prescription tranquilizers or narcotics, which they unknowingly or openly shared with their sons. Many of these mothers suffered from an agitated depression whenever their child "acted out" in destructive ways. Mothers who took prescription tranquilizers or abused alcohol frequently increased their intake whenever the identified patient (IP) acted out. Such enmeshed mothers will do absolutely anything for their addict sons except leave them alone. A large percentage of mothers of drug addicts experienced their own alcohol abuse, suicide attempts, and severe psychosomatic symptoms, which were invariably blamed on the addict, thereby reinforcing a pattern of guilt and mutual manipulation.

Siblings

Brothers and sisters of drug abusers tend to fall equally into two basic categories: "very good" and "very bad." The "bad" group is composed of fellow drug abusers whose drug use is interwoven with that of the IP. The "good" group includes children who assume the role of an authoritarian parent when the father is absent, or disengage from the problem, or are highly successful in their own lives and careers. Some of these successful siblings do manage to individuate from the family, but many remain enmeshed even into adulthood.

Another small group of "good" siblings I have encountered in my own work was quite passive and not involved with substance abuse. Some of these siblings developed disorders such as depression, nervous tics, and headaches, all of which are related to holding in anger. The "good" child in these families conscientiously obeys family rules and works hard in school, attempting to meet the parents' high expectations. They bear the burden of the behavior of the sibling IP and their "incompetent" parents. They feel that if they can only be *good* enough, they will erase the effects of the IP on the family and make their parents look good. These "good" children are rigid, lonely, and suffer guilt and remorse, often for the rest of their lives. They are vulnerable to codependency in adult life.

Enmeshed drug-abusing siblings may provide drugs for each other, inject drugs into one another, set each other up to lose face in the family or society, and even pimp for one another. At times, a large family may show both good and bad types of sibling relationships.

Several of the young drug abusers whom I have treated fuctioned as parents in their own families and had no way of asking for or getting relief from overwhelming family responsibility except through drugs. More commonly, they were the youngest children, and their drug abuse maintained their roles as the babies of the family. They were frequently the children who got the most attention and drug abuse kept them from ever having to abandon the parental nest.

A woman who is married to this type of perennial child will always find herself in competition with his mother for his attention and affection. He often plays mother against wife in a sort of contest for who can and will best support his drug habit.

Family Variations Associated with Different Drugs of Abuse

Since there are so many variables that affect families, it is difficult to sift out those that result from a reaction to specific drugs. It is even more difficult to find family patterns that predispose a drug user to specific drugs of choice and abuse. Most of the work done on this question has been by Spotts and Shontz and describes drug abusers' families of origin, as well as their off-spring. According to these authors, male chronic amphetamine users tend to grow up in homes with strong, dominant, and manipulative mothers, and passive, ineffectual fathers. As adults, these amphetamine users fear women and deal with them by attempting to conquer, overcome, use, and exploit them. Narcotic addicts tend to come from homes in which the father was either absent or was an overpowering tyrant. As adults, they are seriously disabled by poor egos. They frequently are quiet, lonely, and unambitious people.

According to Spotts and Shontz, most cocaine users describe their mothers as warm and caring and their fathers as strong and encouraging. They develop an extreme need for complete self-sufficiency in order to compensate for their strongly denied unmet need for dependency gratification.

Barbiturate users usually decribe neglecting fathers, who are uninterested in their sons' lives, and dependent, ineffectual mothers. They tend to alternate between extreme denigration and overevaluation of relationships with rapid overinvolvement followed by equally rapid detachment.

Spousal and Parenting Relationships

This section has dealt mainly with the families of male heroin abusers and other heavy illicit drug users. As stated before, most abusers of prescription drugs do not fall into the same group as hardcore drug abusers, but rather share similarities in parent and spouse relationships with alcoholics as described in Chapter 4.

Most of the male heroin addicts with whom I have worked have been able to dominate their female spouses or partners through a combination of intimidation and manipulation. If the woman is also an addict, he generally controls her supply and administration of drugs. He may also prostitute her to pay for drugs for both of them, invariably taking a greater share of money or drugs for himself. If the spouse or partner is not an addict, he coerces her into giving him money or steals the family's food and rent money, without a qualm, to pay for his drugs.

The male heroin addict often feels that his family has never given him permission to leave home and that they are repeatedly encouraging him to return if he does leave. As a result, he never fully commits to his marriage(s) or partner(s), and he continually returns home between relationships. In another variation of this theme, he brings his wife and children home to his own parents so that his family of origin can take care of everyone. When he does get off of heroin, becomes sober, and attempts to live away from his parents, it is still extremely difficult for them to give up control of the grandchildren. This is particularly true when they have become the primary parents as the result of their son's abdicating the parental role when he was using drugs.

It is difficult to understand why the marital relationships of these hardcore drug abusers continue when the positive payoff for the abuser's partner seems so minimal. However, a wife or girlfriend may have little hope of surviving on her own when her other options are limited due to lack of education, psychological passivity or because she herself is an addict. Therefore, she continues to stay in a destructive, unhappy relationship out of fear.

References

Kaufman, E. Family structures of narcotic addicts. *International Journal of the Addictions*, 16(2):273-282, 1981.

Spotts, J. V., & Shontz, F. C. A lifetime theory of chronic drug abuse. In D.J. Lettieri et al. (Eds.), *Theories in Drug Abuse*. NIDA Research Monographer, no. 30, 1980.

Stanton, M. D., & Todd, T. C. *The Family Therapy of Drug Abuse and Addiction*. Guilford Press, New York, 1982.

▽   ▽   ▽

C H A P T E R

6

Understanding and Evaluating Co-Dependence

Not everyone who is married to an alcoholic or a drug user, or who is otherwise emotionally close to a substance abuser, is co-dependent. And not every woman—wife, girlfriend or mother—who is co-dependent suffers from the symptoms and behaviors of co-dependence to the same degree. One person's co-dependence may have minimal impact on her life and her relationships; for another, co-dependence may rob her of any real life of her own beyond her involvement with a substance abuser.

Co-dependence is progressive, just like alcoholism and drug addiction. The stages of co-dependence and its progression are discussed later in this chapter. In its early stages, co-dependence may be difficult for a layperson to even recognize. Sometimes the denial, which is almost as prominent a hallmark in co-dependence as it is in substance abuse, makes it nearly impossible for people who are co-dependent to recognize it in themselves. To compound the problem, co-dependence may be hidden behind the guise of the "normal" concern or loving behavior expected from a caring wife, girlfriend, or mother of someone with a substance abuse problem. With all of these variables clouding the picture, how can those close to substance abusers, who suspect that they might have a problem with co-dependence, figure out whether they do and whether it is severe enough to be a problem for themselves, their family, and the substance abuser?

The Signs and Symptoms of Co-dependence

Co-dependence has signs and symptoms just like alcoholism and substance abuse. A good start in making a decision about co-dependence is to understand first what the term "co-dependence" means, and then to be able to recognize some of its signs and symptoms. Experience and studies show that individuals are co-dependent (Co-D) when and if they are so involved in the life of the SA that (a) they cannot enjoy life or (b) they are so crippled by reactive behavior that they are unable to live their own life. Two other major signs of co-dependence are (c) a need to blame the SA for their own unhappiness and (d) a need to control the other person's behavior and actions, particularly those aspects of the SA's behavior that are related to substance abuse.

Joan, whose dilemma with her alcoholic husband, Stan, was discussed in the preface, wanted to know what she could read to gain insight into the disease and how to cope with it. A good way to start, according to an Al-Anon pamphlet directed to the family of an alcoholic says, "The family's best defense against the emotional impact of alcoholism is gaining knowledge and achieving the emotional maturity and courage needed to put (that knowledge) into effect." The person most responsible for the alcoholic or drug abuser may need more asistance and counseling than the alcoholic if an effective recovery program is to be undertaken. Members of the family may be quite capable of assisting substance abusers *outside* their family, but if their own husband or wife is the SA they become so confused and their emotions become so distorted that their interactions may and often do become destructive rather than helpful.

It is not necessary for all four of these particular characteristics of co-dependence to be present for a person to be a Co-D. Most often, however, all four are more or less present and the determination of co-dependence is based on how much an individual's life is damaged by each characteristic.

Claudia Black, Tim Cermak, Jael Greenleaf, and Sharon Wegscheider are considered pioneers in co-dependency work, particularly with adult children of alcoholics. They were part of the initial group that founded the National Association of Children of Alcoholics (NACOA). Although their work has been done primarily with families of alcoholics, the term "substance abuser" can be used interchangeably with "alcoholic" in the following discussion of the results of their studies.

Greenleaf defines a co-dependent as someone who assists in maintaining the social and economic equilibrium of a substance abuser. Cermak defines a relationship as co-dependent when one person's failure substantially lowers another person's self-esteem. He describes the problem with a touch of humor: "When a co-dependent is dying, it is their *partner's* life that passes before their eyes."

Sharon Wegscheider describes five characteristics of co-dependency: (1) delusions about or massive denial of the alcoholic's behavior, and their own behavior as well; (2) compulsions, or acting in repetitive ways without choice; (3) "frozen" feelings—especially anger—which are held under tight rein for fear that the barriers protecting them will be broken down; (4) low self-worth resulting from their own self-esteem being based on the behavior of the alcoholic, rather than on their own behavior; and (5) medical symptoms and complications related to stress (e.g., headaches, high blood pressure).

How can those involved with SAs and who recognize signs of co-dependence in themselves or other family members know if *they* need help for *themselves*? Help for co-dependents can come in many forms: learning how to deal more effectively and constructively with the SA with whom they are involved, learning how to relieve their own emotional pain, or learning how to take responsibility for enhancing their own lives despite the behavior of the substance abuser. How to get appropriate help and more about what it is designed to do is discussed in detail later.

I have modified a questionnaire designed by Don and Nancy Howard that focuses on evaluating family reactivity and overinvolvement with substance abuse, as well as the SA's behavior, to determine if there is a family substance abuse co-dependency problem. Two or three "yes" answers to the eight questions listed are strongly indicative of spousal co-dependency, and four or more "yes" answers are considered diagnostic, a definite indication of co-dependence. In the case of significant others, rather than spouses, ignore the word "spouse" and insert the term that applies (girlfriend, lover, sister).

	Yes	No
1. Do you worry about your spouse's drinking or drug abuse?	____	____
2. Have you ever been embarrassed by your spouse's drinking or drug abuse?	____	____
3. Are holidays more of a nightmare than a celebration because of your spouse's drinking or drug abusing behavior?	____	____
4. Does your spouse deny a substance abuse problem because he or she drinks only beer or smokes just a little pot?	____	____
5. Do you find it necessary to lie to employer, relatives, or friends in order to hide your spouse's drinking or drug abuse?	____	____
6. Do you ever feel guilty about your spouse's drinking or drug abuse?	____	____
7. Are you afraid of physical or verbal abuse when your spouse is drinking or using drugs?	____	____
8. Do you fear riding in a car with your spouse at the wheel when he or she is drinking or using drugs?	____	____

Another predominant identifying feature of most co-dependent people is that they have a strong, perhaps misguided, belief in will power. They feel certain that they can accomplish anything by wanting it desperately enough and by exhorting those around them—particularly the SA—to *make* something happen. If this is true, then they also must believe in the ability of will power alone to make the SA stop drinking or using drugs and to change his behavior.

Unfortunately, will power alone is not sufficient to stop drug or alcohol abuse or addiction.

A common characteristic of most co-dependents is their lack of a clear sense of self-identity, which results from neglecting or giving up their own needs and interests for the sake of others. They concentrate so excessively on the SA in their lives that they cease to explore their own interior life, and they lose the ability to examine their own values and motives. Since emotional individuation from the SA is nonexistent, they have no clear sense of the psychological and emotional boundaries between themselves and others, particularly the SA. Their own identity is derived almost completely from their relationship to others, and their self-esteem is gained from how they carry out their responsibilities to and for other people. They are "mirrored" through other people and by how they respond to them; they only see themselves as reflected in the responsibilities for others that life provides for them. Their sense of success or failure in life is derived not through their own performance in life but from the successes or failures of those for whom they feel responsible.

A majority of co-dependents are extremely frightened of being abandoned by others. In order to prevent abandonment, they live their lives holding back their feelings—particularly anger and aggressiveness—and not expressing their needs. They develop people-pleasing behaviors and manipulations rather than honest dialogue or communication, in order to hold others close to them. This complete dedication to meeting the needs of others and suppressing their real needs and feelings leaves them chronically exhausted physically as well as emotionally. Repeatedly being deprived of having their own needs met contributes further to their low self-esteem.

Although co-dependents may share the characteristics discussed above, they can be further broken down into categories or types. One basic type of co-dependence is based on the history of how the co-dependency developed. This first type of co-dependent has exhibited co-dependent characteristics since he or she was a child or adolescent and, in marrying an SA, continues a lifelong pattern of co-dependent behavior. Stan's wife, Joan, who was discussed in Chapter 1, is one of these types of co-dependents. Such individuals are often adult children of alcoholics like Joan, but many have grown up in other types of dysfunctional families of origin including parent(s) with clinical depression, borderline personality disorders, or severe medical illness.

The second type, referred to as "late-onset co-dependents," have not grown up in dysfunctional families of origin, but have developed co-dependent behavior only after living with an SA as a spouse or significant other. Generally speaking, this type has a better chance of being able to change their co-dependent behavior because the pattern is not a lifelong pattern, which is far more difficult to change.

Many severe co-dependents are themselves adult children of alcoholics (ACAs). In his studies of ACAs, Cermak at one time viewed the syndrome of characteristics and problems affecting most ACAs as quite similar to post-traumatic stress disorder PTSD seen in Vietnam vets or concentration camp survivors. He still includes some PTSD characteristics in his description of ACAs today. Cermack's identification of a co-dependent syndrome includes certain characteristics already discussed to some degree.

Those qualities that constitute the co-dependent syndrome in ACAs, Co-Ds, and to a lesser or more modifiable extent late-onset co-dependents, include:*

1. A *continuous investment in controlling themselves and others* that extends to three primary areas: (a) the need to control situations in order to decrease their own anxiety and minimize chaos, (b) a need to control close personal relationships mainly to avoid abandonment or suppress anger, and (c) the need to control their emotions out of fear that the release of even the smallest bit of emotion such as anger would lead to a calamitous "emotional" explosion.

2. An *overassumption of responsibility in relationships* so that attempts to meet the other person's needs are more important than gratifying their own. Co-dependents also exhibit an enhanced ability to give, but a minimal ability to take in relationships, which is consistent with this tendency to put others before themselves.

3. *Experiencing intimacy and separation in relationships are both very threatening.* Either can lead to severe anxiety and emotional problems, because the Co-Ds' lack of individuation presents them with difficulty in knowing where they leave off and their spouse or other intimate begins.

4. When close *relationships* are achieved they *have an "enmeshed" quality* in which the Co-D appears "stuck" to the SA because the need for closeness is so great. They constantly want to be with, and do everything with, the other person at the expense of their own autonomy and independent activities.

5. There is *excessive denial of* the *stress* to which they are subjected as well as of the stress created by the difficult behavior of the SA.

6. *Depression*, with its resulting loss of appetite or increased eating, along with feelings of hopelessness and helplessness, poor sleep, lack of energy, and suicidal thoughts or acts, is very common.

7. Co-dependents are *overly vigilant*. They are always on the alert for signs of substance use or abuse or related behavior. They are ever watchful for anger, behavioral slips, or any deviance from maintaining their high standard of normal appearance.

8. *Compulsions* often become more pronounced, including overeating, excessive exercising, working, housekeeping and other tidying up activities, and other repetitious behaviors.

9. *Substance abuse by the Co-Ds* themselves may begin at first to share the experience of the SA, and then to relieve their own pain and finally out of habit or actual substance dependence.

---

*Modified from Cermack.

10. If there was *verbal, physical, or sexual abuse* in the family of origin, Co-Ds may duplicate this abuse pattern in which they were abused by their parent(s) or siblings. For example, if they were physically abused by a parent, they might be physically abused by their spouse.

11. Signs of *stress related medical illness* may be present, such as headaches, high blood pressure, ulcers, rheumatoid arthritis, and heart disease.

12. They are convinced that *life is a no-win situation*. If they follow the SA around trying to prevent or intervene in substance abuse, the SA will defy the Co-D and use even more. If the Co-D purchases alcohol to prevent the shakes or help relax the SA, she will feel guilty about continuing or supporting the substance abuse process. The Co-D may want to obtain a job to get away for a while or to help with strained finances but cannot leave the kids alone. Or the SA will not let the Co-D work because it is too threatening to him. The Co-D may want to leave the SA, but is afraid to or cannot afford it. No matter what Co-Ds do, or what position they take, they feel they cannot win.

The very act of reading these 12 criteria, in an honest effort to decide if co-dependency is severe enough to warrant seeking help, is a difficult one. It takes a great deal of courage for people to admit even to themselves that they or someone in their family has a problem with alcohol or drugs, or that their family may need outside help in coping with their problems.

If you are married to or deeply involved with an SA and several of these criteria are very familiar to you, then it is strongly indicated that you and your entire family need help in addressing substance abuse and co-dependency. You may already know from painful experience that denying the problem doesn't make it go away. You may already realize that the solution does not lie in just loving the SA enough that he will stop using, and it isn't a matter of your will power or anyone else's—neither is sufficient to bring about change in a family that is overwhelmed with the problems created by substance abuse. However, there is help and it does work. The critical first step in solving the problem is recognizing the signs of substance abuse and co-dependence in the family. You may be one of the lucky ones who gets off at the first floor. But— like many others—you and your family may be in for a longer ride.

The Stages of Co-dependence

Co-dependency behaviors intensify as the SA's condition deteriorates and he sinks further and further into substance abuse. But co-dependence actually starts with the SA's very first episode of intoxication, and it continues and increases in severity throughout the early, middle, and late phases of alcoholism or drug abuse. Co-dependence often becomes so severe that the Co-D needs treatment just as badly as the SA, regardless of whether or not the SA ever seeks help himself. Recognizing and understanding the various phases of co-dependence can help families to recognize their own behavior and understand how to modify it. These phases are not always passed through in sequence; often families move back and forth between stages. However, the phases lead almost inevitably to ever increasing deterioration of the substance abuser, the co-dependent, and the family.

Not everyone in the family will develop co-dependence, but anyone who is close to the SA will more or less experience the feelings and behavior associated with its stages to some degree. For instance, the oldest sibling may leave the family before parental drinking becomes problematic.

Anticipatory Stage

In this first stage, the family is embarrassed and confused by the drinking, drug taking, and related behaviors of the SA. Family members respond by tending to deny the existence of the behavior or by trying to rationalize and justify it. However, partially outside awareness where thoughts and feelings can lie unrecognized or unacknowledged, they begin to be apprehensive and frightened by the SA's behavior. They also start to become openly irritated and frustrated with the substance abuser and they sometimes express these feelings.

Initial Stage

The family's emotional mechanism of denial leads them to repeatedly feel hopeful, encouraged, and confident that the SA's drinking or using and related behaviors will improve, particularly whenever he promises he will stop his substance abuse. If family members are actually successful in denying the substance abuse, they may even experience elation and cheerfulness. Ultimately, however, once they begin to recognize that the problem is really worsening or has become recurrent and is not just going to go away, they become discouraged and disappointed. They start to feel guilt, shame, and responsibility for the SA's drinking or drug-taking behavior. In reaction to their guilt, they pull away from the SA, which leads to feelings of isolation, alienation, and withdrawal.

Intermediate Stage

The co-dependent family's symptoms are now present whether the SA is using or sober. His provocative behavior elicits overt anger and resentment and his pitiful actions when intoxicated bring out disgust and loathing. But the family still defends and protects the SA by making excuses for missing work or not showing up at important events in the lives of his children. They further protect him by searching out alcohol and drugs in various hiding places in the house, car, and garage, and by pouring out alcohol or getting rid of drugs. In spite of underlying anger and resentment, the family continues to display pity, sympathy, and compassion toward the SA. The family now begins to be obsessed and preoccupied with the SA's behavior.

Advanced Stage

Preoccupation with the SA's behavior permeates every aspect of each family member's life in the advanced stages of co-dependence. Family members often panic and worry about themselves and the rest of family, as well as the SA. Some may have started drinking with the alcoholic or snorting a line with the cocaine addict to avoid their feelings of isolation or having to deal with their own anxieties. They may purchase drugs and dole out alcohol to minimize the SA's withdrawal symptoms. The family feels completely helpless, inadequate and ineffective in dealing with the situation. Anger spills over outside of the home, as well as within the family. Despair, hopelessness, self-pity, and remorse become pervasive and dominate all aspects of family life. Family members have begun to mistrust everyone and feel persecuted by others. Attempts at communicating with other relatives, friends, and associates diminishes markedly.

Final Stage

Assuming responsibility for the SA and his behavior, and frequent altercations with him, are now all-encompassing aspects of family life. Participation in meaningful outside interests declines. The Co-Ds neglect taking care of themselves, and their own needs are disregarded. Medical problems or drug and alcohol abuse and dependence may occur in other family members. The family tries to take complete control of the SA and his drinking and drug taking. They attempt to control every drop of alcohol or every pill he consumes, constantly nagging and scolding him for his infantile behavior. They assume all of his household responsibilities, rendering him totally useless and unneeded in the home. The family may compulsively and frantically seek short-term outside interests to divert themselves from thinking about the SA. At this stage, separation from the SA is frequently threatened. However, this kind of threat is not effective unless the family is actually ready to follow through and leave or ask the SA to leave, and is able to effectively communicate their determination to do so.

When a co-dependent is fully capable of detachment in this final phase, the SA will often become sufficiently motivated for treatment. This sequence of co-dependency stages has been supported by two scientific studies. The first of these, done by Wiseman, involved the study of 76 wives of alcoholics. Wiseman found that these wives first tried to influence their spouses with direct approaches, including logical persuasion, nagging, emotional pleading, and threats to leave. When the direct approaches failed, the wives resorted to indirect methods, including acting normal and uninvolved (detachment), preventing any upsets to the SA, and finally, (often with the help of Al-Anon or Narcanon) taking a complete hands-off approach.

Moos, Finney, and Gamble conducted a study of alcoholics and their spouses as contrasted with nonalcoholics. They found the following characteristics in the spouses of alcoholics: more alcohol consumption; more negative life events; fewer social and recreational activities; less family cohesiveness; more depression; more medical conditions; and more job changes. When the alcoholics stopped drinking, their wives' symptoms actually improved.

An Al-Anon pamphlet entitled "A Guide for the Family of an Alcoholic" states: "Unfortunately many families suffer repeatedly from drinking and its consequences, thinking this is required if they love the alcoholic. The tragic result is that alcoholism is thereby encouraged and fear and resentment take over human emotions." The wife, husband, or other close family member needs to take a close look at his or her own involvement with the alcoholic or drug abuser. "In most instances a change in the family is necessary before a change in the alcoholic may be anticipated. To do nothing is impossible. As a general rule to do nothing means to give in to the situation, to be run over and exploited and to fight back in quiet, passive, destructive ways. The important thing is to learn which interactions are destructive and which might be creative and then have the courage to attempt a creative approach. The change must begin with the nonalcoholic. The alcoholic will not seek help in recovery as long as the alcoholic's needs are met within the family."

This chapter has provided guidelines for recognizing co-dependency. Some co-dependent behaviors exist in all human beings, particularly in those who are in love. However, co-dependency of a sufficient degree to warrant outside help or support occurs in every individual who is in love with a chemically dependent person. Coping, surviving, and overcoming co-dependency is a difficult but obtainable process that is explained in the following chapters.

References

Black, C. *It Will Never Happen to Me*, M.A.C., Denver, 1981.

Cermak, T. L. *A Primer on Adult Children of Alcoholics.* Health Communications, Inc., Pompano Beach, Fla., 1985. Diagnosing and treating co-dependence: A guide for professionals who work with chemical dependents, their spouses and children. Minneapolis, Minn.: Johnson Institute Books, 1986.

Cleveland, M. Treatment of co-dependent women through the use of mental imagery. *Alcoholism Treatment Quarterly* 4:1, 27, 41, 1987.

Greenleaf, J. L. *Co-Alcoholic, Para-Alcoholic: Who's Who and What's the Difference?* Joel Greenleaf, Los Angeles, 1981.

Howard, D., & Howard N. The Howard Institute Family Counseling Center, Columbia, Mo., 1976.

Moos, R. H., Finney, J. W., & Gamble, W. The process of recovery from alcoholism, II. Comparing spouses of alcoholic patients and matched community controls. *Journal of Studies on Alcohol*, 3(9):888-909, 1982.

Wegscheider, S. *Another Chance: Hope and Health for the Alcoholic Family.* Science and Behavior Books, Palo Alto, Calif., 1981.

Wegscheider-Cruse, S. Thirst for freedom. In S. Wegscheider-Crus & R. W. Esterly (Eds.), *Alcoholism and the Family: A Book of Readings.* Health Communications, Hollywood, Fla., 1985.

Wiseman, J. P. The "home treatment": the first steps in trying to cope with an alcoholic husband. *Family Relations*, 29:541-549, 1980.

▽   ▽   ▽

C H A P T E R

7

Strategies for Coping with Male Substance Abusers

At the beginning of the chapter on alcoholics, it was pointed out that although there are many similarities between alcoholics and drug abusers, there are enough differences to warrant discussing each in a separate chapter. In this chapter, which is devoted to helping concerned loved ones learn to cope in more constructive ways with chemically* dependent men, we return once more to the similarities in dealing with alcoholics and drug abusers.

There are so many similarities in the family dynamics of all chemically dependent men that a set of workable, constructive coping attitudes and strategies have evolved that can be successfully utilized by spouses and other family members, as well as friends, employers, and therapists. These strategies are appropriate regardless of the age, overt behavior, or substance of choice of the SA. The universal, generalized principles of coping strategies are emphasized and described first in this chapter. Variations in coping successfully with different types of substance abusers are discussed in the latter part of the chapter.

Regardless of what type of substance abuser may be involved, when someone has finally reached a point at which they are willing to look at the options available for dealing and coexisting with a substance abuser in ways that are healthier for herself and the family, the process should start with the acceptance of a basic truth. No one is ever responsible or to be blamed for the drinking or drug intake of another individual.

It is a fact of family life that many uncomfortable feelings are provoked as family members interrelate. Sadness, anger, anxiety, irritability, tension, frustration, and grief are common byproducts of everyday family interaction.

---

*The terms chemically dependent and substance abuser are used interchangeably with each other and with drug and alcohol abusers.

A substance abuser *chooses* to deal by self-administering drugs and/or alcohol. The other family members who are not chemically dependent do not cope with family stress in this particular way. When substance abuse begins to occur, families develop predictable reactive patterns that perpetuate use and abuse. When and if substance abuse stops, the families may still be locked into conditioned patterns of response that often reactivate substance use and abuse. An example of this is when the family has formed a supportive network that does not include the SA; when he tries to reenter the family, he finds a wall has been built that excludes him and his loneliness leads him back to drinking. However, only the person who bends his elbow to drink, or puts the pills in his mouth, or the needle in his vein, is responsible for substance abuse—not the family. But because the family's dialogue and actions appear to be related to or seem to provoke alcohol or drug use, they *learn* to feel guilty. The SA plays into this guilt and readily accuses the family of responsibility for his substance use. The family in turn responds to these repeated attributes by accepting progressively more blame. Therefore, the family must learn and utilize techniques and strategies for countering feelings of guilt, self-blame, over-responsibility, and overinvolvement in the life of the SA.

Techniques and Strategies for Coping

Unfortunately, a lot of family members may not be willing to use these new techniques until they themselves have "bottomed out" (e.g., reached a level of sufficient pain that they are willing to risk changing their own behavior). Remember, your need to keep blaming the SA for your problems may be because you need an external issue to keep you from looking at yourself and your own intrapersonal difficulties. Or perhaps you need to maintain your role in reprovoking crises to avoid the boring sameness of your life. These may be difficult issues to face at first. Co-dependents have almost as tough a job cracking through their denial as the SAs do. Even though their desperate need for help is obvious to everyone around them, Co-Ds resist getting help for themselves with the same tenacity that they cling to trying to change the SA. Perhaps this resistance is rooted in their need to always put themselves second, or in their false belief that the SA can stop tomorrow, if only they can make him want to stop, and then everything will be okay.

Two important basic attitudes to develop on the road to recovery from co-dependence are accepting powerlessness and realizing your lack of responsibility for the chemically dependent man in your life. These changes in your way of thinking can bring about basic attitudinal shifts that can facilitate the relief of guilt and self-blame.

Powerlessness versus Guilt

It is important to start by accepting the fact that *you* are powerless to control the SA's use of chemicals and his related behavior. Learning to accept that you are not responsible for and, therefore, are not guilty of causing the alcoholic's drinking or the drug abuser's intake of drugs removes a heavy, unnecessary burden you have been carrying around.

Telling someone not to feel guilty is easy. The difficulty lies in putting this into practice and convincing yourself that you are really not guilty, no matter what the SA or anyone else tries to tell you. Guilt is a basic, deep-seated human emotion. It serves many legitimate, healthy purposes in our lives, but sometimes it can be falsely triggered and used in self-destructive ways. Following are several ideas that can serve as techniques for removing guilt about the SA and his behavior:

1. Accept that alcoholism and drug abuse are diseases that have a biological and hereditary basis, as well as social and psychological causes. There is now abundant and persuasive medical evidence to support this perspective. Family behavior does not cause substance abuse any more than it causes other diseases like diabetes or cancer.

2. No one is perfect. We have all done things for which we are sorry. Our human errors do not cause others to abuse alcohol or drugs. If you are feeling guilty, ask yourself, "Why do I need to feel badly right now?" If nothing comes to mind, why waste the effort in feeling badly? If you can pinpoint some real source for your present guilt, work on forgiving yourself, because you cannot cause substance abuse. If you are focusing on guilt from the distant past, isn't it about time you stopped punishing yourself for old baggage? Remember that taking the guilt upon yourself absolves the SA of responsibility—and this is just what he's looking for though, in fact, it only weakens him and doesn't help either of you.

3. Borrow a technique from behavioral psychology. Each time you begin to feel guilty and responsible, repeat to yourself, "I cannot make anyone drink or use drugs. I cannot stop anyone from drinking or using drugs. Only he, himself can." If the SA or his parents accuse you of being responsible for his problem, state your own version of this quote to them in a clear, firm voice. Say it only once. Do not repeat yourself or you run the risk of getting drawn into a power struggle.

Accepting powerlessness and lack of responsibility over the behavior of others may sound easy, but it is not. Have you ever tried to change an adult's behavior by repeatedly urging, cajoling, pleading, or ordering? It doesn't work. The only technique that may work is accepting your powerlessness. This consistent attitude of not taking responsibility for an SA permits the other person to decide to change his own behavior.

As you practice these strategies, you will probably be confronted with a number of dilemmas. One common problem in learning new coping techniques is being able to distinguish between punishing the SA and allowing him to experience the natural consequences of his untreated disease. There is often a delicate balance between the two. If an attitude or action that you take appears to be punishment to him, he may react by feeling that he has already suffered enough so why shouldn't he just repeat his behavior. He may respond to perceived punishment by escalating his actions and creating a crisis to which he responds with self-destructive behaviors in retaliation or escape. Though you run the risk of appearing to punish him when you no longer take on guilt or rescue him, permitting him to feel the consequences may be the only way the SA will accept sufficient responsibility for himself to change his behavior.

Accepting powerlessness and absolving yourself from guilt are two major themes that are interwoven into many other coping strategies. Another important attitudinal shift that is vital in working a program of new coping skills is learning to accept and acknowledge that change is gradual. You must reward yourself for little changes and not be too disappointed by the inevitable setbacks that are normal occurrences in trying to change family dynamics.

Detached Concern versus the Police and the Protector

When the family feels responsible for substance abuse, its members are inevitably drawn into assuming the role of protector or police, or both. These roles present no-win situations for everyone involved.

The protector calls employers and makes excuses for absence and tardiness. Protectors undress the intoxicated SA and put him to bed, purchase alcohol and prescription drugs to alleviate or avoid withdrawal, and provide money and lawyers for legal defenses against minor or serious scrapes with the law. The policewoman berates the SA, screams at him, and chronically criticizes his behavior. When suspicious of substance abuse, the policewoman searches the house for drugs and alcohol repeatedly and compulsively, and destroys all substances found hidden away. Calls are made to doctors asking them not to prescribe or refill drugs. The policewoman is constantly on the alert for any sign of drug or alcohol intake.

It is often difficult to tell if a family member is playing the protector or policewoman role because many behaviors are suggestive of both and because often individuals or families will shift back and forth, from one role to the other. Neither posture is helpful to the family or the SA. If you recognize yourself playing policewoman or protector, you must abandon this behavior and substitute loving, detached concern. How to do this is discussed later in this chapter.

There is only one situation in which the family has no choice but to be both protector and policewoman—when the SA is too intoxicated to drive, but is about to get behind the wheel. The clear and easy decision called for is to keep yourself and all family members out of the car. However, it is impossible not to consider the SA's life and the safety of others on the road if he is allowed to drive. Although the ultimate goal is to give the SA total responsibility for his life and his own actions, not intervening is contraindicated in this specific situation. The best thing to do is to hide or take away the car keys. This is most easily accomplished when you have achieved sufficient emotional distance at the moment to avoid being drawn into a power struggle with him. Taking the keys must be done casually and calmly, with emotional detachment and a minimum of fuss and excitement. You may have to leave the scene after hiding or taking the car keys, if the SA is overly reactive or violent.

This same calm, rational attitude must be practiced whenever the SA's actions are dangerous to others or if he is suicidal. Obviously you must try to protect the lives of loved ones whenever possible. However, responding repeatedly to his dangerous threats by providing protection only reinforces the SA's inability to learn to save his own neck in the long run. Even when a situation is life threatening to him, you must be cautious when intervening. You should only rescue him in a way that does not push you into greater involvement with him. If you rescue successfully once, you will be faced with having to rescue again and again, in progressively more difficult situations. For example, if the SA is arrested for driving under the influence of drugs or alcohol and is thrown into jail and he calls you to bail him out. Harm may come to him while locked up with thieves and rapists, so you want to protect him. If you bail him out, however, he is denied the frightening experience that just might result in his deciding he needs help with his substance abuse problem. It also gives him the clear signal that if it happens again, you'll rescue him again, so why should he worry or change his behavior.

Constantly policing and protecting the SA is not only exhausting for the family, it is bad for their own mental health and emotional well-being. It is only as you are able to withdraw from the role of protector or police that the SA will assume responsibility for his own actions and, ultimately, his own sobriety. Every time you refuse to save him from the natural consequences of his actions, you are permitting him to be confronted by the disease and its destructive effects. Only then will seeking appropriate help become an option to the SA.

Detachment versus Enmeshment

SAs are experts at drawing others into their chaotic lives and destructive behavior. Family members often get sucked in and literally almost stuck to the SA as if he were a "tar baby." Another common reaction for spouses or family members is to go to the other extreme and pull away from the SA totally by leaving home or living with him in stark silence. Never threaten to pull away from the SA for a minute, a day, or a lifetime *unless you are completely prepared to follow through on your threat.* Threats are only productive when you follow through on them or when they are employed to accomplish a helpful goal such as motivation for the SA to enter treatment. However, taking as much distance from the SA as needed on a daily basis is helpful as long as this does not pull you back into a struggle. If you can get the emotional freedom you need while staying in the home, do it. If leaving the house is necessary to get your distance, then follow that course. When you know what action or decision is right for you, express your needs to the SA at once, but do not repeat yourself and do not get into an extended discussion about it. If you are not heard the first time, or you do not get what you want, asking again and again only produces further anxiety and crisis—it never gets your needs met.

One helpful and proven rule of thumb for any family system is "never pursue a distancer." In substance-abusing families, the wife who is enmeshed becomes a pursuer who is constantly moving in on the SA to tell him how he must change. The SA then becomes the distancer who repeatedly moves away and at the same time criticizes the family's behavior and ignores his own. The more the SA is pursued for change or intimacy, the further and faster he runs. The solution is neither pursuit nor angry disengagement—it is loving detachment.

In practicing detachment, we do not criticize the SA's drinking and drug abuse. Rather we become responsible for our own reactivity regarding his behavior. This reactivity is very difficult to control solely through will power. One beneficial way to control overreactivity is through attendance at meetings of Al-Anon, Co-dependents Anonymous (CODA) or Cocanon (described later in this chapter). Al-Anon helps you to convey to the SA, "You can live the way you want to; I also have that right. I will not let your drinking be the most important thing in my life."

If you choose to remain in the relationship with a practicing substance abuser (one who is still drinking or using), you must make yourself as emotionally comfortable as possible. You must create this emotional relief for yourself outside of your interactions with your SA spouse. You must find a way to be good to yourself if you are going to be able to detach. It is extremely helpful for spouses or partners to develop careers, hobbies, and friendships that are rewarding and nurturing to ensure the ability to detach from the SA without great suffering. Being good to yourself means that you don't have to suffer as the SA suffers from his disease. It is his disease and his suffering. Your pain doesn't help him at all. As a matter of fact, it actually makes matters worse.

Discounting the SA's input regarding family matters even when he is sober is a common reaction, but it is not always a good practice for the family. Appropriate assertiveness, limit-setting punishment, or valid concerns on the part of the SA are often ignored in family discussions out of habit or attributing his speaking up to the influence of drugs or alcohol even if he is not drinking or using. When this happens, the SA may become angry or depressed and he will often reengage the family in the old combative cycle that leads again to substance abuse. It is very helpful if the family can detach from their immediate emotional overreaction to the SA, and accept his input as appropriate in cases when it is. Although this type of support may prevent him from bottoming out in this area of family life, the family's recognition and acceptance of his participation may help the SA to feel part of the family again. He, in turn, may then be more receptive to accepting their input about his getting the help he so badly needs.

Confrontation versus Pity

Confrontation can be helpful if done correctly. By confrontation we mean telling the SAs calmly and matter of factly about his behavior. Pity is never beneficial. Confronting SAs when they are intoxicated is invariably ineffective. Confronting is best done when the SA is withdrawing from alcohol or sedative use or "crashing" after taking stimulants. At this point, he is feeling sick, guilty, and repentant, and he may be willing to really hear an empathic statement about the family's concerns or fears. Confronting an intoxicated person is not really dealing with the person, and it can even be quite dangerous. Do not confront when either of you are frightened, angry, or out of control. Instead, confront calmly and with the facts. An example of an appropriate response would be something like, "Amy's graduation is tomorrow, and she would like you to be there because you mean so much to her." As opposed to the provocative, "Well, don't do it again. You miss a family graduation again and Amy will cry all night and I won't be able to calm her down." State your case only once and refuse to enter into a mutual discussion about it. He may become very angry. Try to remember that his anger at you is out of his own need to reassure himself that he is not all bad or the only one who behaves badly. Try not to respond to his anger with your own as this only escalates the situation. One type of confrontation can be done when the alcoholic is concerned about what he did during a blackout. He should be told quietly, without anger or reproach, what happened. You should avoid saying anything that can be construed as picking on him such as talking about how he looked or acted, or what you think of him for what he did.

There are several rules of thumb that are very helpful to keep in mind when a family feels that confrontation is necessary. These suggestions are derived from Al-Anon literature.

• *Do not attack—discuss.* Criticism only makes the SA feel defensive and he is apt to react emotionally.

- *State your point* clearly and do not repeat it.
- *Keep your voice low and pleasant.* When voices become high pitched or loud, feelings run higher. If his voice is too loud, you should leave the room.
- *Stick to the subject.* Particularly stick to the present topic and do not add in past grievances or issues.
- *Listen to his complaints.* Let him know that he has been heard and evaluate what he says for your own growth.
- *Do not make demands.* State your case without suggesting how any issue or problem should be resolved. Let him come up with the way the problem should be solved.
- *Be supportive of his healthy, sober changes.* When he changes behavior positively, do not ask why he could not have done it before, or without AA, or without counseling, or without being reminded.
- *Be courteous.* Unfortunately most of us reserve courteous behavior for strangers, but an attitude of courtesy can be beneficial in the most intimate of relationships. In fact, family members deserve it even more than strangers.

Pity is generally an ineffective response to any person's behavior. It is even less effective with a SA. Pity reinforces his inability to grow up and function as an adult. It communicates to the SA that he does not have to change and it puts him in the position of a child who can get infantile gratification from never growing up.

If there is anything more counterproductive than pitying the SA, it is indulging in *self*-pity. When family members wallow in self-pity, they stay ineffectual and maintain the old, dysfunctional behavior that stands in the way of learning positive new coping techniques that can relieve their own suffering.

Dyads and Threesomes versus Triangulation

Triangulation is the displacement of a problem from between two individuals to a third person, issue, or thing. It happens when individuals become incapable of resolving issues between themselves. A "threesome" is when two people bring in a third person to work together with them. In this case, we're talking about the couple (dyad) as the chemically dependent man and his wife or girlfriend. SAs tend to involve everyone around them, particuarly family members, in triangles. Perhaps not surprisingly, the most frequent issue that is triangulated is the use and abuse of drugs and alcohol by the SA. The SA and significant other commonly argue over whether the SA has had any drugs at all, is intoxicated, has spent too much money on drugs or alcohol, or is too intoxicated to be responsible. Such arguments never achieve resolution. The family should avoid this type of triangulated argument at all times. If you must get into the guessing game of how much alcohol or drugs are consumed, try the following exercise. Make a daily list on a piece of paper and compare your estimates with those of another family member. List-making will take the emotion out of the guessing or it will ensure that you tire of this fruitless game.

Children are commonly used as the third person in a triangulation. A spouse may become overly involved with her eldest male child, or the SA may participate in overinvolvement with a daughter. Such triangles are common in the families of chemically dependent men. If the SA is working toward sobriety and the family is working toward becoming cohesive again, the child must be removed from between the two parents. As long as a child is between you and your mate, or as long as one of you gets your needs for affection and attention met by your child instead of your spouse, your family will be nonfunctional and prone to repeated substance abuse. Furthermore, triangulation is unhealthy for the children, because it does not allow them to seek out and obtain appropriate kinds of gratification associated with their age such as time to be with their friends and taking part in recreational activities with their peers.

Another kind of triangulation takes place when a spouse or the SA takes a lover. Chemically dependent men married to nonalcoholic or non-substance-abusing spouses commonly find lovers with whom they can share drugs and alcohol. The lovers further support the SA's substance abuse and lack of responsibility. These affairs generally are terminated when substance abuse ceases. If the affair continues, substance abuse will probably only stop temporarily, if at all. The wives of SAs may also triangulate their conflicts with their spouses or attempt to ignore them through involvement with a lover. Their lovers may take care of their unmet sexual needs and provide confirmation of their femininity or they may offer consolation about their unhappy marriage. But the guilt experienced over the affair can be disabling to either spouse. The wife's contentment with a marriage that includes a lover may contribute to the SA's satisfaction with the status quo, so that nothing happens to rock the boat and his drinking or using continues. Once the SA is working successfully toward sobriety and both partners become committed to the survival of the marriage, it is essential that any affairs be ended.

A male SA also often triangulates his spouse and his mother. The mother may collude with the son by blaming her daughter-in-law for the SA's problem. Mothers and wives must try to recognize and resist this self-destructive triangle. Spouses also collude with their own mothers and siblings. Remember, a marriage will only work if the dyadic marital relationship is clearly established as the most important relationship in both of your lives.

Celibacy versus Sexual Gratification

A lot of SAs initially use drugs and alcohol to help their sexual performance. But these augmenting effects from alcohol or drugs are always temporary. Addiction ultimately leads to a virtual absence of any sexual needs or desires and an inability to perform sexually.

SAs frequently use sex as a substitute for love and as a way of manipulating their partner to obtain instant forgiveness for all of their inadequacies, including their substance abuse. If a spouse or partner has this awareness of the SA's motives for having sex, she may choose to continue to engage in sex or to abstain. When she does refuse, the SA—potent or not—will beg, plead, cajole, and coerce for sexual favors. When and if the spouse chooses to participate sexually, she must realize that the SA may feel he has been forgiven for all transgressions, and that he is entitled to restoration of all previous rights, privileges, and role functions in the family.

If the spouse has chosen to deal with the SA through detachment and has included not having sex with him as an integral part of that detachment, ground will be lost by resuming sexual relations. Successfully detaching from an unsatisfactory sexual relationship with the SA is a major step toward achieving the level of emotional disengagement necessary for the spouse's own well-being. In addition, the absence of sexual gratification may exert substantial influence on the SA to get the help he needs. When the SA uses sexuality manipulatively, the spouse is truly in a bind. The woman who gives up sexual contact with her husband is left with few satisfactory choices. There are affairs, with all of their attendant problems, or celibacy, or self-pleasuring. The last alternative can also include nonsexual but sensual pleasures such as massages, manicures, pedicures, and lotions.

Acceptance versus Will Power

Effecting any kind of change through will power alone is very difficult and often impossible. Changing through will power is also emotionally exhausting and depleting. However, it is often possible to first change one's own behavior and have the underlying emotions change later. Letting go and acceptance, as opposed to attempts through will power alone, are effective means of changing, but somewhat difficult to explain. Acceptance is a state of letting things happen to you and flow past you without feeling a need to overreact or control events or people. It is best done by taking life one day at a time because viewing all of life's problems at once and wondering how they will all be worked out can be overwhelming.

This idea of letting things happen naturally, without controlling people or events in an effort to make things turn out your way, can be greatly augmented and facilitated by adopting or renewing spirituality. Al-Anon calls this spirituality, a "higher power." This higher power is usually, but not always, conceived of as God. If one does not believe in God, other higher or greater powers than one's self can be substituted, even the idea of fate. The most available alternative higher power and one that is commonly used in facilitating change with co-dependency is the support of the Al-Anon group whose collective power can facilitate and strengthen the state of letting go and acceptance. The AA and Al-Anon serenity prayer is the embodiment of letting go and acceptance: "God, grant me the serenity to accept the things I cannot change, the courage to change the things I can, and the wisdom to know the difference." If you do not believe in God, this serenity may come from meditation or other relaxation techniques. These states are helpful spiritual supplements that are often used to successfully achieve the emotional detachment coping techniques that we have been talking about in this chapter.

Staying or Leaving: Helplessness versus Choice

In families attempting to deal with the effects of substance abuse, the best outcome for the entire family's mental health and well-being is for the SA to achieve sobriety and the family to remain intact and working their own program of recovery. The next best result is for the SA to leave the family or the family to remove the SA from the home. The least desirable alternative is for the family to continue to live together while the SA is seriously abusing drugs or alcohol. There are only two choices available to the family that seems stuck in this latter mode: they can remain the same or they can change.

Once given the tools to change, remaining the same becomes a *choice* not an inevitability. If the family can accept the fact that they are *choosing* to remain the same then they may regard their behavior as a choice rather than something done out of helplessness. Accepting that you are choosing to stay in your misery is a helpful way to emerge from a painful state. By acknowledging that you have been choosing misery, you can opt instead to attempt the alternative of emotional detachment. Techniques for achieving emotional detachment were described earlier in this chapter.

Emotionally detaching from a serious substance-abusing spouse while living in the same household is still an extremely difficult feat, despite having knowledge of these techniques and putting them to work. If you are not successful with this approach of emotional detachment, you still have a choice—working toward a physical separation. The most satisfactory way to accomplish this for all concerned, especially the nondrinking or using spouse, is to leave the SA behind in the house and for the family to move. This is the only method that depends solely on you and does not require any cooperation from the SA. The sober spouse leaving is generally the most workable plan, because the SA is an expert at frustrating the attempts of others to get him to do anything, much less leave. He will refuse to leave. He will disobey court orders of protection and return home. He may threaten to destroy the house and your valuable possessions if you kick him out. He will maintain the passive-aggressive power techniques (behavior that appears passive, but is actually aggressive) so well employed by most chemically dependent men.

One problem encountered with moving the family out is that it presents the often formidable reality of establishing a new geographical identity for family members, particularly if done suddenly. In order to be most effective, all aspects of moving out should be well planned to reduce future problems and anxiety. Financial matters should be carefully planned in advance. The potential financial difficulties of being on your own, and their potential solutions, should be carefully assessed before making a decision to leave. Even with logistical contingencies, such as finding a place to live provided for, moving out is difficult because it means facing the emotional issues of independence which many spouses have denied throughout their marriage.

Making a clear choice between staying the same, emotionally detaching, and leaving is extremely difficult. Therefore, many spouses will find following through on any decision they make, or even making a decision, impossible at first. The wife may also have to "hit bottom" before she stops trying to change the SA or finally reaches a point at which she is ready to leave. When the spouse begins to detach emotionally, the SA will often react by escalating abusive, substance abusing, behavior in an effort to keep the spouse enmeshed. Often, the escalation will consist of job loss, driving under the influence, being arrested, and suicide attempts. If faced with this behavior, the spouse should sincerely communicate that she strongly prefers that the SA not kill himself, but that she is powerless to stop him from doing so. Once the spouse is able to communicate this level of detachment, the SA is likely to enter treatment and stay in it.

A wife has the power to facilitate effective treatment when she can say, with conviction, "I love you, but I will not tolerate your behavior any longer. If you enter and complete a treatment program, I will stay by your side. If you do not enter or complete treatment, I will leave you regardless of any immediate consequences." Because it feels so risky and frightening, taking this approach is acutely painful for most spouses. However, if she can remember that the risk of any single suicidal threat the SA makes is minimal to moderate, whereas the risk of his fatal deterioration if untreated is very high and almost inevitable, she may be armed with enough courage to follow through on a tough decision.

Al-Anon and Other Support Groups

Support groups, such as Al-Anon, are extremely helpful facilitators to the positive steps outlined above for the families of substance abusers. Without the encouraging support of others, taking these steps may seem overwhelming and almost impossible to achieve. Other support groups include Narcanon, Cocanon, Alateen, Alafam, Alatot, Families Anonymous, CODA and ACA. There are groups that deal with specific segments of the family, such as children or wives, as well as those that relate to specific drugs. Significant-other groups, led by recovering SAs—with or without professional co-therapists or professional/recovering SAs—may also be extremely helpful. Information about these groups can be found in the Appendix.

Al-Anon, one of the best known of these groups, is a self-help program that arose in the late 1940s as a parallel but separate movement to AA. The other support groups have developed much more recently, particularly Cocanon, CODA and ACA, which did not become important factors in the area of treating substance abuse until the mid 1980s. The group meetings conducted by all of these organizations are similar to AA in their format of self-help with a spiritual emphasis. Successful Al-Anon members are encouraged to accept the disease concept of alcoholism. This concept maintains that the alcoholic is not behaving out of irresponsibility, low morals, or lack of will power, but has a progressive, fatal disease that is totally out of his or her control. Al-Anon espouses the concept of family co-dependence and follows a 12-step program of recovery for co-dependents, just like AA's 12-step program for alcoholics. Family members are taught not to take the disease "personally." Al-Anon members follow three basic principles: (1) a loving detachment from the alcoholic, (2) the reestablishment of self-esteem and independence, and (3) reliance on a higher or greater power than themselves.

Several slogans have also been adopted from AA by Al-Anon. These are helpful to employ as a part of the program and they embody the Al-Anon philosophy described in this section. They include: "First things first," "Easy does it," "Live and let live," "But for the grace of God," "Keep an open mind," "Let go and let God," and "Just for today."

Al-Anon members are encouraged to recognize themselves in the many similar stories shared in meetings by other group members and to try to adjust their attitudes and behavior to the principles of the group. It is critical that the co-dependent spouse have a group of people in her corner who are applauding and cheering her on. Al-Anon can provide at least part of this support.

Al-Anon recognizes that its members are not equipped by training or experience to advise, judge, or counsel other members in complex family relationships. They acknowledge that such counseling when needed is the function of professionals in the field of substance abuse. Al-Anon and other support groups provide support, relief, and guidance for family members regardless of whether the SA is particpating in rehabilitation. However, these support groups are more effective for the whole family when the SA is himself in a program of recovery like Narcotics Anonymous (NA), Cocaine Anonymous (CA), or AA.

Varying the Coping Strategy with Different Types of Substance Abusers and Families

The coping strategies we have been talking about are generally helpful to the families of all kinds of substance abusers and chemically dependent men.

However, every SA is a unique individual and every family system reacts or adjusts differently to a substance abuse problem. How to vary coping strategies based on the categorically different family systems discussed in Chapters 4 and 5 is the subject of the last section of this chapter.

Separated Families

Most of the written materials that suggest coping strategies for substance-abusing families have focused on the enmeshed family. Generally speaking, separated families are enmeshed families whose pain has been so great that the family has parted ways. Separated families have experienced so many miscarried attempts at uniting that they have given up all hope. Often, the SA will come back to the separated family in a sober state, begging and pleading for the family to reconcile. I would suggest that these families not attempt any efforts or discussion of reuniting until the SA has experienced *at least* six months of sobriety and has proven his vocational stability. Families like these who have suffered so much should not attempt to reunite without the aid of a therapist who understands the special problems of separated alcoholic or drug abusing families.

"Functional" Alcoholic and Drug Dependent Families

"Functional" families are generally better off when they do not examine their family too closely, because their sense of well-being depends on denial of their difficulties. However, education on substance abuse and attendance at AA and Al-Anon meetings can be quite helpful. Rarely does this type of involvement harm a functional family or tip it over into dysfunction. It may help them overcome their denial and gradually work toward sobriety.

Different Stages of Co-Dependence

One way of determining the most effective coping devices to employ in a given family is to first identify and appreciate the family's stage of co-dependence described in detail in Chapter 6.

As stated the *anticipatory stage* is characterized by denial and confusion. This is an excellent time for the entire family to become educated about the medical and psychological aspects of alcoholism or other substance abuse. Generally, Al-Anon is not accepted by families at this stage. However, many substance abuse treatment programs offer excellent education sessions that would be appropriate and helpful for these families.

The initial stage is characterized by further denial or by depression and emotional withdrawal. The spouses in this stage either need to obtain further education about substance abuse or develop alternatives to their loneliness and emotional estrangement from the SA. They may be ready for Al-Anon. The high level of overinvolvement with the substance abuser during the *intermediate stage* necessitates all of the techniques for disengagement and not protecting the SA described earlier in this chapter. In the *advanced stage* the substance abuser should enter treatment, and intervention (described later in Chapter 8) may be necessary to facilitate this process.

In the *final stage* of co-dependence, the need for intervention and treatment is paramount. At this stage, the spouse and other family members may require intensive personal psychotherapy if Al-Anon is not sufficient by itself or is not properly utilized by attending enough meetings and working a program. At this point, the co-dependent spouse may even require hospitalization. If so she should be placed in a program that specializes in treating the families of alcoholics or drug abusers.

Differences and Similarities in Coping Skills with Alcoholics and Drug Abusers

The differences in coping skills required with drug abusers versus alcoholics depends surprisingly little on whether the SA's substance of choice is drugs, alcohol, or a combination. The determination of what may be the most effective coping skills to use is based more on the family's life history, socio-economic status, and the personality of family members rather than on choice of drug or drink. The SA's life history will also determine the probable success of various kinds of interventions. The best strategy will be different for the successful executive than the skid row bum. If the SA is an antisocial personality (formerly called sociopath or psychopath) with a long history of legal and prison involvement or domestic violence, then moving out will usually be the only workable solution for the family. If an SA is motivated to change, is gainfully employed and the employer is supportive of treatment, the prognosis for entering and completing a comprehensive treatment program is excellent. Generally speaking alcoholics are more likely to be gainfully employed and heroin addicts are more likely to be antisocial personalities. Prescription drug and marijuana users are categorically similar to alcoholics and, therefore, require similar coping approaches. Intravenous drug abusers of all types are like heroin addicts and non-IV cocaine addicts fall somewhere between the alcoholic and the heroin addict in predicting the appropriate choice of a coping approach.

Coping Techniques for Children
in Substance-Abusing Families

All of the coping techniques that have been described for spouses or girlfriends can and should be used by the children in these families. If the wife detaches successfully, many SAs will then shift their enmeshing, provocative, and reactive behaviors to the children. This is done in an attempt to engage the children in triangles, power struggles, guilt, and responsibility for his substance abuse now that the wife has refused to be a part of it. It is important that all family members receive information about the medical and psychological effects of substance abuse. Younger members may especially benefit from education in these areas.

A child can frequently be even more successful than the non-SA parent in a loving confrontation with the SA parent about his substance use and behavior. Children need help in learning to respect the substance-abusing father when he becomes sober, and they must be encouraged to follow the limits and guidelines that he establishes as an active parent once again.

SAs frequently make promises to their children that they are unable to keep. The SA often means well and makes each promise with the intent to deliver on it, especially in order to get the love he so desperately needs. Children are particularly vulnerable to broken promises and they are hurt deeply by them. They must be helped to stop relying on the father's promises and to detach when promises are not kept. Broken promises can impair a child's ability to trust people for the rest of his or her life.

The SA father's frequent and unfair criticism can devastate his children's confidence and his insulting and nasty remarks can leave them with repressed fury. The nonusing parent can compensate for the SA's potentially damaging behavior by keeping her own promises to her children, and complimenting and acknowledging their appropriate behavior. Most of the SA's insults and criticisms come during his periods of substance use and intoxication. It is, therefore, best to get the children out of the house during these episodes and to have them spend time with peers or extended family who can help meet their needs for love and encouragement.

Children in substance-abusing families should be protected from being triangulated (a topic that was discussed earlier). They should, at all costs, avoid getting into their parents' arguments. They should particularly not be asked to defend one parent against the other or to make a decision about which parent is right and which is wrong.

Alateen, which is the teenagers' version of Al-Anon, is extremely helpful to children in these families, whether they live with the substance abuser or not. Alateen offers support to children while they are living in a substance-abusing family and helps to prevent some of the common complications associated with becoming adult children of alcoholics. The problems of growing up in a home with an SA, regardless of the substance being abused, are so similar that Alateen is indicated for all children of SAs. ACA groups are often very helpful to adult children of alcoholics and drug abusers even years after they have grown up and left home.

Summary

The key to coping with an SA is to realize that substance abuse is a chronic disease that requires long-term treatment. No one is responsible for this disease, particularly not the family. However, the SA *is* responsible for his behavior and for every drop of booze, every pill, and/or every drug he puts into his body. When the SA interrelates with others in the family, there is anger, fear, and tension that reinforces cycles of substance use and abuse. It is important to understand the family's role in these cycles, but it is also vital to recognize that the family does not *cause* them. The decision to drink or use drugs is solely the responsibility of the SA. The family is not responsible and the family should not feel guilty.

Lois W., founder of Al-Anon, has said, "We [wives] can't get into someone else's head and turn the wheels that will make him behave in the way we think is right."

You must accept your powerlessness to control the SA's use of drugs. You must be neither protector nor police. You must learn how to detach with love, not anger, and refuse to be pulled back into repeated enmeshing. You must abandon pity and self-pity and learn to confront succinctly—and only when you are calm and the SA is not intoxicated. You must avoid triangulation and make a firm decision about your sexual relationship with the SA. Finally, you should be willing to adopt a system for leaving the SA, if substance abuse continues or else your strategies for coping will be unsuccessful, because you won't have any leverage to use if the SA doesn't respond to detachment.

It is difficult to practice these coping techniques completely on your own. You will need all the help you can get from Al-Anon or other support groups. A professional therapist is generally helpful only when specifically skilled in dealing with the families of substance abusers. Therapists who are inexperienced in working with these families often have difficulty addressing substance abuse as the primary treatment issue and, therefore, are in danger of becoming enablers themselves. These principles for coping with substance abusers can be useful to therapists, as well as to educators and employers who invariably find themselves dealing with substance abusers on a regular basis in the business and professional world.

References

Ablon, Joan, Al-Anon Family Groups. Impetus for change through the presentation of alternatives. *American Journal of Psychotherapy*, 28:111-130, 1974.

Ackerman, R. J. *Let Go and Grow, Recovery for Adult Children of Alcoholics*. Health Communications Inc., Pompano Beach, Fla., 1987.

Al-Anon Family Group Headquarters. *The Dilemma of the Alcoholic Marriage*. Al-Anon Family Group Headquarters, Inc., New York, 1985.

Al-Anon Family Group Headquarters. *Al-Anon Family Groups*. Al-Anon Family Group Headquarters, Inc., New York, 1985.

Beattie, M. *Co-Dependent No More*. Hazelden Educational Materials. Center City, Minn., 1987.

Drews, Toby R. *Getting Them Sober: A Guide for Those Who Live With An Alcoholic*. Haven Books International, Plainfield, N.J., 1980.

Hornik-Beer, Edith L. *A Teenagers Guide to Living with an Alcoholic Parent*. Hazelden Educational Materials. Center City, Minn., 1984.

Kaufman, E. and Kaufmann, P. *Family Therapy of Drug and Alcohol Abuse*. Gardner Press, New York, 1979.

Twerski, A. J. *Caution, Kindness Can Be Dangerous to the Alcoholic*. Prentice-Hall, Englewood Cliffs, N.J., 1981.

Valles, Jorge *How to Live with an Alcoholic*. Simon & Schuster, New York, 1965.

▽   ▽   ▽

C H A P T E R

8

How to Get Him to Enter Treatment When He Says No: The Intervention

What Finally Motivates a Substance Abuser to Get "Clean and Sober?"

*T*here are a multitude of factors that can motivate a substance abuser to want to stop using drugs or quit drinking and to seek appropriate treatment. Some SAs will, quite suddenly, stop using drugs and alcohol for no apparent reason and without outside help. In some cases, the parents of an SA will stop their own use or abuse because their child has sought treatment and is abstinent. Others will stop because their child has started to abuse drugs or alcohol. Some alcoholics or drug abusers will stop using when their spouse makes a firm commitment to leaving or detaching as described in the previous chapter.

At the other end of the spectrum, all too many SAs will not stop their drug or alcohol abuse even when faced with serious physical consequences or even the threat of impending death. Intravenous heroin users rarely stop using even when a physician confronts them with the news that they will be dead in two years from hepatitis, AIDS, or other complications. Obviously, the terrifying hold that a drug like heroin has on an addict is extremely difficult to break.

Alcoholics, on the other hand, stop drinking much more frequently when a physician informs them of the physical consequences of continued use or abuse. An alcoholic who is told that he is functioning on only 40 percent of his liver, or that he has a bleeding ulcer that can kill him within a few years, is frequently motivated to get sober by these fatal predictions.

Regardless of what factors ultimately lead to the cessation of alcohol or drug abuse, individuals who stop using chemicals without changing their behavior may present many difficulties to their family, their employer, and their friends, as well as to themselves. Such individuals are considered dry rather than sober. A person who is dry, not sober, is prone to drink again. Stopping substance abuse through a substance abuse treatment program that also helps individuals examine and change their behavior is almost always preferable to merely getting dry. Nevertheless, the critical first step toward achieving sobriety (the term here means free of alcohol or any other substances accompanied by a commitment to relinquishing alcoholic and other immature behavior) is for the SA to admit that he or she has a problem and needs help.

The event, or series of events, that ultimately lead the great majority of SAs to seek help is called "bottoming out." It is helpful to talk about this concept of bottoming out in order to better understand what finally motivates an alcoholic or drug abuser to seek treatment. Some SAs only hit bottom enough to seek treatment and move toward recovery when they have lost everything— family, friends, house, job, and so on. This is called a "low bottom." Others hit their bottom when they are convinced that their spouse is leaving them, or when their job is in jeopardy or their physical health is sufficiently impaired. When life consequences, such as receiving a single drunk driving charge, lead to the decision to stop chemical use, it is considered a "high bottom." Often some combination of these or other factors is necessary before an SA finally becomes sufficiently motivated.

Professional athletes who have used or abused illegal substances like cocaine only a few times often have a very high bottom in terms of substance use. Even the single use of an illegal substance discovered on a urine screen for drugs or alcohol can mean the end of an athletic career. In such cases, a high bottom in terms of a minimum of drug use can rapidly turn into a low bottom when the athlete is faced with the loss of career. Sometimes the publicity about the drug-related death or suspension of another athlete will "shock" an athlete into stopping his or her own substance use before his or her life or career are jeopardized.

There are many paths by which a reluctant SA can become willing to seek treatment. In many cases, it comes about as a result of the influence of other people. These include firm insistence on treatment by a family physician, family, courts, or employers. It also may be necessary that the family not rescue the SA from the consequences of his actions. Thus the family would have to stop behaviors such as providing repeated financial bailouts, making excuses for his behavior, getting him the best lawyer in town to avoid a drunk driving conviction, or dropping charges for family violence. The list of common enabling behaviors is a long one, which was delineated earlier.

Often a counselor, therapist, psychiatrist, or other professional who is knowledgeable about substance dependence can gently confront the SA, in one or only a few visits, with the need to pursue abstinence and recovery. An SA who seems resistant may actually have a desire for recovery, which is near the surface and needs only to be tapped by a professional who knows just what buttons to push. Vernon E. Johnson describes this pattern as "defiant dependence." Here SAs resist the idea of treatment vigorously because of their denial and high level of emotional distress, but immediately after entering treatment they tell their loved ones that they should have made them go into treatment years before.

However, many SAs will not respond to the methods described above with a strong commitment to enter and complete a treatment program. If this is the case, then the only way to facilitate entry into treatment is the technique known as intervention. This method has been widely successful in recent years and among those who have responded positively to family intervention is Betty Ford, wife of President Gerald Ford, who went on to establish her own treatment facility.

Guided Intervention

The technique known as intervention was developed by Vernon E. Johnson at St. Mary's Hospital in Minneapolis, Minn., which opened in 1968. Because all of the methods previously described in this chapter are types of interventions that facilitate entry into treatment, this specific technique developed by Johnson is best termed "guided intervention." The intervention requires about six hours of preparation, and the actual guided intervention itself lasts from one and a half to three hours. Stated very briefly, a guided intervention is a structured, rehearsed meeting led by a professional. Attended by family members, close friends, or other persons who have a significant relationship with the substance abuser, the meeting provides the opportunity for them to relate directly to the SA in a caring and loving manner how his substance abuse and behavior has affected them personally. At the same time, they convey the need for him to pursue abstinence and undergo treatment.

The First Step

The first step in planning a guided intervention is to assess the problem to determine if an intervention is indicated. Basically, if you are certain that the SA in your family is a serious substance abuser or is dependent on drugs, alcohol, or both, and he has consistently refused to seek help, then an intervention is indicated. If you are uncertain about the level of substance abuse or the SA's motivation to get help, then a consultation with a professional who understands the principle of an intervention is indicated.

Choosing an Interventionist

When choosing an interventionist, it is not only important that he or she be well trained in the technique and knowledgeable about substance abuse, it is also important that he or she is not wedded to only one treatment approach or program. Since many interventionists are tied to specific programs, you should remember that you are free to request a second opinion about which one is best for the SA in your family. You may also want to personally visit several programs to find out what is available and how various programs are conducted before making a final decision.

In the assessment, the qualified interventionist should evaluate the following factors: (1) the extent of substance use and its social, behavioral, and health consequences; (2) the motives of the family members or others (the interveners) who have sought the intervention—do they genuinely want to help the SA out of love and concern, or do they have other primary motives, such as inappropriately gaining control of an estate? (Although in some cases the prospect of losing an estate may be a very powerful force to get someone into treatment); (3) whether the interveners possess sufficient emotional control and motivation to follow through and effect the intervention; (4) how to gather together a sufficient number of concerned persons (family members, friends, employer) to participate to ensure that an effective intervention can take place.

Components of a Guided Intervention

The Beginning

In the first or early sessions of an intervention process, the family is made aware that it will be up to them to follow through on certain assignments such as contacting other members of the family and their social network to participate, reading material on substance abuse and attending instructional classes, and attending Al-Anon meetings. The family needs to learn about the physical effects and consequences of substance use and abuse, the nature of the disease process, and the characteristic defense mechanisms and memory distortions displayed by an SA. Defense mechanisms and memory distortions protect the SA from conscious knowledge of his need for abstinence-oriented treatment. The sicker the SA gets, the more likely it becomes that he will be unable to initiate his own recovery and the more he will need an intervention because of overwhelming denial.

The family must also understand that the primary goal is not merely to achieve cessation of the use of chemicals, but to change the behavior of the SA and family so that a workable personal and family harmony is achieved. In addition, they need to recognize how involved the entire family is in the disease process of substance abuse, even the children. The family must understand that for long-term sobriety to take place after treatment, it will be vitally important that they, too, seek appropriate help through counseling and regular attendance at Al-Anon or other support groups. Even if the intervention itself does not take place, or if it is unsuccessful in getting the SA to seek treatment and stop drinking or using, a good consultation with a professional should at least motivate the family to begin their own recovery from the family disease of co-dependence.

After the assessment process has taken place and the family has had its first meeting with a professional interventionist, the business of preparing for the actual intervention with the SA begins. A number of decisions need to be made beforehand and information must be gathered, among other tasks. In general, the components of preparing for and conducting a guided intervention are:

1. Choosing the team
2. Gathering the data
3. Choosing a setting
4. Establishing a nonjudgmental, concerned, loving attitude
5. Figuring out how to get the SA to attend the intervention
6. Deciding on treatment
7. Learning about alternative treatment plans
8. Rehearsing
9. The intervention session
10. Following-up

Choosing the Team

Team size can vary from two participants (interveners) to 12 or more, with an average of six to ten. The team should consist of people who have meaningful relationships with the SA. Normally the people are drawn from the family of the SA, but they can also include an employer or supervisor and close friends. Other valuable resources to tap are neighbors, clergy, physicians, and attorneys. One important criterion for inclusion is first-hand knowledge of the SA's substance abuse and related behaviors. A friend who says, "Gosh, I didn't know he had a problem," is usually not an appropriate candidate for the team. Another criterion is the participant's ability to make an impact on the SA, be it through emotional closeness and need, or through his or her position of authority to the SA.

Children and grandchildren should not be excluded in order to spare them pain or embarrassment. They already suffer from these feelings on a daily basis in living with the SA or in being affected by the SA's behavior. They can very often be quite effective motivators who could make the key difference in penetrating the defenses of the SA. However, if children resist participation, they should not be forced. Instead, they may be willing to contribute by writing a letter to the SA or taping a message that can be presented at the intervention session. These forms of input can also be quite effective.

A "surprise guest" may also be an effective addition to the team. The guest might be an old college roommate or a friend who hasn't seen the SA in years, or a favorite out-of-town relative. This person can serve to keep the SA honest and his or her presence conveys a special feeling of concern and importance to the intervention.

As in any group therapeutic setting, anyone who would be irreversibly damaging to the intervention should be excluded. Individuals who, for example, despite education efforts and hearing the evidence of chemical dependency, continue to deny its existence or the need for treatment should be excluded. People who are themselves SAs or substance dependent can be included under certain conditions. Through their own participation in the intervention, they may well gain insights into their own need for a commitment to sobriety. However, they should only be allowed to participate if they can attend meeting sessions in a drug- and alcohol-free state and if their denial doesn't blind them to the identified SA's need for treatment. In addition, those who are so emotionally vulnerable that they would be harmed by participation should be excluded. This is a very rare situation that would apply only to seriously disturbed individuals such as those with severe mental illness.

Gathering the Data

Data consists of specific instances of behavior, events, or circumstances that illustrate how the SA's substance abuse impacts the lives of the interveners. Data should be very specific describing circumstances in which the interveners had been present and behavior that they actually observed. The SA's behavior should be presented in great detail, and it should be tied directly to drinking or drug using whenever possible. The focus should be on behavior that illustrates the SA's inability to control alcohol and/or drugs, and how this has resulted in the SA's life becoming unmanageable (i.e., the days of work he missed recently, or that he let people down by not attending important family functions or occasions, or that he lost his temper and lost control). The effects of this irrational behavior on the interveners should also be communicated; for instance a wife might state, "The night of Tommy's birthday, your drunken behavior in the restaurant embarrassed and humiliated me." Changes in the SA's character, personality, and actions as observed by the interveners can be given as data if they are presented accurately and clearly, not in a generalized or vague manner. Recent events are best related as they are fresh in the SA's memory and not easily rationalized away. Gossip, generalities, and pejorative terms including "addict" and "alcoholic" should be avoided.

Each intervenor should try to recall and present as many as five or six incidents. These incidents should be written down beforehand to be referred to as the person is speaking so the SA is presented with accurate facts. Details like, "You forgot everything you said the night before," "You kept falling down," and "Your eyes were glassy," provide information that the SA may not recall or easily refute. Audio or videotapes provide statements that are hard to deny, and they are acceptable for use.

Choosing a Setting

The office of the interventionist or another team member, preferably a professional or employment supervisor or boss, has proven to be the best setting for the intervention itself. There are several important reasons for this that can affect the successful outcome of the intervention. It is rarely a good idea to hold the intervention in the SA's home. He has too much power in his own home, including the legal right to ask nonfamily members to leave. In addition, there may be frequent disturbances and interruptions in a home that should be avoided or at least minimized. The home of another family member or a close friend can also provide an appropriate setting.

Attitude and Why It Is Important

Each team member should make eye contact with the SA and speak directly and matter of factly to him when presenting data. There should be no expressions of anger, moral judgments, or talking "down" to the SA. It is extremely important that the SA hear and feel each team member's love and concern. The data and facts are presented as items to demonstrate the legitimacy of each member's concern. The SA will become quite anxious when he first realizes what is going on, and he may react quite defensively and negatively until he senses loving concern or gets in touch with his own need to be helped.

Getting the SA to the Intervention

It is important that the interventionist confidently reassure the team that there will not be any problems getting the SA to the intervention, and that the only issue to decide beforehand is which of several proven methods to use. One method that is possible if the SA's employer is part of the team, is to arrange to call a business meeting at the office that will be attended by the SA if he is at work. Another option is for a family member who is on the team to invite the SA over to discuss a "crisis." The SA could be told that the family is seeing a professional therapist for problems in dealing with his substance abuse, and the SA could be asked to attend "just" one meeting.

If it is anticipated that the SA will not attend a meeting labeled as addressing his problem, he should not be told that he is being invited to any sort of therapy or intervention. Instead, he might be told that some people are getting together or some other vague reason. In discussing possible methods for getting the SA to the intervention, the one method best suited to the circumstances always becomes apparent.

The best time of day for the intervention also requires thought and planning. The SA should be free of drugs and alcohol at the time chosen, so early morning is often the best time. If the team is planning to insist on hospitalization, admission has to be cleared in advance to take place immediately following the intervention. If hospitalization is warranted and does not take place immediately, an intervention that results in the SA carrying through with treatment will almost always fail. A delay of more than a day or so will turn into long-term procrastination as the SA balks at the idea of treatment.

Some SAs will be totally surprised and shocked when they enter the intervention meeting and realize what is happening. But many will have suspected something was going on because of the shift away from enabling behaviors on the part of team members in the weeks during which they have been preparing for the intervention session.

Deciding on Treatment

In the chapter that follows, the many different treatment options for substance abuse now available are described in detail. For the purposes and goals of the intervention, it is essential that medical insurance and other sources of funding be explored thoroughly beforehand, so that there is realistic financial input into the final decision. Similarly, it is necessary to establish the effects that a prolonged leave of absence will have on the SA's present job or career. Generally speaking, treatment requires about two weeks to one month for inpatient hospitalization and one year for a therapeutic community (discussed in the following chapter). It is extremely helpful if the employer can use the ultimatum that if the SA completes a program and follows up on all recommended after care, he will always have a job, but that if he does not enter treatment, he will be terminated. This is obviously a powerful intervention tool by itself. Even though the team has made certain decisions prior to the intervention, the SA should be included in certain aspects of the final decision, such as which hospital or which outpatient program he will enter. However, nonworkable proposals made by the SA should not be accepted. Dealing with this issue is described in the following section.

Alternatives to Recommended Treatment

It is not uncommon for the SA to refuse the recommended treatment program, insisting that he can stop on his own. The team should be prepared for this type of response in advance. First, team members should be able to recite specifically and accurately the many examples of how this approach has already been tried and has failed, if this is the case. Second, the team should decide before the intervention if it will accept an alternative method of achieving sobriety. No alternatives should be accepted unless they are truly workable. For example, a vague promise to attend NA or AA is not an acceptable alternative. However, an agreement to attend such meetings daily for three months may be effective, even if it is carried out without a period of hospitalization.

If an alternative plan is accepted, the team must be prepared to insist that if it does not lead to sobriety, the SA must agree to immediately implement the team's original recommendation. In order for this kind of delayed response to be successful, a new meeting of SA, team, and therapist may have to be held or strong ultimatums immediately reinforced. The family can give an ultimatum very similar to that of the employer: "If you do not agree to and carry out the terms of treatment we have presented, you will have to leave, or I will leave you. If you do complete treatment, I will stand by you all the way."

The Rehearsal

The rehearsal is the last meeting of the team held right before the intervention session. Everyone on the team should attend this crucial meeting. The rehearsal is an opportunity for team members to role-play and to get the feeling of what the intervention will be like by utilizing an empty chair or another recovering SA as the identified patient. The role-play permits members to experience a preview of the powerful feelings they will have during the intervention, and it gives them an opportunity to anticipate and control any feelings, such as anger, that would be potentially destructive in this setting. The practice also serves to focus on the team participants' love and concern for each other, giving them a special bond and energy that contributes enormously to the success of the intervention.

The rehearsal helps each team member to define his or her role and to gain confidence in his or her ability to present the data in a helpful and caring way. The rehearsal also allows members to deal with any final fears or concerns they may have about the intervention. It provides an opportunity to discuss all expected difficulties and contingencies and it helps to put the members at ease. Even details like the seating arrangements and order of presentations should be planned in advance. The more everyone knows about what to expect at the intervention, the more comfortable they are going to be when it finally takes place.

The Intervention Session

At last—the big day has arrived! Even just reading the preparatory material in this chapter should give the reader a sense of anticipation and excitement about the intervention itself. If the team is well prepared and rehearsed, this excitement will give added impetus to the success of the intervention. The goal of the intervention is to break through the denial in order for the SA to accept enough of the reality of his alcohol and drug dependence and related behaviors so that, no matter how much he protests, his need for help is recognized and will be acted upon.

Introduction and Ground Rules: After introducing him– or herself and briefly describing his or her function in the group, the interventionist should play a minimal role in the well-rehearsed group. In the introduction, the interventionist demonstrates both verbally and nonverbally the attitude of caring, support, and concern that is necessary for the success of the intervention. The interventionist should establish the ground rules of the meeting and ask the SA to agree to them. The ground rules should include letting each person speak without interruption, listening carefully to each person, and, of course, cautioning against any physical violence. Spontaneity should be minimized, sticking rather to the prepared data. Any free, unhelpful expression of emotion by any participant should be gently curbed by the interventionist.

The Planned Scenario: Data sharing should begin immediately after the introduction is completed and the ground rules are established. Members should look the SA directly in the eye as they glance at their prepared list to assure the clearest possible presentation of facts. The order in which everyone shares is based upon prior agreement. The SA should be requested not to respond until after the individual has finished. It is expected that the SA's initial response will be denial, but this will progressively wear away as the confrontation continues.

Ultimatums or specific conditions may be shared, even if the SA agrees to enter treatment, to ensure follow through, or they can be withheld and only used if pressure seems necessary. Ultimatums have been described previously in this chapter and in other parts of this book. Briefly, they communicate to the SA that he will be left by his wife or girlfriend, asked to leave, or that he will be out of a job if he does not stop abusing drugs and alcohol. They bring about the type of crisis that will push the SA to accept treatment. Ultimatums also frequently help team members to recognize and give up their own enabling behaviors.

But any ultimatum is only going to be effective if the team members are certain that they will be able to follow through, and they are able to communicate this certainty to the SA. Members should offer brief, clear, pragmatic, and honest statements of consequences, and not simply emotional threats. The group support and ceremonial aspects of the intervention help make ultimatums more believable.

If the SA leaves the room during the session, one or two prearranged team members should follow him and ask him to return. This is usually successful, but if it fails, other family members can follow and deliver their ultimatums. If the SA refuses to return to the session or enter treatment, the team is encouraged to continue the cessation of their enabling behaviors. This permits them to feel better, in spite of the outcome, and it definitely enhances the likelihood that the SA will eventually enter treatment.

If the intervention team has been adequately prepared, and everyone is filled with hope, love, and concern, the intervention will most likely be successful. The success rate of experienced interventionists for getting SAs into treatment is over 75 percent.

Follow-up

Although, in most cases, the intervention breaks down the wall of family denial and lack of communication, this wall will rapidly return if the family does not continue to pursue open, honest communication with the SA and within the family. To do this may require continued professional help and/or continued attendance at Al-Anon or other support groups.

A follow-up visit should be scheduled with the intervention therapist to ensure that open, honest family communication continues and to support the homeostasis of a new family reorganization based on more effective ways of coping with substance abuse. When indicated, the therapist may also deal with the family's guilt about pushing the SA into something he said he did not want. Some families need continued support to avoid returning to rescuing behavior and attempting to pull the SA out of the "cruel, confronting" mode of the hospital or other program he has entered. This type of support and insight for the family may be provided by the treatment program the SA enters. However, regardless of what treatment program the SA is involved in, extensive aftercare of one or more years is often necessary. The importance of reestablished equilibrium in the family as a necessary part of treatment for substance abuse is discussed in Chapter 10.

References

Johnson, V. *I'll Quit Tomorrow.* Harper & Row, San Francisco, 1980.

Krupnick, L. B., & Krupnick, E. *From Despair to Decision.* CompCare Publications, Minneapolis, Minn., 1985.

9

Factors to Consider in Choosing
A Treatment Program

*T*his chapter provides comprehensive information about the many kinds of substance abuse treatment programs available today. Using this knowledge, the family of the substance abuser—and, it is hoped, the willing SA himself—will be able to participate actively, intelligently, and in an informed manner in the decision about what type of treatment will be the most helpful and successful. This extremely important decision should be made with the assistance of an informed, impartial expert on substance abuse and not based on a newspaper or television ad for a treatment program. Such a counselor, therapist, or physician will be able to provide the family with the latest information about treatment programs, including what they have to offer, how much they cost, and other critical information. By far the best approach is an integrated one that employs several modalities that taken together meet the SA's particular needs for treatment. The decision is a complex one; there are many issues to be considered and questions that need to be asked and answered. Not only is the SA's health and welfare at stake but so is the future of his family.

Some of the issues that need to be addressed include whether treatment should be: (1) in- or outpatient; (2) duration—for a period of three days, three months, or three years; (3) drug free or facilitated with substances like naltrexone, methadone, or Antabuse®; (4) combined with AA or other self-help groups.

an expert in intervention, then the family has probably already decided on what type of treatment is best. Although inpatient treatment is not always necessary, it is probably indicated if a full scale intervention was necessary in order to get the SA into treatment. However, interventionists can have their own biases about which specific program to choose that is often based on the treatment philosophy of the particular program with which they are affiliated. The choice of a treatment program should be based on the unique needs of the individual and his family. It should not be selected solely on the basis of what insurance coverage is available or what has worked in the past for the referring professional. On the other hand, finances usually need to be considered. A $30,000 treatment program may be located in a nicer or more hospital-based setting but is not necessarily more effective than a program costing $5,000. During and after treatment, the SA and his family must deal with the financial challenges of everyday life, as well as having to repay the cost of treatment and often facing the monetary consequences of the SA's substance abuse behavior in the past, such as debts or attorney's fees.

The purpose of this chapter then is to help you decide which program will be best suited for the SA in your family, as well as the entire family. There are several steps in making the decision about a complete and comprehensive treatment program that will ensure maximum success.

1. Assessing the extent of drug and/or alcohol abuse and the particular substances abused.
2. Initiating a substance-free state.
3. Achieving a method to establish permanent abstinence.
4. Arriving at a decision on a treatment program.
5. Aftercare.

Assessing the Extent of Substance Abuse

The first step in deciding what treatment will be most successful is *assessing the extent of the chemical dependency.* The great majority of SAs will minimize or deny the true extent of their use of chemicals. Some will be honest with their family, particularly if they recognize their need for help. Others will be truthful when confronted by an impartial expert who is familiar with the behavior of SAs, and who understands and can recognize the behavioral and physical effects of drugs and alcohol. Quite often the SA's truthfulness with an expert is enhanced by the family's presence and their participation in a nonhostile, loving confrontation about his chemical dependency and related behavior. In some cases the SA will be much more honest and open when he is given the opportunity to meet alone with the expert; this is particularly true if the SA is too embarrassed or ashamed to let his family know about the real extent of his substance abuse and how self-destructive he has been.

In my experience, about half of the SAs are surprisingly honest in their first interview with a professional. Some unconsciously resistant SAs will see a physician and allow a physical examination or laboratory tests that wind up revealing a great deal of information about what substances he is using and the extent of physical damage the chemicals have caused. On the other hand, many individuals whose lives are seriously impaired by the use of drugs and alcohol may show no overt signs of abuse or dependence upon a physical examination or in laboratory tests and may even use this lack of concrete findings to further their denial and "prove" to the family that they don't really have a substance abuse problem.

When the expert takes a substance abuser's history, there are many issues that must be covered. The lifetime history of use and abuse of every type of drug and alcohol must be revealed and ascertained, as well as the SA's present use. A determination about substance use and related behavior should be made that will reveal the following:

- Quantity used;
- Quality of substances used—whether street drugs, dealer's cut, cheap wine;
- Duration of use;
- Expenditure of funds and how intake was financially supported;
- The extent of involvement with drug- and alcohol-abusing cultures and relationships;
- The extent of impairment of vocational and educational functioning, and relationships;
- Physical effects and medical complications;
- Drug tolerance;
- Potential withdrawal severity.

It is also important to determine what types of treatment have failed in the past and why they failed, as well as what approaches may have worked temporarily and for how long. If prior treatment efforts have been successful for a period of time, it is also helpful to determine why those treatments stopped working and the SA returned to using or drinking.

How to Achieve Cessation of Substance Abuse

The second step is to determine how best to *initiate a substance-free state.* A substance abuser can only be treated after he has first stopped using drugs or drinking. The specific methods that are best employed to achieve abstinence vary according to the extent of the SA's use, abuse, and dependence as revealed in the first assessment step. Cessation of mild to moderate use in individuals who have no prior history of being physically dependent on chemicals may be achieved simply by the family informing the SA that his continued use of chemicals will not be tolerated. In some cases, the family's firm threat to leave the SA if he continues to abuse chemicals will be sufficient motivation for a nonaddicted individual to stop using. Some SAs will stop when they are informed by a physician of the extent to which they have damaged their body or of the dire consequences of continued chemical dependency. As already stated, alcoholics tend to be much more likely to stop than hardcore drug addicts when confronted with the physical consequencs of their substance use. When substance abuse is more severe in quantity and duration, then more drastic measures are usually necessary to initiate abstinence.

When more severe abuse is not yet characterized by physical dependence, with the possibility of severe withdrawl symptoms, then measures short of hospitalization may be sufficient. Some examples of a level of abuse that may not require hospitalization include binge drinking that is limited to weekends, and occasional use of marijuana, amphetamines, cocaine or even heroin. Regular attendance at a relevant self-help group, such as AA, CA (Cocaine Anonymous), or NA (Narcotics Anonymous) may be successful in initiating a substance-free state in such cases as these. Alcohol abusers may be able to utilize daily Antabuse doses to enable them initially to refrain from drinking. Heroin abusers may be able to use Naltrexone, a narcotic antagonist, successfully to refrain from heroin use. Both of these specific pharmacologic treatment measures are described in detail in the latter part of this chapter. Some mild to moderate substance users find that relaxation techniques, an exercise regimen, or devotion to their religion provides a sufficient system around which to begin to organize a drug-free existence.

Again, it is important to emphasize that individuals who stop using drugs *without a self-help program or therapeutic experience that changes their behavior* are much less likely to stay off drugs for more than a brief period of time. They are also more likely to continue much of their prior substance abuse-related behavior, even when not drinking or using.

When an individual is physically dependent on chemicals, hospitalization is generally necessary to achieve abstinence. However, there are some exceptions to this rule. Narcotic addicts on occasion can be detoxified with the utilization of methadone or clonidine followed immediately by relevant psychotherapy on an outpatient basis. Most individuals who have been addicted to narcotics for more than a year or two rapidly return to addition after detoxification if not engaged in further treatment. If they are going to be able to remain abstinent without hospitalization or a stay in a residential treatment program, they may require methadone maintenance in order to stay sufficiently drug free to participate in a therapeutic program.

Those abusers of drugs that produce minimal physical withdrawal that is not life threatening, like amphetamines or cocaine, can sometimes also be initiated into a drug-free state without hospitalization. However, severe abusers of these kinds of stimulant drugs do best when treatment is begun in a comprehensive, intensive inpatient program.

Recently, psychiatrists at Yale University found that antidepressant drugs such as Norpramine® may block the craving for cocaine in some individuals, as well as serving to treat underlying depression. Such a study suggests that the use of antidepressants may enable some cocaine abusers to stay off of cocaine. For the past 15 years, I have tried using antidepressants with cocaine addicts with little success; generally because the addicts have been unwilling or unable to take the antidepressants and forgo using cocaine for the two-week period it generally takes for the antidepressants to take effect.

If the decision is made to treat a severe drug abuser on an outpatient basis, an intensive program will be required rather than one or two hours weekly. The criteria to use for deciding if an SA can be treated on an outpatient basis are:

1. Moderate to excellent motivation (solid family or legal pressure can achieve this);
2. The ability to stop drinking or using drugs;
3. The presence of a family, work, and peer environment supportive of a drug- and alcohol-free state;
4. Appropriate employment or jobs which would be threatened by the prolonged absence involved in most inpatient or residential treatment programs are indications for non-residential treatment.
5. Absence of medical conditions or the potential of serious withdrawal problems.
6. Absence of serious psychiatric disorders;
7. Absence of prior outpatient treatment failures.

A period of hospitalization is usually helpful, if not necessary, in order to achieve abstinence with most physically dependent SAs and with most severe drug abusers. Hospitalization should be insisted upon if: the SA is unable to attend counseling sessions without being on drugs or alcohol; he is physically violent or poses a suicidal risk; he has failed in prior outpatient therapy; or he is unwilling to participate in the necessary aspects of a comprehensive outpatient program.

In many cases, non-hospital-based social detoxification (detox) centers are a legitimate alternative to hospitalization for achieving cessation of substance abuse, and they are equipped to handle most moderately severe alcohol detoxification. However, hospitalization is absolutely necessary if the individual is physically dependent on a drug or alcohol to the extent that withdrawal may be life threatening. This is the case with those who are dependent on sedative hypnotics, or when an individual is using any of the many combinations of tranquilizing drugs and alcohol. Hospitalization is also usually necessary when repeated attempts at outpatient detoxification have failed or when prior attempts at detox have resulted in life-threatening situations such as seizures or delirium tremens.

It has been my own experience that it is never advisable to attempt to provide medication in order to withdraw SAs from sedative hypnotic drugs, minor tranquilizers, or alcohol on an outpatient basis. There are two good reasons for this. Any medication that may be effective in treating withdrawal can itself be abused by SAs. Doctors who do prescribe sedatives for outpatient withdrawal frequently wind up becoming drug suppliers themselves helping to maintain a patient's addiction. Secondly, the withdrawal symptoms produced by these substances are too dangerous to permit treatment on an outpatient basis. A few specialized programs nationally are able to perform outpatient detox under the supervision of an expert in the field and with a great deal of structure.

Achieving Permanent Abstinence and Sobriety

Once the individual is detoxified from substances, the next treatment decision that needs to be made is *how to keep him off of these chemicals permanently.* Many of the methods available to accomplish this have already been mentioned (self-help groups, methadone maintenance, Antabuse, etc.). In my experience, a commitment to total abstinence as opposed to attempting controlled substance use is the best approach if treatment is to be successful.

Most individuals are overwhelmed by the prospect of a commitment to a lifetime without drugs or alcohol. However, the "one day at a time" approach of AA can help them overcome this initial stumbling block. It has proven both feasible and effective. The formerly chemically dependent person is encouraged to refrain from drugs and alcohol one day at a time, and with each new day, he renews this intention. Generally speaking, if individuals have been dependent on drugs or alcohol at any time in their lives, they are vastly better off if they totally stay off of all chemicals. This is really the only way they can guarantee that they will not return to addiction. There is one other distinct advantage to total abstinence: it is an integral part of, and the foundation for, a commitment to AA, CA, or NA, without which rehabilitation is rarely successful.

Self-Help Groups

Active involvement and regular attendance at AA has proven to be an effective method for maintaining long-term sobriety for drug abusers as well as alcoholics. However, many cocaine abusers have difficulty in relating to AA at first and feel much more comfortable in CA initially. In my experience, former cocaine addicts who successfully maintain sobriety shift their emphasis from CA to AA after a few months in the program. This may well be attributable to the fact that CA is a relatively new group, so there are few former cocaine addicts who attend CA meetings with a sufficiently long enough period of sobriety to provide a solid and stable program of support to newly sober persons. In contrast, AA meetings provide examples of people who have achieved long periods of sobriety—some with 30 to 50 years.

Newly sober individuals are encouraged to find AA groups in which they personally feel comfortable. I strongly encourage a variety of kinds of meetings including 12-step study groups that require more active member participation; small, intimate discussion groups like men's stags; as well as inspirational, or larger, speaker's meetings. Working the 12 steps of AA, found in the book *Alcoholics Anonymous*, can achieve a great deal of meaningful personality change, as well as provide a means of staying substance free, even without a psychotherapist.

As already stated, it is often helpful to shop around for meetings at which the SA will feel comfortable. Finding meetings made up of people like him helps cut through the early denial mechanism of, "I'm not like them." One of the most important influences in overcoming resistance and denial is for a person to be able to identify with and relate to others who have admitted their problem and gotten sober. A person is much less likely to identify with and feel comfortable in a room full of homeless people or low socioeconomic groups if he has a good job and still has his family. The opposite is just as true. SAs may also choose from smoking or nonsmoking groups, mens' and womens' stag groups, and couple-oriented groups, young people's groups, or gay and lesbian groups. The AA directory of meetings in an area usually indicates the type of meeting as well as the day, location, and time of meetings. In Orange County, California, for example, there are several hundred different meetings held each week, so finding a comfortable meeting presents little problem if the SA is willing to "shop around and attend a few different meetings.

Obtaining an AA or CA "sponsor" is an essential part of working a successful, full AA program. The sponsor helps the newcomer structure a workable commitment to AA and is available in times of crisis. Some recovering SAs initially need to overcome their conflicts about dependency before they will seek out and accept a sponsor. "I can do it myself" and "I don't need or trust anyone" are not uncommon sentiments of the SA in the early stages of seeking help. Most members of AA are generally willing to sponsor several individuals at a time, in part because the AA philosophy stresses that working with newcomers to the program is a crucial part of maintaining their own sobriety.

Drug-Aided Abstinence*

I personally prefer that Antabuse not be given to a family member by a physician for daily dispensing to the alcoholic, because it tends to contribute

---

*See also section in this chapter on drug-aided treatments.

to the family's continuing involvement in the alcoholic's decision to drink or not to drink (and it must be clear that it is his decision only). Benzodiazepines such as Valium®, Serax®, or Ativan are discouraged from being used for outpatient treatment of alcoholics. All too frequently, the use of these drugs becomes a contributing factor in the SA's mixed sedative drug and alcohol problem rather than a solution to alcoholism.

Heroin addicts can be successful in establishing a method to remain free of abusable substances through naltrexone or methadone treatment. The latter is only effective if the SA does not drink heavily or use other drugs while on methadone. My ultimate goal with every SA in methadone maintenance is achieving a totally drug- and alcohol-free state.

28-Day Inpatient Program

A very effective method that can provide a basis upon which to build a lifetime commitment to sobriety is an intensive 28-day inpatient program. These programs provide total immersion in treatment that includes detoxification, learning about substance abuse and health education, individual and group therapy, family therapy, and daily meetings of AA, CA, or NA. Although such short-term residential programs are generally reserved for addicted SAs, this total immersion in treatment may be effective and even necessary for as yet nondependent individuals in order to help them turn their lifestyles around toward a commitment to a sober existence. Alcoholics do quite well in 28-day specialized, chemical dependence hospital programs particularly if they continue with active AA involvement after discharge. SAs who have become dependent on illicit drugs often require even more intensive and longer periods of residential treatment than 28 days. These drug addicts may require long-term therapeutic community treatment programs of six to 18 months.

This concludes the general section on principles of establishing and maintaining abstinence from chemicals. The following section deals with descriptions of the *various types of treatment* for chemical dependency. This section will be divided into drug-free and drug-aided treatments.

Drug-Free Treatment

Alcoholics Anonymous and Other Self-Help Groups

The origins of Alcoholics Anonymous are generally agreed to have been in meetings in Akron, Ohio, beginning in 1935, under the leadership of a man known until recently only as Bill W. Part of the impetus for the formation of AA came from a mystical experience Bill W. had while being treated for alcoholism in Towns Hospital in New York City in 1934. The original concept of AA began in a 1932 conversation between an alcoholic American patient and his Swiss psychiatrist, Carl Jung. AA also has substantial roots in the Oxford Group Religious Movement of the same era.

Every successful treatment program for alcoholics with which I have been associated has used AA principles as an integral part of the program, regardless of its other orientation. The 12 steps and 12 traditions of AA found in the book *Alcoholics Anonymous*, first published in 1939, also serve as the basis for NA, CA, and other 12-step groups such as Pills Anonymous (PA), Gamblers Anonymous (GA), an Overeaters Anonymous (OA). Although only AA is described here in detail, much of the description applies to all of the other 12-steps groups, including Al-Anon.

The 12 steps of AA can be summarized in five basic principles: (1) the admission of alcoholism and the total inability to drink like other people; (2) dependence upon some kind of higher power or power greater than oneself; (3) personality analysis and catharsis; (4) positive behavioral modifications and adjustment of personal relations; and (5) helping other alcoholics achieve and maintain sobriety.

Passive participation in the AA program by merely attending large speaker meetings, for example, is generally not sufficient for rehabilitation. Speaker meetings are, however, particularly helpful in providing new members with an initial inspirational model that motivates them for achieving abstinence and recovery. The message is: AA worked for the speaker because he wanted it to, and if the new member wants it, it will work for him too. Generally speaking, a more active AA involvement and participation rather than just going to large, anonymous meetings is necessary if the SA is to achieve long-term sobriety.

There are six stages of recovery through AA: (1) hitting bottom; (2) identification with AA or with another AA member; (3) conversion or full affiliation with AA; (4) "the honeymoon"—an intense experience of elation and enhanced self-confidence, and a heightened sense of belonging that often occurs during the first few months of sobriety; (5) successful coping with the reemergence of life's problems; and (6) perpetual recovery—a lifetime commitment one day at a time to working the AA program and principles.

Spirituality is an important aspect of AA. Some alcoholics react to this aspect by using their own lack of belief in God or a Higher Power, as a reason for not joining AA or working a program. This is actually quite common but can be overcome. Such doubting newcomers are urged to think of their higher power, or a power greater than themselves, as the power of the millions of alcoholics who have stayed sober through AA or the power of a particular meeting group.

The subject of sponsors in AA has already been touched on elsewhere in this chapter, but further mention may be helpful. Sponsors act as AA "advisors'' who help the new member plan a course for sobriety and provide one-to-one support. They also help with day-to-day problems and the reinforcement of the daily decision not to drink or use other chemicals. Sponsors are not trained therapists, but rather AA members who have a successful substance-free period of time in the AA program. In rare instances they may also be therapists. The style of some sponsors is to respond with the brief, ritual-type cliches often used in AA, such as: go to 90 meetings in 90 days; if you don't want to slip, stay away from slippery places; one day at a time; keep the plug in the jug; the first drink is the one that gets you drunk; and easy does it. These sayings, though clear, simple and often helpful, when used by the sponsor without additional guidance, may be insufficient for the newcomer. On the other hand, certain sponsors can be rigid and overcontrolling in their opinions about how to work the program. If the member/sponsor ''fit'' is not working, the new member should feel free to check this out with other AA members and change sponsors. Finding the right fit may require going through several sponsors before the appropriate one is found. The success rate of individuals who commit to AA after a 28-day hospital program is better than 50 percent.

Although NA has been very helpful to many heroin addicts, as well as sedative/tranquilizer dependents, it has never had quite the success of AA. Cocaine Anonymous (CA), which first began to take hold in 1983, has the spirit and vitality of a new approach and is presently meeting with some success. A drug-free approach to drug abuse that is also often successful is the therapeutic community (TC).

Therapeutic Community (TC)

Although the TC was initially developed for British psychiatric patients in the late 1950s by Maxwell Jones, it was first applied to drug abusers in 1958 by Chuck Dederich III. Dederich, who began Synanon, was greatly influenced by his own participation in Alcoholics Anonymous. Although Dederich had ideas of his own from the very beginning, initially there was a close rapport between AA and Synanon. After about nine months, however, Synanon moved away from AA and began to develop an identity and approach of its own. However, all TCs still show the significant impact of AA on their basic principles and techniques as well as the imprint of Synanon.

The TC—like AA—operates on a principle of self-help with a majority of the staff being recovering drug abusers who have themselves graduated from TCs. A few professionals have been involved with TCs almost from their inception, though not many. Two large national TCs are headed by psychiatrists, and over the past decade TCs have dropped their more or less antiprofessional stance and have incorporated mental health professionals into their programs.

Almost all TCs are residential. Residential treatment has two distinct advantages over outpatient programs. It provides a drug- and alcohol-free environment along with an intensive therapeutic experience every waking hour. It also provides a less clinical environment, which helps to ease the "shock" of moving from the hospital setting back into the community.

Most TCs require a minimum stay of 12 months and many are 18- to 24-month programs. The long-term TC is the best treatment method that has been developed to date to deal successfully with the ingrained pattern of antisocial, criminal behavior that is commonly associated with long-term illicit drug use. TCs utilizing more professionals on staff provide excellent treatment modalities designed for polydrug abusers who have severe personality impairments requiring major professional support and personality reconstruction.

The treatment approach of therapeutic community programs embodies the following techniques and principles.

The Role Model: In the process of maturing in a TC program, a substance abuse client identifies at different stages with staff members and therapists. In most programs the first therapists the clients encounter are recent graduates or advanced members of the program. These individuals may share emotion-charged stories of their own struggle to give up drugs with which the client can identify. They relate the difficult and painful experiences in their own lives prior to giving up drugs. By example, they demonstrate that they have arrived where they are through hard work and the slow, painful process of turning around their attitudes and behaviors. This kind of identification facilitates confrontation through mutual empathy, which permits the therapist to join with the client supportively as the client begins the process of recognizing and relinquishing undesirable aspects of his own personality, which has been damaged by drug use.

Loving Concern: An atmosphere of genuine loving concern and caring must pervade the treatment program. This attitude, together with identification, allows the SA's defenses to be stripped away. Love and concern are given in return for adult, responsible, giving behavior, painful insights, and emotional release.

Confrontation and Encounter: In this technique, addicts are confronted with their manipulativeness, selfishness, dependency, and irresponsible behavior. One type of confrontation is called the "haircut." Several significant figures, such as therapists and other addicts, "take apart" a member. All of a member's behavior is reviewed in a rather brutal manner, although the interaction is totally verbal. The individual is stripped of his sick patterns of behavior, and this is followed by an attempt to "put the person back together" by the end of the meeting.

Stratified Responsibility: This approach uses what is called "the graduated gains of learning theory," in which the individual is assigned and accomplishes progressively more responsible tasks that place him on ascending levels of responsibility. At most TCs these levels are accomplished through the work and tasks necessary to maintain the house. Kitchen and service crews, for example, are low status levels, building and administrative crews enjoy moderate status, and those individuals who acquire material goods and pursue community relations have higher status. Each work crew also has its own hierarchy, with department "heads" assisted by "ramrods" followed by lowly crew members.

Acting As If: The principle of "acting as if" is a simple one: (1) one sets a goal of the sort of person one would like to be; (2) one acts and behaves "as if" one actually were that person; (3) gradually, through the practice of acting that particular way, one actually changes and feels like that person. Even before any internal personality change has occurred, people who are trying to stop abusing drugs or alcohol must perform "as if" change has already occurred and as a result, change eventually happens.

Although the proportion of entrants who actually graduate from TCs is rather low (10 to 20 percent), most of those who stay more than 12 months do quite well. For those who stay in TCs more than three months, each additional month in treatment at the TC leads to longer periods of happier, drug-free lives. It is an interesting fact that SAs who are court-committed to a TC do as well as those who participate voluntarily.

Outpatient Treatment

As described in the beginning of this chapter, outpatient treatment for substance abuse may have potential success with nonsevere abusers or nonaddicted individuals. With more severe cases, outpatient therapy is only successful after detoxification and with the aid of a drug-free or drug-aided method of maintaining abstinence such as AA or Antabuse®.

Generally, individual outpatient therapy does not work well with SAs, particularly without a supportive abstinence method. Group therapy is always preferable to therapy that consists only of individual sessions. Individual therapy alone simply cannot provide the total support system that a newly recovering individual requires. Another hazard of individual therapy is that often an intense transference to or dependence on the therapist may develop, which frequently leads to frustration resulting in a return to substance abuse. An individual therapist who treats a serious SA who continues to use drugs while undergoing therapy for any extended period of time is an enabler.

Individual psychotherapy, when combined with a 12-step program and/or group therapy, can prove to be quite successful. Outpatient programs, on the whole, tend to be more succssful as they become more comprehensive. The addition of other treatment modalities such as vocational programs and family therapy enhance greatly the overall success rate of outpatient programs.

The model that I prefer to use for a newly abstinent individual who is an appropriate candidate for outpatient treatment consists of one individual session, one group therapy meeting with other SAs, one couples group (if appropriate), one family session or multiple family group session, and three to seven AA/NA/CA meetings *weekly*. I also recommend an active Al-Anon program for the spouse and 12-step groups for the children (Alateen or Alatot depending on their ages).

Individual Therapy

One-to-one psychotherapy treatment for substance abuse follows phases similar to those that are outlined as the general stages or steps for comprehensive treatment discussed earlier in this chapter. In the first phase of individual therapy the focus is on achieving sobriety. The second phase emphasizes the maintenance of sobriety. At this stage the therapist who understands substance abuse will place great importance on the various mechanisms needed to establish and maintain sobriety. The third phase, known as early recovery, begins after sobriety is well established and may last for six months to two years.

Early on, psychotherapy focuses on the cognitive and behavioral aspects of substance abuse. An examination of the causes and effects of substance abuse allows for the suggestion of alternative behaviors that can avoid triggering relapse. Encouraging and presenting opportunities to practice drug-free behavior provides coping strategies for the sober patient. Focusing on "why" the SA uses is not helpful, because it feeds into excuses from the SA and stirs up his need to defend himself as a good person. Rather, we focus on how and when he uses drugs or alcohol. Replacing destructive and dysfunctional actions with behavior that maintains sobriety is an appropriate treatment goal of early recovery. Developing substitute activities and behaviors of all kinds are helpful and should not be confronted or discouraged at this stage. Smoking or eating sweets can be addressed later, for example. The therapist may suggest and help the SA to participate in active alternative pastimes such as regular exercise or education. A commonly heard cry from SAs in the beginning stages of treatment is, "What am I going to do with all the time I have on my hands or what will I do for recreation if I don't use or drink?"

Substance abuse psychotherapy during early recovery should not confront the person's defenses too quickly or attempt to remove them prematurely. These defenses are instead redirected positively and supported by the therapist to help maintain abstinence and continued treatment; for example, when denial is used for coping or adjusting to former triggers of substance abuse (like "When my wife nags me I need a drink.") or some previous inappropriate behavior of the SAs is attributed to the disease (by projection and rationalization), rather than to other people or self. Once comfortably sober, the patient has a lifetime to recognize that not all of his difficulties can be explained by alcoholism and/or other substance abuse.

During the early supportive phase of psychotherapy with substance abusers, psychodynamic therapy still has a place. Considering psychological conflicts and forces with dynamic approaches is often helpful in reinforcing the principles of Alcoholics Anonymous or other 12-step groups. For example, these approaches are useful when resolving conflicts over dependency needs that prevent obtaining a sponsor, or in reducing a sense of entitlement that impairs commitment to AA as well as pushes other supportive persons away. Dealing with the antecedents of conflict may be helpful in resolving present difficulties even at this phase of the therapy. The phase of advanced recovery follows the therapy of early recovery with a more traditional in-depth psychotherapy that gradually shifts from supportive to reconstructive or uncovering psychotherapy. Here the goal is insight and personality change through the exploration of transference, dreams, and defense mechanisms.

Intense anxiety or anger can and often do surface when an SA's defenses are lowered and the process of uncovering psychotherapy is attempted. For the patient to tolerate this anxiety or anger without resorting to chemicals for relief, his identification as an alcoholic or substance abuser must be solid. The SA's controls on substance abuse must be intact and ready for reimplementation as needed. A heightened desire to use substances may be a warning signal to stop uncovering, but when interpreted and acknowledged as such, the reconstructive psychotherapy may resume.

By the time the final phases of successful treatment have been reached—almost regardless of the method of therapy—SAs usually drop their defenses and become open to intimacy and sharing. They frequently voluntarily drop defenses such as compulsions to overeat, overwork, overexercise, or engage in excessive sexual behavior. They may stop smoking, consuming caffeine, and generally begin to take better care of their bodies. They are able to develop their capacities for pleasure and build their self-esteem.

Finally, the formal termination of reconstructive psychotherapy is a beneficial process contributing to a final resolution of the SAs' difficulties in separation and individuation from significant people in their lives. Nevertheless, although this resolution may take place, the door should always be left open for the SA to return if substance abuse and/or other life crises threaten him or his sobriety.

Family Therapy

The model of family therapy that I use is an integration of several other treatment systems with structural family therapy, a method developed by

Salvador Minuchin and others that emphasizes restructuring family roles, rules, closeness, flexibility, and adaptability. My model is also influenced by the vastly different systems of psychoanalysis and ex-addict psychotherapy. Most family therapists with chemical dependency experience use an integrated, personally derived method of therapy and when drug abuse is severe, insist on a method for achieving and maintaining abstinence. My own model of family therapy has been described in detail in my book, *Substance Abuse and Family Therapy.*

The goal of family therapy is to restore the SA to his role as an effective, loving husband and father. The steps that serve to accomplish this goal are:

1. Education about the physical, social, and psychological effects of alcohol and drugs;
2. Education about the family's behavior that has enabled the SA to justify, rationalize, and continue substance-abuse-related behavior;
3. Education about the family's unhealthy role realignments in response to substance abuse, by which other members have taken over the SA's rightful role as parent and spouse;
4. Teaching and practicing new coping strategies, rules, and bonding with others;
5. Reinforcing the necessary boundary around the marital dyad that protects the spouses from adverse and threatening influences in the world outside them and that can threaten the marriage—including in-laws, lovers, work stresses, etc.;
6. Facilitating the children's return to a world of peers where they belong, a world that exists apart from their fear of the SA or their past role in providing protection of the mother.

Multiple Family Therapy

Many of the steps in family therapy that were just described can be taken in multiple family therapy (MFT) or in couples groups. Both should be available as they are quite useful in restoring the health of the family of the SA.

A multifamily group is a stimulating and rejuvenating experience for the therapists and the overall treatment program, as well as for the families who participate. The therapeutic team used in MFT should include the primary therapist who is experienced in group and family therapy and who is comfortable in working with large groups. There should also be at least one co-therapist, preferably a recovering substance abuser. A proportional male-female balance in the therapy team is also preferred and is usually most effective.

MFT provides an opportunity for the SA and his family to form a new supportive network—a "family of families" that offers a healthier alternative to a network of substance abuse enablers and substance abusers.

The group is usually seated in a large circle with co-therapists distributed at equal distances around the circle to provide good observation of the total group. Families ordinarily sit together, and the way they seat themselves should be carefully observed by the therapists, as they usually follow common patterns of family interaction and reveal a lot about the family's dynamics. MFT group meetings are usually long, often lasting up to three hours.

These groups can be used to educate families as well as to support them in practicing new behaviors. When one family is worked with extensively in a session, many other families and their members will identify with the conflicts going on, and will express their own feelings, offer support, and, in turn be stimulated to work on similar conflicts in their own family.

The group frequently functions as adjunctive family therapists. Usually family members take their cues from the primary therapists and will be appropriately confronting, reassuring, and supportive. It is quite common for families to share experiences and offer help by acting as substitute extended families to each other outside of the actual therapy hours. Many family members recognize problems in other families that they can readily apply to themselves.

In the early phases of treatment, the families begin to support each other by expressing the pain they too have experienced through having a substance abuser in the family. The family's sense of loneliness and isolation in dealing with this major crisis is greatly lessened just by the fact of sharing the burden with other families.

Many families are able to express love and anger directly for the first time in MFT groups, and thereby learn that doing so is okay. Deep emotional pain is commonly expressed, when appropriate, and other family members are encouraged to support these expressions of feelings rather than to nullify or deny them. When families like these have become emotionally isolated because of substance abuse, encouraging the mutual exchange of physical affection is very helpful and healing to them.

Couples Groups

Many of the basic principles of multifamily groups apply to couples groups as well. Participation in couples groups serves to solidify the boundary around the marital dyad and permits couples to work on their problems without interference from other members of their family or network of friends, whose input has often been neither constructive nor helpful. Frequently, the kinds of issues worked on in the couples group can subsequently be tested in the multifamily group, where they may also prove to have merit and usefulness in resolving problems. The support of other couples who attend both couples and MFT groups helps the spousal pair follow through with their contracts and alliances and deal better with other family members. Couples groups should never be the only family treatment modality offered, however. By virtue of their specific concentration on the couple, they neglect dealing with the essential three-generation model of family treatment that is a vital area of family dynamics in substance-abuse families.

Couples groups are generally smaller than multifamily groups, consisting of three or four couples, although somewhat larger groups are often seen in inpatient settings. Couples groups are offered more frequently in outpatient settings and private practice than are MFT groups, perhaps because couples groups are less complex, involve fewer people, and require less space. Couples sessions are also usually shorter, conforming more to the traditional group therapy period of 90 minutes, but groups are usually based on a long-term commitment of about six months to two years. Since most of these couples require extensive therapy, a long-term commitment is often warranted.

Spousal and Significant-Other Groups

Co-dependent and significant-other groups are designed to deal with the special problems of living with a substance abuser, as well as serving to provide the opportunity for individual personal growth to the members of alcoholic or drug-abusing families. Al-Anon and Alateen self-help groups also encourage the development of an attitude of loving, detached acceptance that is so important for family members to strive for. Al-Anon is described in detail in Chapter 6. Attendance at its meetings provides a learning experience derived from the candid personal exchange of feelings and problems and the sharing of typical family reactions, while offering appropriate strategies for behavior that have worked for others in the group related to living in a household with a problem drinker or drug abuser. The experience of other members of the group provides a basis for comparison, as well as stimulation of self-examination leading to new insights in all areas of life, not just substance-related experiences.

However, Al-Anon alone is sometimes not enough for the spouse, perhaps because the approach is not sufficiently individualized to deal with all of the spouse's unique needs. The Al-Anon organization recognizes this limitation in its declaration that, ''It is important for the newcomer to realize that our fellow members are not equipped, by training or experience, to advise, judge or counsel in intimate personal problems, and particularly not in those involving complex family relationships.'' Supplementary professional individual and group therapy may also also be necessary for some. Some spouses will do better in significant-others groups led by trained professionals, because the group fit is better, or they resist the concept of a higher power, or because they are ready for more in-depth change, e.g., personality reconstruction which some of these groups provide.

Those family members who continue on in support groups, even when the SA does not enter or stay in treatment, not only experience relief from their own stress and problems, but also find that the SA will often enter or return to substance abuse treatment as a result of the changes that are taking place in the family's attitudes and behavior toward him.

Group Therapy

The beginning phase of group therapy for substance abusers should be educational, and both directive and supportive. It should impart information about alcohol and drugs, as well as introduce effective coping skills to deal with the anxiety and depression inherent in stopping substance use.

In the middle phases of group therapy, substance abusers learn how to work through their feelings, accept responsibility for their behavior, gain a better understanding of interpersonal interactions, and learn how to recognize the functions and secondary gains of their behavior. They become able to analyze typical mechanisms like defenses, resistances, and transference. The success of this middle phase depends on the substance abuser developing the ability to relieve anxiety without the use of alcohol and drugs. In this vein, it is extremely important not to end a session with any members in a state of unresolved conflict which leaves them vulnerable to possible urges to drink or use. This can usually be avoided by bringing some kind of closure when troubling issues are raised. Closure can be achieved by the group offering concrete suggestions for problem resolutions so that the SA will be better armed in facing his problems outside of the group. When this is not possible, group support, including extra-group contact by members, can be offered as a means of allowing the member to feel safe and protected when he feels anxious.

In the closing phase of a course of group therapy, the substance abuser has usually accepted sobriety without resentment and is well on the way to freeing himself from counterproductive underlying personality problems.

Hospitalization

Hospitalization should almost always take place in a medical facility that has a special unit that deals with substance abuse. The exceptions to this rule are when severe complicating medical or psychiatric illness is also present. In these cases, the medical or psychiatric illness should first be brought under control, perhaps by hospitalization in a psychiatric unit; then the patient can be safely transferred to a substance-abuse specialty hospital or unit.

Specialized hospital substance abuse units have the capability of providing the comprehensive treatment required for SAs and their families. They provide safe, medically supervised detoxification, if needed, and offer attention to most health needs. However, the most important and crucial service provided is a 24-hour complete immersion in the principles of substance-abuse recovery that lays the foundation for a commitment to a sober recovery.

Psychiatric hospitals have long been a haven for SAs, but they have rarely produced any successful results. It wasn't that long ago that they constituted practically the only form of hospitalization available to alcoholics and drug abusers in a time when no one really knew what to do with them or how to treat them. As a rule, SAs should never be treated as inpatients in a traditional psychiatric unit. The reasons that support this abound. When substance abuse is treated without specialized techniques and without implementing a system to achieve and maintain abstinence, such hospitals may well be said to serve as co-dependents, perpetuating alcoholism and drug abuse by inhibiting a commitment to sobriety and becoming expensive drug suppliers. One of the major objections to psychiatric treatment for substance abuse is that it often does not concentrate on the "primary" problem of substance abuse. Antisocial personalities constitute a minority of alcoholics, but represent a larger group of drug abusers. These antisocial substance abusers can all too easily manipulate a psychiatric hospital ward environment in a manner and to such a degree that prevents others from getting the treatment they need. Likewise, passive SAs frequently become dependent on inpatient treatment units and the drugs they provide, or pass through without changing at all or being helped with their primary problem.

There are some other alternatives to hospitalization that are less costly though they are not always available or as effective. These include social detoxification homes (for alcoholics only), day hospitals, shelters, rehabilitation centers, and halfway houses. Outpatient treatment as an alternative has been described above. Although geared more to alcoholics than drug abusers, there is a broad national network of information and referral centers.*

Drug-Aided Treatment

Drug-aided (pharmacological) methods of treating substance abuse include: Antabuse®, aversion therapies, methadone maintenance, naltrexone, and some antidepressant drugs.

---

*The local office of the National Council on Alcoholism can be extremely helpful. The national office is located at 12 West 21 Street, New York, NY 10010. The national office of Narcotics Anonymous is located at P.O. Box 622, Sun Valley, CA 91352.

Drug-Aided Treatment for Alcoholics: Antabuse® and Aversion Therapies.

Antabuse®

Antabuse®, which is the trade name for disulfiram, causes a severe physical reaction when it interacts with alcohol. At one time, patients were instructed to drink alcohol at least once while they were on Antabuse® to allow them to actually experience the severe physical reaction so that the ordeal acted as a deterrent to future drinking. This is no longer done because the alcohol/ Antabuse® reaction is severe and can be dangerous. Currently, the reaction is explained in detail and the patient is asked to cooperate by not drinking. The signs and symptoms of an alcohol/Antabuse® reaction include: flushing of the skin, throbbing headache, respiratory distress and hyperventilation followed by respiratory depression, heart palpitations and chest pain, blood pressure drops, and sweating, nausea and vomiting. Severe reactions can progress to death, but this is rare. After 30 years of broad use of Antabuse® in treating alcoholism, only 20 cases of death have been reported, which includes incidents of suicide. *Any* severe reaction to Antabuse® and alcohol requires immediate emergency medical treatment.

To be successful, Antabuse® treatment requires that the alcoholic commit himself to sobriety and to the Antabuse® method of maintaining it. Ideally, he must only make one commitment a day to abstinence, the moment that he takes his Antabuse® pill. Nonetheless, by itself, administering Antabuse® does not constitute a treatment of alcoholism. It must always be given under careful physician's monitoring and is best employed as only one part of a comprehensive therapeutic program. Some physicians permit it to be dispensed on a daily basis by a clinical nurse or a company nurse at the SA's place of employment. It should not be given to the alcoholic by his spouse or any other family member as it tends to put the dispensing family member in the no-win position of assuming a degree of responsibility for the alcoholic's drinking. In some instances, the Antabuse® could be taken at breakfast in front of the family as a ritual act of commitment to sobriety, if the family is nonreactive and able to refrain from reminding the alcoholic to take the pill or checking up on him to see that he has taken it.

If someone has taken Antabuse® regularly and then stops taking it, he will experience a gradually decreasing alcohol/Antabuse® reaction for about a week after his last dose. However, an individual can be started on Antabuse® only 18 to 24 hours after his last drink. When taking Antabuse®, alcohol fumes, shaving lotions containing alcohol, and food with wine sauces should be avoided as they can trigger the reaction.

If the alcoholic decides to stop taking Antabuse®, particularly without therapeutic discussion, then he is taking a major step toward drinking and a return to alcoholism. When this happens, the family should use the coping techniques they have learned, such as detachment, or they should begin making plans for an intervention.

Aversion Therapies

Treatments using aversion therapy for alcoholism are presently done mainly in special hospital settings that also offer a comprehensive program incorporating other therapies, including AA. There are presently two hospital chains that offer aversion as a major modality. The basic principle of aversive therapy is the technique called "conditioning" where the sight, smell, or taste of alcohol is paired with an aversive stimulus such as an electric shock or a drug that causes nausea (Emetine®). The aversive stimulus replaces the formerly pleasant stimulus associated with alcohol to a degree that the unwanted behavior of alcohol ingestion is eliminated.

The average patient receives five aversion treatments, each lasting three hours, on alternate days during a ten-day hospital stay. The aversion treatment days alternate with pentothal-facilitated interview days. The purpose of the pentothal (sometimes called "truth serum") interview is to relax the patient sufficiently so that he is able to talk about any psychological or environmental factors that contribute to drinking problems. Two reinforcement conditioning sessions are recommended, taking place 30 and 90 days after the initial treatment, and constituting two follow-up hospital stays. The pentothal interview is also given during each of the two follow-up periods. Comprehensive, continuing aftercare provided by the hospitals is recommended for up to two years following the aversion treatments. Follow-up studies of the results of this approach claim a 64 percent rate of abstinence over a four-year period.

Drug-Aided Treatment for Drug Abusers:
Naltrexone and Methadone

There are several drugs that are used to assist in the treatment of heroin addicts. Naltrexone and methadone are the two major drugs utilized. There has been little, if any, documentation of drug-aided treatment success with any other drug of abuse besides heroin until some recent treatment of cocaine abusers.

Naltrexone Therapy: Naltrexone is a narcotic antagonist that blocks the effects of narcotic drugs on receptor sites throughout the body. It was made available for general prescribed use at the end of 1985. Most narcotic addicts have a disaffinity for this drug, because it produces no euphoria of its own and prevents the desired pleasant effects of heroin, which is exactly what it was designed to do. As a consequence, naltrexone is only effective on highly motivated patients or with those who are required to take the drug through rigidly enforced court rulings. If given to someone who has been using a narcotic drug regularly, naltrexone can cause sudden and severe withdrawal symptoms. This kind of a reaction can still take place up to one week after the last dose of narcotics, although there is no withdrawal from naltrexone itself.

Methadone Maintenance: Detoxification and maintenance using methadone can only be used in specially certified programs by federal law. Methadone causes its own euphoria that is similar to that of heroin, but patients maintained on it rapidly develop a tolerance for the euphoric and sedating effects of this drug. Since methadone is administered orally and is sufficiently long acting that it need be given only once a day, it is easily substituted for heroin. Methadone is most often used to detoxify heroin addicts over a 21-day period in registered detoxification programs.

By law, methadone maintenance cannot be used unless the patient has at least a one-year history of narcotic dependence. It should not be used unless other methods of treatment have failed or been exhausted. Methadone is a highly addicting substance itself, and given the weak potency of street heroin (often as low as 0.5 to 2.0 percent though newer forms may be quite potent) it is often more potent than heroin. Detoxification from methadone is even more difficult than heroin. Any narcotic, including methadone, is extremely difficult to detoxify from if taken daily for six months or more.

All too often, methadone-maintained patients resume or move to heavy use of alcohol or non-narcotic drugs. One way to prevent this nonproductive shift to other harmful substances is for intensive individual, group and family therapy to take place with the methadone considered only an adjunct to treatment. This approach stabilizes an individual or family so that meaningful therapeutic change can take place.

A substitute called L-alpha acetyl methadol (LAAM or long-acting methadone) is only given three times weekly and is generally less abused than methadone. LAAM provides the patient with more flexibility because he or she doesn't have to show up somewhere everyday for its administration. It has not yet been approved by the Federal Drug Administration (FDA) for general use even though it was used successfully in the late 1970s.

Narcotic addicts can also be detoxified by using clonidine, a drug customarily used to lower blood pressure. This can be done on an in- or outpatient basis.

Drug-aided detoxification from narcotics rarely has any long-term successful effects unless it is accompanied by intensive efforts to enlist the patient in long-term treatment.

Antidepressant Drugs

The use of antidepressants has had some success in blocking craving and preventing relapse with cocaine addicts. It may be more effective if given with the amino acids tryptophane and tyrosine. Ritalin® successfully blocks cocaine craving only in those cocaine abusers who had an attention-deficit disorder (hyperactivity or ADD) as children. Minor tranquilizers should never be given by a general physician or psychiatrist as treatment for dependence on any drug. They should also not be given for outpatient detoxification. In both of these cases, they are readily abused, contribute to cross-addiction, lead to drug overdoses, or become a part of multiple physician-supplied drug dependence.

Aftercare

Aftercare is generally defined as the therapeutic program that follows hospitalization for substance abuse and the implementation of an abstinent state. Many specific aspects of aftercare treatment programs are discussed in other sections in this chapter—Family therapy, AA, NA, CA, intensive individual therapy, and group therapy.

The critical point that needs to be made is that the therapeutic process applied in treating a formerly chemically dependent person and expected to bring about successful results is *not* a six-hour intervention or a 28-day hospital stay. *It is a lifelong process.* What happens therapeutically *after* the substance abuser leaves the hospital is far more important than what occurred while he was there. Aftercare cannot be casually relegated to participation in a single group or individual session or attendance at a few AA meetings. It is a complex ongoing process requiring a detailed, integrated program that is strictly adhered to and carried out by the substance abuser and his family. This program should be managed and coordinated by a single qualified person, preferably a professional who is highly skilled and experienced in substance abuse. The concept of aftercare for the spouse as well is discussed in detail in the following chapter and is as important for maintaining long-term sobriety, achieving harmony in the home, and furthering the well-being of all the family members, including the children.

References

Ablon, J. Alanon family groups. *American Journal of Psychotherapy.* 28(1):30-45, 1974.

Al-Anon Family Group Headquarters. *The Dilemma of the Alcoholic Marriage.* Al-Anon Family Group Headquarters, Inc. New York, 1984.

Alibrandi, L. The fellowship of Alcoholics Anonymous. In E. M. Pattison and E. Kaufman (Eds.), *Encyclopedic Handbook of Alcoholism.* Gardner Press, New York, 1982, pp. 979-986.

Blume, S. B. Group psychotherapy in the treatment of alcoholism. In S. Zimberg, J. Wallace, and S. B. Blume (Eds.), *Practical Approaches to Alcoholism Psychotherapy.* Plenum Press, New York, 1978.

Brown, S. *Treating the Alcoholic: A Developmental Model of Recovery.* John Wiley & Sons, New York, 1985.

Brown, S., & Yalom, I. D. Interactional group therapy with alcoholics. *Journal of Studies on Alcohol,* 38(3):426-456, 1977.

Ewing, J.A. Disulfiram and other deterrent Drugs. In E. M. Pattison and E. Kaufman (Eds.), *Encyclopedic Handbook of Alcoholism.* Gardner Press, New York, 1982, pp. 1033-1042.

Fox, R. Group psychotherapy with alcoholics. *International Journal of Group Psychotherapy.* 12:50-63, 1962.

Kaufman, E. Group therapy for substance abusers. In M. Grotjohn, C. Friedman, & F. Kline (Eds.), *A Handbook of Group Therapy.* Van Nostrand, New York, 1982, pp. 163-191.

Kaufman, E., & Kaufmann, P. Multiple family therapy: a new direction in the treatment of drug abusers. *American Journal of Drug and Alcohol Abuse,* 4(4):467-478, 1977.

Kaufmann, P., & Kaufman, E. From multiple family therapy to couples therapy. In E. Kaufman & P. Kaufmann (Eds.), *Family Therapy of Drug and Alcohol Abuse.* Gardner Press, New York, 1979.

Nace, Edward P. *The Treatment of Alcoholism.* Brunner/Mazel Publishers, New York, 1987.

Rodin, M.B. Getting on the program: a biocultural analysis of Alcoholics Anonymous. In L. A. Bennett & G. M. Ames (Eds.), *The American Experience with Alcohol.* Plenum Press, New York, 1985, pp. 41-58.

Smith, J. W. Treatment of alcoholism in aversion conditioning hospitals. In E. M. Pattison & E. Kaufman (Eds.), *Encyclopedic Handbook of Alcoholism.* Gardner Press, New York, 1982, pp. 874-884.

Wilson, B. *Alcoholics Anonymous Comes of Age: A Brief History of A.A.* Alcoholics Anonymous World Services, New York, 1957.

▽   ▽   ▽

C H A P T E R

10

The Job is Not Over When He Stops Using and Abusing Chemicals

Congratulations! You and your family have finally achieved what you've worked toward for years—no more drugs and alcohol. At last he has admitted that he has a substance abuse problem and has stopped drinking or using, and he has agreed to enter a treatment program. Or perhaps he is already in such a program or has just completed one. It seems that your personal war against drugs or alcohol is finally at an end. The great majority of wives and families who have been battling substance abuse feel much better right after the SA stops using chemicals. However, it is quite common and even expected that most families continue to experience some family and personal difficulties after the SA gets sober. Sometimes these problems are quite severe.

SAs frequently experience a honeymoon period shortly after they stop using drugs and alcohol. This is especially true of those who have been working an AA, CA, or NA program or who have employed some other treatment method that promotes psychological growth and/or a spiritual reawakening. These heightened experiences and strong feelings of exceptional positive changes within the SA are often temporary, particularly when he begins to deal with the everyday stresses of work and family life. Some who are newly substance-free experience a devastating plummet from the high of the honeymoon period back down to earth and the problems of living. At this point, they must have a recovery program firmly in place to get them through this critical transition period. This is equally true for the family.

As pointed out before, there is a definite distinction between being "dry", which applies to the former SA who is just not drinking or using drugs, and being "sober", which denotes a substance-free state in which there also is a commitment to changing the old destructive and dysfunctional behavior in a meaningful, positive fashion. AA members sometimes explain this important distinction by saying, "Do you know what you have when you sober up a horse thief? You have a sober horse thief." Sobriety is not achieved by merely halting substance use and abuse. It is not achieved in a few weeks or a few months. Solid, real sobriety requires a *lifetime commitment* to self-examination and behavioral change. The tasks required to achieve and maintain sobriety are not short term nor are they easy. AA refers to their program of 12 steps of recovery: "It's a simple program, but it's not easy."

What to Expect After He Stops Drinking or Using

In the newly dry alcoholic's or drug abuser's first few months of recovery, the family is faced with the difficult task of dealing with a multitude of new adjustments. During the years of chemical dependency, the wife and family have established defenses, family roles, alliances and ways of communicating that excluded the SA. Now that he's substance free, he wants to return to the position he formerly enjoyed in the family system often before the family is willing or able to give up the roles and attitudes they developed during his drinking and using days. The family system will adjust much better if he gradually finds his way back to the way it was before he became a substance abuser. Nevertheless, it is often the case that right off the bat he expects his children to follow his commands and his wife to carry out his orders. In addition, he demands their immediate and total trust after but a few days or weeks of abstinence. Now that he is dry, he often feels threatened by the independence and autonomy of his wife and children. Moreover, when the wife and children are faced with beginning to give up their old roles they question what will replace them. After the initial honeymoon phase of relief and joy for the whole family, frustration, anger, and anxiety may take their place as the problems and adjustments of reality begin to take over. At this juncture, each person in the family will be required to be patient with each other if the conflicts of adjustment and transition are not to escalate rapidly and compound an already difficult time in the family's life.

New Ways of Relating Within the Family

The SA who is dry and unprepared or reluctant to be sober, remains psychologically "drunk." Expecting but not receiving exceptional rewards from everyone for giving up alcohol and drugs, he punishes the people around him, especially the family. As the romance of new-found sobriety rapidly wears off, a period known as "mourning" sets in and the slightest stress or obstacle may tip him off again, sending him into bouts of temper, depression, and verbally punishing those closest to him for his loss. The mourning process of giving up alcohol and drugs may last for months or sometimes years. During this period of prolonged grief and unfulfilled expectations, the recovering SA who continues alcoholic-type behavior is referred to as a "dry drunk." Dry drunks may also show signs of irritability, impulsivity, and many other left over behavioral patterns from their days of substance abuse. It is essential at this point that the family learn new patterns of relating that will replace those developed during chemical dependency, and that can be firmly entrenched. If healthy new patterns are not developed, the pull of the old family system can draw the SA and his family back into prior nonproductive interactions that often lead the SA back to drug and alcohol abuse.

The spouse and family members may be surprised and extremely puzzled to find that what they have so looked forward to can instead cause them so much pain. Spouses may continue to blame the SA for many of their own difficulties. Without their accustomed object of blame—the using or drinking partner—they may well have to look within themselves for the source of their disappointments and failure. On the other hand, they are being presented with a wonderful opportunity to concentrate their efforts on endeavors of their own, *if* they can turn their focus from the former SA to themselves. Achieving this change of focus can be a painstaking process of self-revelation, as well as admitting and accepting their own responsibility for disappointments or failures.

If the SA has fallen very far down (bottomed out) emotionally, spiritually, vocationally, and socially, the spouse has probably let him drag her down with him. In that case, up is a long way and she, as co-dependent (Co-D), may resent the SA for how far she now has to climb back up. She wants to express her anger, yet feels if she lets it out, she may provoke the SA back to abusing drugs or alcohol again.

The SA may not only want to resume all of his old responsibilities but also assume some new ones, which he may or may not be prepared to handle. The spouse and other family members may not really want to give up the important family roles they have adopted during substance abuse, because they enjoy the sense of power and competence that being in charge gives them.

The Phases of Recovery

As the SA goes through varying phases during recovery, so too will the spouse and family go through comparable phases. Generally speaking, the SA's recovery progression—or lack of it—will set the tone for the family's phases of recovery and their success or lack of success of completion of the phases. On the other hand, when the spouse or Co-D works a strong program of her own through some combination of family therapy, individual therapy, and Al-Anon, her growth will have a strong effect on the rest of the family's phases of recovery.

The Early Phases of Recovery

The early phases of recovery are usually characterized by the SA moving back and forth between closeness to and distance from the family, particularly the spouse. The passivity and neediness that evolved during his substance dependence frequently remains for a long period after the onset of abstinence. With the progression of sobriety, the SA becomes more aware of his obvious as well as hidden emotional dependence and passivity toward his wife. Threatened by this awareness, he may react by moving away from her emotionally or by becoming more possessive of her. Either of these reactions may, in turn, cause a parallel distancing from his spouse. He may try to intimidate his wife into a submissive position that also serves to drive her further away from him. He may repeatedly ask for her caretaking while denying that taking it leads him to feel he is in a one-down position. Remember, it is common for the SA to feel "entitled," in other words, that everything he wants is now due him just because he has given up his prized possession of alcohol or drugs.

In many instances, the spouse and children adjust to the SA's "push-pull" distancing maneuvers by setting up their own barriers to closeness. The spouse who is used to distance may be threatened by the SA's need for closeness. A spouse who fought constantly with the SA about his drinking and drug intake often continues to use arguments in order to achieve distance. She looks for any reason to start a new series of disagreements. A common argument revolves around whether he has really changed, and the likelihood that he will inevitably return to drug and alcohol use. This type of dispute may actually serve to trigger a return to chemical abuse.

Every family member experiences a need to maintain his or her own sense of personal space and separateness in the early stages of sobriety. The SA can be helped to find this sense of self through AA, NA, and CA and the family through Al-Anon and Alateen. Each individual member can find solace, understanding, and communication within a peer group such as Al-Anon, where the emphasis is on the unique and special needs related to his or her position within the substance-abusing family.

One risk inherent in participation in such supportive self-help groups is that the recovering SA may use his own AA program to distance himself in a way that ultimately leads to further family conflict or disruption. For example, though frequent attendance at AA meetings is encouraged, especially when the SA is new to the program, he may use this as a way to escape from the intimacy he fears or as a means of excluding his spouse from his life in AA. This risk is more likely if his family does not share in the 12-step program with the SA (by attending Al-Anon or open AA meetings with him). AA is rarely used to distance the family in a major way if the family members are unitedly involved in their own recovery. Specific AA aphorisms can also be misused by family members as a way to prematurely cut off necessary and helpful discussion or to make hostile demands that a family member change in an abrupt or inappropriate manner: "Don't bother me—just take one day at a time," or "Don't interfere in my program, just work your own."

In some cases, spouses may already have developed sufficient strengths, support systems, and new ways of coping so that they have not felt their mental attitudes or ability to function dragged down by the SA's substance abuse. However, even the successfully detached spouse should still be involved in the SA's process of recovery now that he is sober. The adage "If you're not a part of the solution, you're a part of the problem," is indeed relevant here. It is difficult for me, not only as a therapist but also as a human being, to comprehend how any woman married to a man who has pulled himself out of the abyss by using a recovery program would not be curious to learn about the program that has had such a deep impact on his life as well as hers. Yet some women do not get involved. Perhaps because they hang onto a resentment that someone or something other than themselves has made such a difference in his successful recovery from substance abuse. Some of this kind of anger or resentment, and a feeling of being left out of a part of his life, is common in the early stages of his recovery, but it usually quickly dissolves. An uninformed or uninvolved spouse is often a contributing factor associated with recurrent returns to substance abuse, called relapses or "slips." On the other hand, an involved and supportive spouse can contribute significantly to the prevention of relapse.

Many co-dependent spouses and their SA husbands have become used to and even "hooked" on the emotional intensity of the past repeated crises created by the SA and his chemical dependency. The relatively sudden absence of these crises in sobriety and the need for the old excitement is another possible precipitating factor in a slip. Because of the many reasons for dysfunction in the family that are still present after the SA sobers up, the spouse is often disillusioned, unhappy, or angry at a point when she had anticipated only bliss and joy. Her problems are then magnified because, in addition to all the adjustments required in recovery, she now also feels guilty that she isn't happy.

In some cases the newly sober couple finds they are doing things together that they used to do, but suddenly with a new set of feelings. Now, when together, there is less excitement and intensity. Instead there is comfort and stability and a new sense of vigor and drive. It is not unusual for the spouse to feel some confusion about her identity at this point.

The Mourning Phase

As the SA moves into a stage of stable sobriety, the Co-D may experience a stage of mourning or grief for the old ways, which is perfectly natural and normal and needs to be acknowledged and allowed to happen in constructive ways. An important aspect of this grief work is arriving at a clear understanding of what it is that she is giving up in order to recognize and appreciate how she and the family can grow. A successful metamorphosis requires seeing how the old ways were harmful and counterproductive to a happy, rewarding life and being able to envision how the new ways will serve to enhance and enrich her relationships with everyone, not just her partner.

The *first phase* of mourning or grief is one of experiencing confusion and feeling a lack of clear direction. This feeling of chaos is based on the fact that one is being pushed back and forth between new ways and old ways of doing and thinking.

The *second grief stage* is anger. This anger may be directed at recollections of all the old substance abuse-related punishments the Co-D experienced and endured. It is important at this point to expect and accept some degree of mood swings and feelings of being unprotected and vulnerable. A lot of things *are* still changing and change always involves a certain amount of chaos. Allowing for some confusion while sticking to her recovery program and regularly attending her support group will give the spouse the steadiness and validation she needs as change is happening.

Anger may also be the result of the Co-D feeling deprived of unrecoverable, lost years because sobriety did not take place sooner. She might feel resentment because she couldn't cure the SA herself, or because the fact that he became sober did not make him what she wanted or expected him to be. This kind of anger may be overwhelming to the Co-D, as well as to the SA. It is best dealt with by the woman discharging these strong emotions with a trained therapist in a protected environment of individual or group sessions, without the SA present. After the sting is out of the anger, it can then be shared constructively with the SA as part of meaningful discussion that can enhance rather than harm communication in the marriage.

The stages of grief do not occur strictly consecutively; there may be back and forth movement from stage one to three and then back to two, etc. The *third stage* is sadness over old memories and new disappointments. There is sadness about the loss of old ways and old roles. In spite of the pleasure of seeing her husband becoming stronger and less needy, the wife may miss the many ways in which she felt important, in charge, responsible, or admired.

There is also sadness that so many precious years of life had to be spent in pain and deprivation. There may be repetitive thoughts and preoccupation with "Why did this have to happen?" or "Why me?" These recurring thoughts, if not properly dealt with and dispelled, can impair growth. A shift should eventually occur from "Why did the co-dependency occur?" to "What can I learn from my need to have participated in this experience, so that I can be a fuller and more self-knowledgeable person?"

As the sadness is experienced, the spouse learns compassion and understanding that in turn helps to relieve the feelings of sadness and loss. Unfortunately, experience has erroneously taught many of us that sadness is to be avoided at all costs and as a result we have become reluctant and afraid to feel sadness. We may want to quickly throw our sadness away so that we can look ahead. But sadness, like other human emotions, is natural, and it is actually an enriching experience. When hastily brushed aside or buried it can lead to a feeling of despair or smoldering depression. Grief over loss is normal. When not processed and understood, buried grief can lead to depression, which is not normal and usually requires professional help. In some cases, a shortcut to discharging sadness is to go back to phase two of grief work and release anger that may have been held in.

The *last phase of grief* has to do with a new and different sense of aloneness as the spouse of the sober alcoholic learns about and discovers a new sense of self through individuation. In the process of individuation, she will become her own person: expressing her own needs, wants, and desires yet respectful of those of others. The individuated person possesses self-respect, self-esteem, and self-identity all of which exist independently of the praise of others and do not rest upon the need to take care of others. Yet the individuated person is able to love others and receive their love without being overwhelmingly threatened. With the struggle gone and without the hostile current against which to battle, life takes on a new meaning. Boredom can be replaced by contentment on one hand, and new adventures on the other.

The process of fully resolving grief in this growth-producing way can take months or even several years. It is hoped that during this period, the former SA is also involved in a program that enhances his growth so that the couple can build together toward an intimacy that permits each partner a distinct and separate sense of self while developing their identity as a couple. In this manner, working through the grief process completes the cycle of giving up the old ways of being together and reinforces the new, more rewarding and satisfying ways. Couples who have worked with me in this way call their new language of communication "newspeak."

Finally, in completing the grief work there needs to be a realization and acknowledgment that at times of stress all of the old patterns may return. If or when this takes place, and the mutual recovery process is working well, the couple soon realizes what stressors drove them away from supportive behavior so that they can deal with these stresses together and return to "newspeak." Thus, the grief work serves as a bridge to establishing the individuation of each partner while serving also to strengthen the couple's bond.

Mothers also may have deterred their adolescent children from individuating because of a need for them to gratify their own unmet needs for closeness and communication. One of the family's tasks in sobriety is to let the adolescents individuate so that they can catch up to the autonomy level of their peers. In order to achieve independence and autonomy, adolescents, as well as parents, must work through the stages described above. If the adolescent is not given the opportunity to individuate, then he or she runs a very high probability of becoming a substance abuser or marrying one.

I find it most helpful if family therapy is not only accompanied by a comprehensive program for the SA, but for the spouse and children as well. With this in mind, the ultimate goal for each individual in the family is accepting sobriety without resentment and a commitment to a life time of growth. Another goal for all family members, which is as important a goal as abstinence for the SA, is the realization and acceptance that they cannot be responsible for the behavior of another family member nor can they blame others for any aspect of their own life's difficulties. One of the parents in a family group for recovering SAs was heard to respond to their teenage child when accused of being to blame for all their problems: "I may be responsible for a lot of the problems you have, but you are the only one responsible for the solutions."

Relapse

A discussion of relapse is appropriate as we near the end of this book. Yes, SAs do relapse—and often. This frank statement may sound frightening and ominous, but relapse is part of the disease. However, if dealt with constructively, relapse can also be a vital part of recovery. I recall a fine chemical dependency therapist, with 15 years of sobriety, who had a one-day "slip" in reaction to some major changes taking place in his spouse during the process of her individual therapy and their own couple work. He bounced back from the slip immediately and has been sober again for the past five years. He did not let the slip throw him off course. Rather, he learned from it. If the SA is changing too fast, or if he is subjected to too much stress too early in his recovery, then a relapse is certainly possible. There are many other potential causes of relapse, but it is important to recognize that a slip is his, and it doesn't necessarily have to be the spouse's or family's as well.

My policy as a therapist is to view a slip as part of the disease of chemical dependency. However, when slips occur frequently, or in someone who is not working a comprehensive recovery program, then I insist on instant commitment to an adequate substance abuse treatment program or hospitalization— or else termination of therapy. I suggest that the family adopt the same policy with the bottom line being that the wife will leave if the SA doesn't seek immediate treatment. I know how difficult this decision is and how hard it is to carry out because of how difficult it is for me to end therapy with one of my patients in such cases of relapse, particularly after several years of a relationship. However, my patients know I mean it when I state emphatically that they either work a program or the therapy will be interrupted. They invariably either begin to work a program immediately or stop seeing me for a while. After a few days or weeks, they almost always return to therapy willing to enter a hospital treatment program or else ready to dedicate themselves to a full therapeutic approach rather than a half-hearted attempt at sobriety. The SA will respond as well, or even better, to a spouse who sends a similar clear message.

Many families of sober SAs need intensive restructuring family therapy to overcome the many difficulties that have been described in this chapter. After the first few months of sobriety and therapy, these families can gradually shift the emphasis from an educative approach, which teaches material similar to the contents of this book, to one that restructures family roles and relationships.

Substance abusers and their families should know how to recognize the signs of relapse so that they can be alerted to early warning signals, whenever possible, in an effort to avert the relapse. This does not mean, however, that the family should react overprotectively when these signals arise. They should be responded to as signs of a need for increased communication and for a return to a more intensive therapeutic program if there has been a slacking off of the attention and work required to maintain sobriety.

Signs of Relapse

The approach of relapse is signaled by a reversal of gains, particularly of integrity and honesty, with a return of the old denial. Another key sign is a sudden lowering of attendance at AA meetings and other therapeutic endeavors, such as individual or group therapy. Many AA members need fewer and fewer meetings as the years go by in order to maintain quality sobriety, but increase their attendance at times of crisis. Generally speaking, if the SA stops attending meetings significantly—he has been going to five meetings a week and drops back to one or two, or to no meetings—in the first two or three years, it could well be a warning sign of relapse or impending relapse. If he cuts back substantially, or stops attending meetings in the first six months to a year of sobriety, this behavior should trigger an immediate danger signal.

Other obvious warning signs include drinking or using drugs, or taking a drug that is not the chemical of choice (beer instead of whiskey, Xanax® instead of illicit Quaalude®, etc.), associating with prior substance-abusing peers, expressing a personal conviction that they are "cured" and need not work on themselves any longer, missing work or losing jobs, or overt signs of depression. More subtle signs include irritability, overreacting to stress, overconfidence, little white lies, "benign" compulsive behaviors like overworking, overeating, or overexercising, diminished pleasure, joy, or capacity for fun, and beginning to care about things less and to blame others more.

"The Game's Not Over 'Til It's Over"

There are common adages that are applicable to the family of the recovering SA. "The game's not over 'til it's over" or "The opera ain't over 'til the fat lady sings," reflect a spirit and drive to win and a capacity to come from behind. They apply to SA families as well.

Substance dependence and recovery from the disease does not end with the first day or the first year of sobriety. It lives on in the individual recovering alcoholic or drug abuser, and forever affects his life. The effects of his chemical dependence live on with each family member as well. However, if you and your spouse have succeeded in developing the level of self-understanding and honesty that we have described in this book, your lives will be deeper and more meaningful than that of the person who has not gone through a similar experience. Furthermore, your mutual intimacy can reach a profoundly rewarding level as a result of the work you have both done individually and together. This work can serve as a solid base of knowledge from which each of you can continue to grow as individuals and within your marriage.

It is my hope that this book provides each member of the family of a chemically dependent man with the information necessary to understand chemical abuse and dependency, the family's participation in it, and how to cope with it whether the substance abuser is wet, dry, or sober. This information can also be helpful to friends, employers, counselors, and others in the SA's life. Further, it is my hope that upon reading *Help at Last* those who live with substance abusers will be motivated to seek assistance or treatment for themselves. Family members can find support in their own community. They can dispel some of the loneliness that comes from living with an alcoholic or drug abuser and realize that there are many others just like them. In this way, they too can start on the road to recovery.

Most of all, perhaps it will instill hope for the many who have felt abandoned to the seemingly unsolvable and devastating problems of alcoholism and drug abuse and show them that they are not alone with the problem—that there is, indeed, help at last.

References

Bepko, C. Pride and paradox: Dealing with resistance to change. In C. Bepko & S. Krestan, *The Responsibility Trap: A Blueprint for Treating the Alcoholic Family*. The Free Press, New York, 1985.

Gorski, T. *The Relapse Dynamic*. Alcohol Systems Associates, Hazel Crest, Ill., 1982.

Schroeder, E. Reorganization of the family after aftercare. In S. Wegscheider-Cruse & R. W. Esterly (Eds.), *Alcoholism and the Family: A Book of Readings*. The Caron Institute, Wernersville, Pa., 1985.

Appendix

Publications and Information Sources

1. AA World Services, Inc.
   P.O. Box 459
   Grand Central Station
   New York, NY 10017

   Al-Anon and Alateen Literature
   P.O. Box 182
   Madison Square Garden
   New York, NY 10010

   Literature outlet for Alcoholics Anonymous and Al-Anon; reflects AA philosophy; literature aimed at people who have alcohol problems or are involved with alcoholics; low-moderate cost.

2. Al-Anon Family Group Headquarters, Inc.
   1372 Broadway, 7th Floor
   New York, NH 10018
   (212) 302-7240

3. Alcohol and Drug Addiction Research Foundation (ARF)
   33 Russell Street
   Toronto, Ontario, Canada M5S 2S1

   Factual, well-researched information; sound reputation for high quality work; pamphlets and books; moderate cost.

4. CompCare Publications
   2415 Annapolis Lane, Suite 140
   Minneapolis, MN 55441   800-328-3330

   Distributes a wide variety of publications on alcohol and "growth-centered" topics. Cost moderate.

5. CLAUDJA, INC.
   301000 Towncenter Dr., Suite 0-211
   Laguna Niguel, CA 92677   (714) 499-4806

   Excellent materials for children of alcoholics of all ages. Moderate cost.

6. Do-It-Now Foundation
   P.O. Box 5115
   Phoenix, AZ 85010   (602) 257-0797

   Casual, for drug using audience; intervention, treatment, drug education; "street" information; quality generally high; lost cost.

7. Hazelden
   P.O. Box 176
   Center City, MN 55012   (800) 328-9288

   A chemical dependency treatment center; alcohol information with AA approach; distributes material written elsewhere; NCA, AA, Al-Anon; general audience and professionals; moderate price.

8. Health Communications, Inc.
   2119-A Hollywood Blvd.
   Hollywood, FL 33020   (305) 920-9435

   General alcohol and other drug materials; moderate cost.

9. National Association for Children of Alcoholics (NACOA)
   31706 Coast Highway, Suite 201
   South Laguna, CA 92677   (714) 499-3889

   National newsletter; excellent low cost publications.

10. National Center for Health Education
    901 Sneath La., Suite 215
    San Bruno, CA 94066   (800) 227-6934

    Publications, advice and assistance in programming.

11. National Clearinghouse for Alcohol Information (NCAI)
    P.O. Box 2345
    Rockville, MD 20852   (301) 468-2600

    Free, federally sponsored materials about alcohol and alcoholism; wide audience range; generally high quality.

12. National Clearinghouse for Drug Abuse Information (NCDAI)
    5600 Fishers La.
    Rockville, MD 20852   (301) 443-6500

    Free, federally sponsored information; wide variation in intended audience.

13. National Council on Alcoholism (NCA)
    12 West 21 Street
    New York, NY 10010   (212) 206-6770

    Alcohol information; Alcoholics Anonymous and other materials; varied audiences—general, hospital, labor and management, psychiatry, youth education; books, pamphlets and periodicals; low-moderate cost.

14. Perrin & Treggett
    Booksellers
    One Madison Street
    East Rutherford, NJ 07073-1604
    (800) 321-7912   (201) 777-2277

    Addiction Specialists

15. Parent Resources & Information for Drug Education
    Robert W. Woodruff Bldg.
    Suite 1000, Volunteer Service Center
    100 Edgewood Ave., N.E.
    Atlanta, GA 30303   (800) 241-9746

    Community support; printed materials and films.

16. Project Pyramid
    3746 Mt. Diablo Blvd., Suite 200
    Lafayette, CA 94549

    Federally funded prevention assistance and resource sharing network; program planning, staff and organizational development, community relations, media techniques; free.

17. Rutgers Center for Alcohol Studies
    New Brunswick, NJ 08903   (201) 932-3510

    Annotated bibliographies of alcohol educational information.

18. Women for Sobriety
    P.O. Box 618
    Quakertown, PA 18951

    Newsletters, books, pamphlets, guidelines for self-help.

Other National Organizations and Information Agencies

1. Alcohol and Drug Problems Association
   1101 15th St., N.W.
   Washington, DC 20007   (202) 452-0990

2. American Council on Marijuana & Other Psychoactive Drugs, Inc.
   6193 Executive Blvd.
   Rockville, MD 20852

3. AMA—Dept. of Health Education
535 N. Dearborn Street
Chicago, IL 60610   (312) 751-6584

4. American Pharmaceutical Association
2215 Constitution Ave., N.W.
Washington, DC 20037   (202) 628-4410

5. Drug Enforcement Administration
U.S. Dept. of Justice
Washington, DC 20537

6. Families in Action
Suite 300, 3845 No. Druid Hills Road
Decataur, GA 30033

7. Fetal Alcohol Syndrome Program
Eunice Kennedy Shriver Center for Retardation, Inc.
200 Trapelo Road
Waltham, MA 02254

8. Food and Drug Administration
5600 Fishers Lane
Rockville, MD 20857

9. Government Printing Office
Washington, DC 20402

10. Narcotics Anonymous — World Services Offices
1346 N. Highland Ave.
Los Angeles, CA 90028   (213) 463-2533

11. National Clearinghouse for Poison Control Centers
U.S. Dept. of Health and Human Services
Washington, DC 20201

Call your local poison control center for any information about an
overdose!

12. National Congress of Parents and Teachers
700 N. Rush Street
Chicago, IL 60611   (312) 787-0977

13. National Federation of Parents for Drug Free Youth
1820 Franwall Ave., Suite 116
Silver Springs, MD 20902

14. National Health Information Clearinghouse
    P.O. Box 1133
    Washington, DC 20013   (800) 336-4797

15. The Office on Smoking & Health
    U.S. Public Health Service
    5600 Fishers Lane, Room 1-58
    Parklawn Building
    Rockville, MD 20857

16. Other Victims of Alcoholism, Inc.
    P.O. Box 921
    Radio City Station
    New York, NY 10019

17. Parents Who Care
    P.O. Box 50663
    Palo Alto, CA 94303

18. Whitman-Walker Clinic, Inc.
    1606 17th St. N.W.
    Washington, DC 20009

    Publications and organizing for gays.

Special Books and Pamphlets*

BOOKS FOR ADULT CHILDREN OF ALCOHOLICS
ALL FROM NACOCA CLEARINGHOUSE PUBLICATIONS:

A Primer on Adult Children of Alcoholics
by Timmen L. Cermak, M.D.

Adult Children of Alcoholics
by Janet G. Woititz, Ed.D.

"Al-Anon is For Adult Children of Alcoholics"
pamphlet by Al-Anon Family Group Headquarters

Al-Anon Sharings From Adult Children
20-page pamphlet from Al-Anon Family Group
Headquarters

An Elephant in the Living Room
by Jill M. Hastings, M.S. and
Marion H. Typpo. Ph.D.

*Please also see references at end of each chapter

*Another Chance: Hope and Health for
the Alcoholic Family*
by Sharon Wegscheider-Cruse, M.A.

*Broken Bottles, Broken Dreams: Understanding
and Helping the Children of Alcoholics*
by Charles Deutsch

*Children Are People Support Group
Training Manual*
by Rokelle Lerner and Barbara Naiditch

*Children of Alcoholics: A Bibliography
and Resource Guide*
by Robert J. Ackerman, Ph.D.

*Children of Alcoholics: A Guidebook for
Educators, Therapists and Parents*
by Robert J. Ackerman, Ph.D.

*Children of Alcoholics Handbook: Who They
Are, What They Experience, How They Recover*
by Herbert L. Gravitz, Ph.D.

*Children of Alcoholics: Meeting the Needs
of the Young COA in the School Setting*
by Ellen R. Morehouse, A.C.S.W., C.A.C.
and Claire M. Scola, R.N., M.W., C.A.C.

Choicemaking
by Sharon Wegscheider-Cruse, M.A.

*Co-Alcoholic/Para-Alcoholic:
Who's Who and What's the Difference*
by Jael Greenleaf

*Daily Affirmations for Adult Children
of Alcoholics*
by Rokelle Lerner

El Secreto de Pablito
by Ronny Figueroa (bilingual)

*Guide to Recovery: A Book for Adult
Children of Alcoholics*
by Herbert L. Gravitz, Ph.D. and
Julie Bowden, M.S., M.F.C.C.

It Will Never Happen to Me
by Claudia Black, Ph.D., M.S.W.

Living with a Parent Who Drinks Too Much
by Judith S. Seixas

My Dad Loves Me, My Dad Has a Disease
by Claudia Black, Ph.D., M.S.W.

Repeat After Me
by Claudia Black, Ph.D., M.S.W.

The Forgotten Children
by R. Margaret Cork

The Secret Everyone Knows
by Cathleen Brooks

BOOKS FOR CO-DEPENDENTS
AVAILABLE FROM HAZELDEN AT PRICE BELOW:

Codependency: A Second-Hand Life
by Stephanie Abbott

Codependent No More
by Melody Beattie

Guidebook for the Family With Alcohol Problems
by James E. Burgin

Help For the Marriage Partner of an Alcoholic
by James E. Burgin

Detaching With Love
by Carolyn W.

Families, Alcoholism and Recovery
by Celia Dulfano, M.S.W.

Do's and Don'ts
Hazelden Family Center

Alcohol, A Family Affair
by John E. Keller

By Joseph L. Kellerman:

   Alcoholism, A Merry-go-round Named Denial

   *El Alcoholismo Un Carrusel Llamado
      Negacion-Spanish*

   A.A. A Family Affair

   Al-Anon, A Message of Hope

   *The Family and Alcoholism, A Move from
      Pathology to Process*

   A Guide for the Family of the Alcoholic

   Guida Para la Familia del Alcoholico

   Reconciliation with God and Family

To Be Somebody
by Evelyn Leite

A Newcomer to Al-Anon
by Evelyn Leite

When Daddy's a Drunk . . . What to Tell the Kids
by Evelyn Leite

Family Denial
by Mary M.

Family Relationships
by Mary M.

Victims No More
by Thomas R. McCabe, Ph.D.

Self-Esteem and the Family
by Charles E. Nelson

When a Bough Breaks
by Mary Ylvisaker Nilsen

Addicts and Families in Recovery
by Cynthia Orange

Alcoholic Family Disorders, More than Statistics
by Roy W. Pickens, Ph.D., and Dace S. Svikis

Hope for Relationships
by Melvin R. Schroeder

Recovery for the Whole Family
by Harold A. Swift, A.C.S.W. and
Terence Williams, M.A.

Recuperation para Toda la Familia
Spanish

Free to Care
by Terence Williams, M.A.

Glossary

AA: Alcoholics Anonymous

ACA: Adult Children of Alcoholics

ADD: Attention Deficit Disorder (hyperactivity)

Al-Anon: Support group for family members and friends of alcoholics

Alateen: Support group for teenage children of alcoholics

Alatot: Support group for young children of alcoholics

Aberrant: Diverging from normal or usual standards

Abuse: A level of drug or alcohol use that interferes with physical health, family/social relationships, or vocational functioning but is not at an addictive level

Addictive, addiction: The condition of taking progressively more of a drug and being unable to stop doing so without adverse effects (withdrawal)

Additive: A condition wherein the effects of one drug are added to those of another drug

Adjunctive: Serving to support or assist

Aftercare: A therapeutic program that follows hospitalization for substance abuse

Albumen: A substance manufactured by the liver that helps regulate the proper amount of fluid in body cells

Alcoholic: Someone whose drinking is out of control and who exhibits the signs or characteristics of physical dependence, who has a preoccupation with drinking, and has impaired work and/or career functioning and relationships, and/or health problems related to alcohol consumption

Amotivational Syndrome: A cluster of symptoms, sometimes associated with marijuana use, that includes a loss of drive and ambition and dropping out of the "establishment

Amphetamines: Synthetic stimulant drugs

Analgesic: Pain-relieving

Analogs: Substances that are similar to other substances

Androgens: Male sex hormones such as testosterone

Anemia: Deficiency of red blood-corpuscles or their hemoglobin

Anorexia: A disorder characterized by an absence of appetite or desire for food

Antabuse® (disulfiram): A drug which is used to prevent alcohol consumption by the feared and unpleasant effects it produces when combined with alcohol.

Antidiuretic: A substance that inhibits the excretion of urine and other body fluids

Antisocial personality (ASP): An individual with aberrant personality patterns beginning before age 15 including: incapacity for loyalty or social values, callousness, impulsivity, irresponsibility, guiltlessness, low frustration tolerance

Aphorism: A succinct statement or general truth

Aphrodisiac: Arousing sexual desire

Aspiration: The process of vomit passing into the airway rather than being expelled orally, blocking breathing which can cause strangulation

Ataxia: Stumbling gait

Atrophy: Wasting away

Autonomic nervous system: Controls life sustaining functions such as heart rate, digestion and breathing. Deals with reactions to fight or flight impulses

Aversion therapy: A method of conditioning where the sight, smell, or taste of alcohol is paired with an aversive, disagreeable stimulus

Barbiturate: A category of soporific and sedative drugs

"Black tar": A form of heroin up to 40 times more potent than usual heroin

Blackout: A period of amnesia despite apparently normal performance to the outside observer

Blood alcohol level (BAL):   The concentration of alcohol in the blood

"Bottom out": A term used to denote when someone has reached a level of sufficient pain and emotional, vocational, and spiritual losses so that they are willing to risk changing their own behavior

CA: Cocaine Anonymous

Co-D: Co-dependent

Cardiomyopathy: Inflammation of the heart

Catharsis: Outlet of emotions

Chemical: Used synonymously with "drug" and "substance"

Chemical dependence: Abuse and dependence on either drugs or alcohol, or combinations of the two. An interchangeable term with "substance abuse"

Cirrhosis: Long-term scarring of the liver tissue caused by repeated episodes of alcoholic hepatitis

Co-dependency: Interchangeable with "co-alcoholic." A disease in which non-alcoholic family members' lives revolve around the alcoholic, yet their responses to the alcoholic perpetuate and protect his drinking and related behaviors

Cognition: The action or faculty of knowing, perceiving

Computerized tomographic (CT) scan: A method of viewing the brain and skeletal structure using a computer program of multiple x-rays

Conjunctiva: White part of the eyes

"Crack": A potent, smokable and extremely dangerous form of cocaine that is made by adding baking soda and water to cocaine powder

Cross-tolerance: A condition when the use of one drug leads an individual to require greater than normal doses of another drug or drugs

Data: Specific instances of behavior, events or circumstances which illustrate how a substance abuser's substance abuse impacts the lives of the members of an intervention team

Debilitating: Poor, feeble health

Defiant dependence: A term used to denote a substance abuser's behavior wherein he resists the idea of treatment, but when subsequently entering treatment tells his family that they should have forced him into treatment even sooner

Delirium: A confused, disordered state of intoxication, often with hallucinations and frenzied excitement

Delirium tremens (DTs): Physiological reaction to alcohol withdrawal characterized by fear, shaking, disorientation, fever, and hallucinations

Dementia: Irreversible, severe deterioration of brain functioning

Denial: A defense mechanism in which the individual disavows reality as well as thoughts, feelings, and behaviors in order to justify, hide, and protect substance abuse, avoid treatment, and preserve self-esteem

Depersonalization: Feeling unreal

Depressants: A class of substances that includes barbiturates, barbiturate-like substitutes, and benzoadiazepines that produces effects of disinhibition, drowsiness, euphoria, drunken behavior and are prone to abuse particularly by alcoholics and other drug abusers

Derealization: A state of mind wherein the world feels unreal

Dermatitis: Skin inflammation

Designer drugs: Drugs of abuse that are made in sophisticated laboratories and are either more potent or less expensive than existing drugs or that have not yet been designated as illegal, e.g., MDMA or XTC (ecstasy)

Detachment: The ability to remain uninvolved in a substance abuser's disease and to lead a normal life and refuse responsibility for the substance abuser and his behavior

Detoxification: The process of removing a poison or toxic substance from the body

Disinhibiting: Reducing or removing inhibitions (emotional resistance to thought or action)

Downers: Drugs like sedatives and narcotics that produce effects of calmness and drowsiness, dampen and lessen drives and feelings like anger, and reduce stressful stimuli

Dry: Used interchangeably with abstinent. Refers to a substance-free state only, not accompanied by an examination of destructive, childish behaviors and a pursuit of personality change

Dry drunk: A term referring to the state of mind and behavior of a recovering substance abuser who continues alcoholic-type behavior

Dyad: A term used to denote a couple (husband/wife or significant other) and their direct communication with each other

Dysfunction: Abnormality or impairment of functioning

Electromyography: A method of measuring abnormalities in muscles by electrical impulses

Emboli: Lumps of bacteria and debris occurring in the bloodstream

Enabler: Another term for a co-dependent which emphasizes more the consequences to the substance abuser than the significant other

Endocarditis: Infection of the inner lining of the heart

Endocrine system: The glands of the body that deposit substances which govern various functions directly into the bloodstream

Epilepsy: A disorder that entails convulsive and other types of seizures with loss of consciousness and control, which may be hereditary or the result from head trauma

Estrogens: Female sex hormones

Etiology: Cause of disease

Euphoriant: Producing a false sense of well-being

Flashback: Spontaneous reexperience of a prior sensation or memory from a hallucinogenic episode

Freebase cocaine: A form of potent, smokable cocaine which is made by extracting it from ordinary cocaine with flammable solvents like ether

Gastritis: Irritation of the lining of the stomach

Globulin: A substance manufactured by the liver that helps the body fight off infection

Grand mal (epileptic) seizures: Described above under "Epileptic," however the seizures themselves may also be caused by drug and alcohol withdrawal

Grandiosity: An exaggerated, pompous belief or claim of importance or greatness

Guided intervention: A structured, rehearsed meeting led by a professional where family members, close friends, and other persons with significant relationships with a substance abuser relate directly to him in a caring and loving manner how his substance abuse and behavior has affected them personally, and the need for him to pursue abstinence and undergo treatment

Habituation: Habit of or being accustomed to (another synonym for addiction)

Hallucination: Perception of external objects, sounds, or smells not actually present

Hallucinogens: Substances, which include LSD, peyote, mescaline, etc., that produce effects of hallucinations and other distortions of reality

Hashish: A concentrated, very potent form of marijuana

Hemorrhagic pancreatitis: A long-lasting, potentially life-threatening condition affecting the blood vessels of the pancreas

Hepatic encephalopathy: Inflammation of the brain occurring when the liver fails to detoxify proteins

Hepatitis, alcoholic: The direct damage of alcohol to the cells of the liver

High bottom: The need for relatively minor consequences of substance abuse, such as the threat of losing a job or career or receiving a single drunk driving charge, that motivates a substance abuser to seek treatment and recovery

Histamine: A chemical occurring naturally in the body responsible for allergies

Homeostatic: A state of being characterized by a placid, content, and integrated sense of well-being

Hypertension: High blood pressure

Hypochondriasis: Excessive concern with one's health

"Ice": A potent smokable form of methamphetamine

IP: Identified patient (as denoted by family or healthcare system)

Identify: The ability to relate to another person by recognizing similarities in feelings, attitudes and use and abuse of drugs or alcohol

Illicit: Unlawful

Individuation: The process of developing one's own individual identity and autonomous life

Inhalants: Substances that are inhaled, including ether, glue, aerosols, etc. that produce effects of excitement, euphoria, disorientation, hallucinations, and other effects

Interveners: Those concerned persons close to a substance abuser who participate in a guided intervention

Intervention: Any act or acts by persons close to a substance abuser, or in a position of authority, of confrontation that is aimed at a result of the substance abuser admitting his problem and seeking treatment

Interventionist: A trained professional who is qualified to facilitate a guided intervention and recommend appropriate treatment of substance abuse

Intoxication: The state of being drunk

Intranasal: Inhaled through the nose

Intravenous (IV): Injected by needle into the veins

Late-onset co-dependent: A person who has not grown up in a dysfunctional family of origin, but has developed co-dependent behavior only after living with a substance abuser

Layperson: Someone who is not an expert in a given field, such as science or medicine

Look-alike drugs: Substances especially manufactured to resemble other drugs in appearance and effect, particularly mock amphetamines

Low bottom: The need to suffer serious consequences, such as losing family, job, and friends, before an individual with a substance abuse problem becomes willing to seek treatment and recovery

MFT: Multiple family therapy

Macropsia: Feeling big

Manipulation: Controlling others by unfair, indirect, or devious means

Megalomania: Grossly exaggerated feelings of self-worth and importance

Megaloblastic anemia: An anemia with the presence of large, inefficient blood cells

Melanoma: Skin cancer originating in the pigment cells of the skin

Metabolize: The process by which a substance is broken down by the body

Micropsia: Feeling little

Misogynistic: An attitude of hatred toward women

Modality: Model; method of procedure

Mutual alcoholism: A term referring to persons, usually husband and wife or significant other, who are both alcoholics

Myopathy: Muscle inflammation characterized by muscle swelling and tenderness in the early stages with muscle paralysis in the chronic stages

NA: Narcotics Anonymous

NACOA: National Association of Children of Alcoholics

Narcanon: A support group for family and friends of narcotics abusers

Narcissism: Extreme self-worship, self-love, and preoccupation with one's image

Narcotics: A class of substances, including heroin, codeine, Demerol®, Percodan® and methadone, that relieves pain, induces drowsiness, sleep, stupor, or insensibility and produces a false sense of well-being

Nasal septum: Wall between the nostrils

Neurotic: Emotional disturbances of all types that are not psychosis, characterized by psychological pain and discomfort and an inability to take a rational, objective view of life

"Newspeak": A language of communication between a couple that encourages an intimacy that permits each partner a separate sense of self while still developing their identity as a couple

Non-alcoholic: Someone whose use of alcohol is mild to moderate, causes no problems in his or her family, and shows no other signs of problems with alcohol

Nystagmus: A symptom characterized by repetitive, rapid eye movements

OTC: Over-the-counter. A substance that can be purchased without a physician's prescription

Omnipotence: Having absolute, infinite power

Pancreatitis: A disease of the pancreas occurring when blocked digestive enzymes "digest" or literally eat up the pancreas

Paranoia: A state of mind characterized by abnormal feelings of persecution and mistrust

Peripheral nervous system: Includes all nerves except those associated with the brain and spinal cord

Passive-aggressive behavior: Aggressive behavior that is manifested in passive ways such as pouting, procrastination, obstinacy, and intentional inefficiency

Pathological: Symptomatic of a disease or abnormality

Pellagra: A vitamin deficiency disease

Pharmacologic: Pertaining to drugs or chemicals

Physiological: Pertaining to the body's parts and functions

Physical or physiological dependence: Occurs when physical tolerance to a substance has developed to the extent that the drug-dependent person's body requires a certain intake level of the substance in order to avoid withdrawal symptoms or to maintain body functions

Polydrug abuse: The simultaneous or sequential use or abuse of more than one drug and/or alcohol

"Popper" (or "snapper"): Euphemism for an inhalant like amyl nitrate, which is in ampule form requiring snapping or popping to open

Post-traumatic stress disorder (PTSD): A syndrome seen in individuals who have been exposed to the severe stress of combat, which is considered similar to the symptoms seen in children of alcoholics

Pot paranoia: A state of mind brought on by marijuana use that includes anxiety progressing to extreme confusion and paranoia, especially about arrest for marijuana use

Pre-alcoholic: Someone who, with a lesser degree of the characteristics of an alcoholic, will most likely develop full blown alcoholism in a matter of years

Precursor: Substance occurring in the body from which another is formed by chemical transformation

Projection: Blaming others, projecting or attributing the source of one's problems from self to others

Prostatitis: Inflammation and swelling of the male prostate gland

Prothrombin: A substance manufactured by the liver, which is necessary for proper blood clotting

Psychedelic drug: One that allegedly produces "mind expansion" effects

Psychoactive: Affecting the mind

Psychodynamic: A knowledge and theory of human behavior and its motivation that emphasizes unconscious determinants

Psychological dependence: Occurs when a drug-dependent person or addict relies upon the change in consciousness and feelings produced by a substance in an attempt to cope more effectively and experience reality differently

Psychological state: Pertaining to drugs refers to how a substance is experienced in the mind

Psychomimetic drug: One which mimics or acts like psychosis

Psychosis: Severe mental derangement involving the whole personality

Pulmonary edema: Fluid backup in the lungs

REM: Rapid eye movement; Stage I of sleep in which dreams take place, this type of sleep provides a necessary, restorative function

Reverse tolerance: A state in which progressively lower doses of a drug are necessary to achieve its desired psychological effects

Rhinitis: Inflammation of the nasal area due to intranasal ingestion of a drug

Rhinophyma: An enlargement of the nose frequently connected to excessive alcohol consumption

SA: Substance abuser

Schizophrenic psychosis: A mental disorder marked by paranoid delusions and a retreat from reality

Scurvy: A vitamin deficiency disease

Sedative-hypnotic: A downer-type of drug that is used for relaxation, anxiety relief or sleep

Septicemia: Infection in the bloodstream caused by contaminated needles used in intravenous drug injection

Shermans: An expensive brand of cigarette that is dipped into a solution of PCP

Slip: A brief return to alcohol or drugs by a recovering substance abuser

Sober, sobriety: A substance-free state in which there is also a commitment to changing old, destructive and dysfunctional behavior in a meaningful, positive fashion

Social detoxification facility: A non-hospital-based facility for the purpose of moderately severe alcohol detoxification and cessation of substance abuse

Somatic: Physical as opposed to mental

Soporific: Producing drowsiness, sleepiness

Spider nevi: Dilated large blood vessels that appear in the skin of chronic alcoholics as a result of liver disease

Sponsor (AA): A member of Alcoholics Anonymous (AA) who helps a new member plan a course for sobriety and provides one-on-one support for day-to-day problems and who helps reinforce the decision not to drink or use chemicals

Stimulants: A class of substances including cocaine, amphetamines, and caffeine that produces effects of increased alertness, excitation, euphoria and others

Subdural hemorrhage: A potentially fatal bleeding under the skull from head trauma that is worsened by a lowered level of prothrombin (see prothrombin)

Substance: Mind-altering drug or chemical, including alcohol

Substance abuse: The use of psychoactive drugs, alcohol, or a combination of the two, to the extent that it seriously interferes with an individual's physical health, social relationships or vocational functioning

Substance dependence: Addiction or habituation to the use of a substance to the extent that tolerance and withdrawal are present in an individual

Sympathomimetic: Mimicking the Sympathetic Nervous System

Syndrome: A cluster of symptoms

Synesthia: The changing of sensations from one sensory perception to another, i.e., from sight to sound

Team: The members (interveners) of the group who participate in a guided intervention or who provide treatment

TENS Unit (Transcutanious Electrical Nerve Stimulation): A device carried by the user which delivers an electrical stimulus causing no pain itself, however blocking painful sensations.

Therapeutic: When applied to the normal dose or prescribed amount of a drug used to treat a condition

Therapeutic community (TC): A live-in facility for substance abusers, that requires a long-term commitment and provides a drug and alcohol-free environment along with an intensive therapeutic program

Threesome: A term used to refer to the situation when a couple bring in a third person to work together with them in discussing issues and problem solving in a relationship (contrasted to triangulation)

Thrombophlebitis: Vein infection

Tolerance: The need for increasing amounts of a drug to experience the same or lessened effects produced by the drug

Tracks: Bluish-black, hard, raised streaks on the skin over veins in which drugs are frequently injected

Tremor: Body quivering, shaking

Triangulation: Communication or conflict between two people directed to a third party or issue

Ultimata(-um): Conditions set forth or consequences to be carried through (i.e., separation, loss of job, etc.) if a substance abuser will not stop abusing drugs and/or alcohol

Uppers: Drugs, like amphetamines, that produce the effects of feeling active and powerful

Varicose veins: A dilation of blood veins, especially in the legs, esophagus, and rectum, caused by backup pressure resulting from a swelling of liver tissue (occurs in alcoholics with cirrhosis)

Varix: An esophageal vein that may rupture in severe alcoholics

Wernicke-Korsakoff syndrome: A common vitamin deficiency seen in alcoholics caused by the lack of thiamine, characterized by a syndrome of symptoms such as mental confusion, paralysis of eye muscles, etc.

Withdrawal: The presence of serious physical and psychological symptoms when drug or alcohol intake is lessened or discontinued

Yellow jaundice: A condition caused by a backup of the breakdown products of bile in the bloodstream characterized by the presence of yellow pigmentation in the skin and whites of the eyes; seen in alcoholic cirrhosis and viral hepatitis of heroin addicts

Index

EDWARD KAUFMAN, M.D., is Director of Family Therapy Training, and Chief of Psychiatric Services at the Department of Psychiatry and Human Behavior, California College of Medicine, University of California at Irvine. Dr. Kaufman is co-editor of *Family Therapy of Drug and Alcohol Abuse* (Gardner Press, 1979) and author of numerous articles on substance abuse. He is also a member of the Alcohol Studies Advisory Board and a special review consultant to the Drug Abuse, Clinical, Behavioral, and Psychosocial Research Review of the National Institute of Drug Abuse. He holds his M.D. from Jefferson Medical College.